Early praise for *Arduino: A Quick-Start Guide, Second Edition*

Buy this book *only* if you don't mind being sucked into an amazing world of Arduino hacking, programming, games, controllers, motors, tweeting, networking, and lots of other mind-blowing things!

➤ **Kevin Beam**

Software engineer, National Snow and Ice Data Center (NSIDC)

Maik Schmidt's writing style is engaging and makes complex concepts accessible. When I finished the book, I was daydreaming about future Arduino projects I could create.

➤ **Matthew Sullivan**

Senior Rails/Ruby developer, Paradigmisr

A very well-written, thorough introduction to the Arduino platform. The second edition is a nice refinement of the first, with much updated as a result of the changes to the platform since the initial release of the book.

➤ **Mike Riley**

Author, *Programming Your Home, Build an Awesome PC,* and *Developing Android on Android*

Arduino: A Quick-Start Guide, Second Edition

Maik Schmidt

The Pragmatic Bookshelf

Dallas, Texas • Raleigh, North Carolina

Many of the designations used by manufacturers and sellers to distinguish their products are claimed as trademarks. Where those designations appear in this book, and The Pragmatic Programmers, LLC was aware of a trademark claim, the designations have been printed in initial capital letters or in all capitals. The Pragmatic Starter Kit, The Pragmatic Programmer, Pragmatic Programming, Pragmatic Bookshelf, PragProg and the linking *g* device are trademarks of The Pragmatic Programmers, LLC.

Every precaution was taken in the preparation of this book. However, the publisher assumes no responsibility for errors or omissions, or for damages that may result from the use of information (including program listings) contained herein.

Our Pragmatic courses, workshops, and other products can help you and your team create better software and have more fun. For more information, as well as the latest Pragmatic titles, please visit us at *https://pragprog.com.*

All circuit diagrams were created with Fritzing (*http://fritzing.org*).

The team that produced this book includes:

Susannah Davidson Pfalzer (editor)
Potomac Indexing, LLC (indexer)
Cathleen Small (copyeditor)
Dave Thomas (typesetter)
Janet Furlow (producer)
Ellie Callahan (support)

For international rights, please contact *rights@pragprog.com.*

Printed in the United States of America.
ISBN-13: 978-1-94122-224-9
Printed on acid-free paper.
Book version: P2.0—March 2015

Contents

Part I — Getting Started with Arduino

Part II — Eleven Arduino Projects

Part III — Appendixes

Acknowledgments

Susannah Davidson Pfalzer was the editor of the first edition of this book. When planning the second edition, I hadn't forgotten how difficult it was to write the first one, but I also remembered how great it was to work with her. Again, she turned this endeavor into a real pleasure. Thank you very much!

This is not the first book I've written for the Pragmatic Bookshelf, so I knew already how professional and nice everyone on the team is. Still, they get even better every time, and I'd like to thank everyone for making this book happen.

This book would not have been possible without the stunning work of the whole Arduino team. Thank you so much for creating Arduino!

A big thank you goes to all the people who contributed material to this book: Christian Rattat took all the book's photos, Kaan Karaca created the Blaminatr's display, and Kassandra Perch improved the JavaScript code in the "Creating Your Own Universal Remote Control" chapter.

I created all circuit diagrams with Fritzing,[1] and I'd like to thank the Fritzing team for making such a great tool available for free.

For the games I developed for this book, I needed some artwork, and I've found amazing things on the OpenGameArt website.[2] I used some graphics contributed by www.kenney.nl[3] and a great song created by Alex Smith[4] for my breakout clone. Thank you for putting these into the public domain.

The background image of the browser game comes from ESA/Hubble, NASA, Digitized Sky Survey, MPG/ESO (acknowledgment: Davide de Martin). The image showing how raster scan works was created by Ian Harvey.

---

1. http://fritzing.org/
2. http://opengameart.org/
3. http://opengameart.org/content/puzzle-game-art
4. http://opengameart.org/content/awake-megawall-10

For an author, there's nothing more motivating and valuable than feedback. I'd like to thank my reviewers: Kevin Beam, Jessica Janiuk, Kassandra Perch, Mike Riley, Sam Rose, and Matthew Sullivan. This book is so much better because of your insightful comments and suggestions!

Finally, I have to thank my wonderful wife, Tanja, and my adorable son, Mika, for being patient and understanding whenever I had to write yet another page.

Preface

Welcome to Arduino, and welcome to the exciting world of physical computing! Arduino[1] is an open-source project consisting of both hardware and software. It was originally created to give designers and artists a prototyping platform for interaction design courses. Today, hobbyists and experts all over the world use it to create physical computing projects, and you can, too.

Arduino lets you get hands-on again with computers in a way you haven't been able to since the 1980s, when you could build your own computer. And Arduino makes it easier than ever to develop handcrafted electronics projects ranging from prototypes to sophisticated gadgets. Gone are the days when you had to learn lots of theory about electronics and arcane programming languages before you could even get an LED blinking. You can create your first Arduino project in a few minutes without needing advanced electrical engineering coursework.

In fact, you don't need to know anything about electronics projects to read this book, and you'll get your hands dirty right from the beginning. You'll not only learn how to use some of the most important electronic parts in the first pages, you'll also learn how to write the software needed to bring your projects to life.

This book dispenses with theory and stays hands-on throughout. I'll explain all the basics you need to build the book's projects, and every chapter has a troubleshooting section to help when things go wrong. This book is a quick-start guide that gets you up to speed quickly and enables you to immediately create your own projects.

Who Should Read This Book

If you are interested in electronics—and especially in building your own toys, games, and gadgets—then this book is for you. Although Arduino is a nice

---

1. http://arduino.cc

tool for designers and artists, only software developers are able to unleash its full power. So, if you've already developed some software—preferably with C/C++ or Java—then you'll get a lot out of this book.

But there's one more thing: you have to build, try, and modify the projects in this book. Have fun. Don't worry about making mistakes. The troubleshooting sections—and the hands-on experience you'll gain as you become more confident project by project—will make it all worthwhile. Reading about electronics without doing the projects yourself isn't even half the battle. (You know the old saying: we remember 5 percent of what we hear, 10 percent of what we write, and 95 percent of what we personally suffer.) And don't be afraid: you really don't need any previous electronics project experience!

If you've never written a piece of software before, start with a programming course or read a beginner's book about programming first. (*Learn to Program, Second Edition [Pin09]* is a good starting point.) Then, learn to program in C with *The C Programming Language [KR98]* or in C++ with *The C++ Programming Language [Str00]*.

What's in This Book

This book consists of three parts ("Getting Started with Arduino," "Eleven Arduino Projects," and the appendixes). In the first part, you'll learn all the basics you need to build the projects in the second part, so read the chapters in order and do all the exercises. The chapters in the second part also build on each other, reusing techniques and code from earlier chapters.

There's one exception, though: in this book you'll create several Google Chrome apps that connect your web browser to Arduino. Appendix 4, *Controlling the Arduino with a Browser*, on page 267, explains in detail how Chrome apps work, so you should read it after you've read Chapter 4, *Building a Morse Code Generator Library*, on page 61.

Here's a short walkthrough:

- The book starts with the basics of Arduino development. You'll learn how to use the integrated development environment (IDE) and how to compile and upload programs. You'll quickly build your first project—electronic dice—that shows you how to work with basic parts such as LEDs, buttons, and resistors. By implementing a Morse code generator, you'll see how easy it is to create your own Arduino libraries.

- Then you'll learn how to work with analog and digital sensors. You'll use a temperature sensor and an ultrasonic sensor to build a very accurate digital metering ruler. Then you'll use a three-axis accelerometer to build your own motion-sensing game controller and a cool breakout game clone.

- At this point you've output data mostly using some LEDs and the Arduino's serial port. Now you'll connect the Arduino to an actual TV set and generate your own video signals. You'll create a graphical thermometer that you can display on the TV set in your living room.

- In electronics, you don't necessarily have to build gadgets yourself. You can also tinker with existing hardware, and you'll see how easy it is to take full control of Nintendo's Wii Nunchuk so you can use it in your own applications. Soon, you'll have everything you need to build your own video game console.

- The Arduino does not have to work in isolation, and it works great with different networking technologies. You'll connect the Arduino to the Internet in various ways, and you'll learn how to send Twitter messages and emails. You'll build a burglar alarm that sends you an email whenever someone is moving in your living room during your absence.

- Using a Nunchuk to control applications or devices is handy, but often it's more convenient to have a wireless remote control. So, you'll learn how to build your own universal remote control that you can even control using a web browser.

- Finally, you'll work with motors by creating a fun device for your next software project. You can connect it to your continuous integration system, so whenever the build fails, it will move an arrow to point to the name of the developer who is responsible.

- In the appendixes, you'll learn about the basics of electricity and soldering. You'll also find advanced information about programming a serial port and programming the Arduino in general. And you'll find an appendix that explains how to control the Arduino using a web browser.

Every chapter starts with a detailed list of all the parts and tools you need to build the chapter's projects. All chapters contain lots of photos and diagrams showing how everything fits together. You'll get inspired by descriptions of real-world Arduino projects in sidebars throughout the book.

Things won't always work out as expected, and debugging circuits can be a challenging task. So in every chapter, you'll find a "What If It Doesn't Work?" section that explains the most common problems and their solutions.

Before you read the solutions in the "What If It Doesn't Work?" sections, though, try to solve the problems yourself, because that's the most effective way to learn. In the unlikely case that you *don't* run into any problems, you'll find a list of exercises at the end of every chapter to build your skills.

Arduino Uno and the Arduino Platform

After releasing several Arduino boards and Arduino IDE versions, the Arduino team decided to specify a version 1.0 of the platform. Arduino's version numbering was counterintuitive before. At the beginning of the project the developers increased the version number by 1 with each new release. They did that up to number 23, and then they decided to use 1.0 as the version number for the next release. That means Arduino 1.0 is more recent than Arduino 23.

Arduino 1.0, released at the end of 2011, has since been the reference point for all developments. The Arduino developers have also released the Arduino Uno board, and they've continued to improve the IDE and its supporting libraries.

In parallel, the Arduino team has created more Arduino boards, such as the Arduino Due,[2] the Arduino Leonardo,[3] and the Arduino Yún.[4] These boards either have more powerful microcontrollers or come with additional hardware, such as a Wi-Fi module.

Most of the new boards use a different processor architecture designed by ARM. This architecture isn't compatible with the architecture of the older board's AVR processors. To overcome this gap, the Arduino team started to develop version 1.5.x of the Arduino IDE in parallel with 1.0.x. This development led to version 1.6.0, which supports the different processor architectures transparently.

In addition to all that, there's a separate IDE for the Arduino Galileo.[5] This board was created by Intel and is compatible with the Arduino.

This book is current for versions 1.0.6 and 1.6.0 of the Arduino platform and up to date for the Arduino Uno board. Most of the projects will also work on other recent boards, such as the Leonardo or the Due. They will also work

---

2. http://arduino.cc/en/Main/ArduinoBoardDue
3. http://arduino.cc/en/Main/ArduinoBoardLeonardo
4. http://arduino.cc/en/Main/ArduinoBoardYun
5. http://arduino.cc/en/ArduinoCertified/IntelGalileo

on older Arduino boards, such as the Duemilanove or Diecimila. All code in this book has been tested with Arduino 1.0.6 and 1.6.0.

Code Examples and Conventions

Although this is a book about open-source hardware and electronics, you will find a lot of code examples. We need them to bring the hardware to life and make it do what we want it to do.

We'll use C/C++ for all programs that will eventually run on the Arduino. For applications running on our PC, we'll mainly use JavaScript and Processing.[6] In *Serial Communication Using Various Languages*, on page 255, you'll also learn how to use several other programming languages to communicate with an Arduino.

Online Resources

This book has its own web page at http://pragprog.com/book/msard2 where you can download the code for all examples. (If you have the ebook version of this book, clicking the little gray box above each code example downloads that source file directly.) You can also participate in a discussion forum and meet other readers and me. If you find bugs, typos, or other annoyances, please let me and the world know about them on the book's errata page.[7]

On the web page you will also find a link to a Flickr[8] photo set. It contains all the book's photos in high resolution. There you can also see photos of reader projects, and we'd really like to see photos of your projects, too!

Let's get started!

---

6. http://processing.org
7. http://www.pragprog.com/book/msard2/errata
8. http://flickr.com

The Parts You Need

Here's a list of the parts you need to work through all the projects in this book. In addition, each chapter lists the parts you'll need for that chapter's projects, so you can try projects chapter by chapter without buying all the components at once. Although there appears to be a lot of components here, they're all fairly inexpensive, and you can buy all the parts you need for all of the projects in this book for about $200.

Starter Packs

Many online shops sell Arduino components and electronic parts. Some of the best are Maker Shed[1] and Adafruit.[2] They have awesome starter packs, and I strongly recommend buying one of these.

At the time of this writing, the best and cheapest solution is to buy the Adafruit Experimentation Kit for Arduino (product ID 170). It contains many of the parts you need to build the book's examples, as well as many more useful parts that you can use for your own side projects. Check the current contents of the kit, but usually you have to buy the following parts separately:

- Parallax PING))) sensor
- ADXL335 accelerometer breakout board
- 6-pin 0.1-inch standard header
- Nintendo Nunchuk controller
- A passive infrared sensor
- An infrared LED
- An infrared receiver
- An Ethernet shield
- A Proto shield
- An RCA (composite video) cable

---

1.   http://makershed.com
2.   http://adafruit.com

All shops constantly improve their starter packs, so it's a good idea to scan their online catalogs carefully.

Complete Parts List

If you prefer to buy parts piece by piece (or chapter by chapter) rather than in a starter pack, here is a list of all the parts used in the book. Each chapter also has a parts list and a photo with all parts needed for that chapter. Suggested websites where you can buy the parts are listed here for your convenience, but many of these parts are available elsewhere also, so feel free to shop around.

Good shops for buying individual components parts are Digi-Key,[3] SparkFun,[4] and Mouser.[5] Over the years Amazon[6] has become an excellent shop for electronic parts, too.

- An Arduino board, such as the Uno, available from Adafruit or Maker Shed.

- A USB cable. Depending on the Arduino board you're using, you will either need a standard A-B cable or a standard A-micro-B cable. You might already have a few. If not, you can order it at Amazon, for example.

- A half-size breadboard from Maker Shed (search for *breadboard*) or from Adafruit (product ID 64).

- Three LEDs. (You need four additional ones for an optional exercise.) Buying LEDs one at a time isn't too useful; a better idea is to buy a pack of 20 or more. Search for *LED pack* at any of the online shops mentioned in this chapter.

- One 100Ω resistor, one 330Ω resistor, two 10kΩ resistors, and three 1kΩ resistors. It's also not too useful to buy single resistors; buy a value pack, such as catalog number 10969 from SparkFun.

- Two pushbuttons. Don't buy a single button switch; buy at least four instead, available at Digi-Key (part number 450-1650-ND) or Mouser (101-TS6111T1602-EV).

- Some wires, preferably breadboard jumper wires. You can buy them at Maker Shed (product code MKSEEED3) or Adafruit (product ID 153).

---

3.   http://digikey.com

4.   http://sparkfun.com

5.   http://www.mouser.com

6.   http://amazon.com

- A Parallax PING))) sensor (product code MKPX5) from Maker Shed.

- A passive infrared sensor (product ID 189) from Adafruit.

- A TMP36 temperature sensor from Analog Devices.[7] You can get it from Adafruit (product ID 165).

- An ADXL335 accelerometer breakout board. You can buy it at Adafruit (product ID 163).

- A 6-pin 0.1-inch standard header (included if you order the ADXL335 from Adafruit). Alternatively, you can order from SparkFun (search for *breakaway headers*). Usually, you can only buy strips that have more pins. In this case, you have to cut it accordingly.

- An Arduino Proto shield from Adafruit (product ID 2077). You'll also need a tiny breadboard (product ID 65 at Adafruit). The Proto shield is optional, but I highly recommend it, especially for building the motion-sensing game controller. Note that this shield comes as a kit, so you have to solder it yourself.

- A Nintendo Nunchuk controller. You can buy it at nearly every toy store or at http://www.amazon.com/, for example.

- An Arduino Ethernet shield (product ID 201) from Adafruit.

- An infrared sensor, such as the TSOP38238. You can buy it a Adafruit (product ID 157) or Digi-Key (search for *TSOP38238*).

- An infrared LED. You can get it from SparkFun (search for *infrared LED*) or from Adafruit (product ID 387).

- An RCA (composite video) cable. You can get it at Adafruit (product ID 863), for example.

- A 5V servo motor, such as the Hitec HS-322HD or the Vigor Hextronik. You can get one from Adafruit (product id 155) or SparkFun. Search for standard servos with an operating voltage of 4.8V–6V.

For some of the exercises, you'll need some optional parts:

- A piezo speaker or buzzer. Search for *piezo buzzer* at Maker Shed (product code MSPT01) or get it from Adafruit (product ID 160).

---

7. http://www.analog.com/en/sensors/digital-temperature-sensors/tmp36/products/product.html

For the soldering tutorial, you need the following things:

- A 25W–30W soldering iron with a tip (preferably 1/16-inch) and a soldering stand.

- Standard 60/40 solder (rosin-core) spool for electronics work. It should have a 0.031-inch diameter.

- A sponge.

You can find these things in every electronics store, and many have soldering kits for beginners that contain some useful additional tools. Take a look at Adafruit (product ID 136) or Maker Shed (search for *Soldering Starter Kit*).

Part I

Getting Started with Arduino

CHAPTER 1

Welcome to the Arduino

The Arduino was originally built for designers and artists—people with little technical expertise. Even if they didn't have programming experience, the Arduino enabled them to create sophisticated design prototypes and some amazing interactive artwork. So, it should come as no surprise that the first steps with the Arduino are very easy, even more so for people with a strong technical background.

But it's still important to get the basics right. You'll get the most out of working with the Arduino if you familiarize yourself with the Arduino board itself, with its development environment, and with techniques such as serial communication.

One thing to understand before getting started is *physical computing*. If you have worked with computers before, you might wonder what this means. After all, computers are physical objects, and they accept input from physical keyboards and mice. They output sound and video to physical speakers and displays. So, isn't all computing physical computing in the end?

In principle, regular computing is a subset of physical computing: keyboard and mouse are *sensors* for real-world inputs, and displays or printers are *actuators*. But controlling special sensors and actuators using a regular computer is very difficult. Using an Arduino, it's a piece of cake to control sophisticated and sometimes even weird devices. In the rest of this book, you'll learn how, and in this chapter you'll get started with physical computing by learning how to control the Arduino, what tools you need, and how to install and configure them. Then we'll quickly get to the fun part: you'll develop your first program for the Arduino.

What You Need

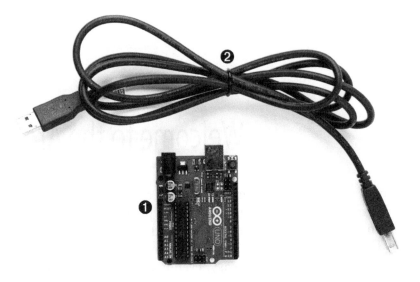

1. An Arduino board, such as the Uno, Duemilanove, or Diecimila.

2. A USB cable to connect the Arduino to your computer.

3. The Arduino IDE (see *Installing the Arduino IDE*, on page 10). You will need it in every chapter, so after this chapter I'll no longer mention it explicitly.

You'll find photos such as this in most of the following chapters. The numbers in the photo correspond to the numbers in the parts list. In later chapters the photos do not show standard parts, such as the Arduino board or a USB cable.

What Exactly Is an Arduino?

Beginners often get confused when they discover the Arduino project. When looking for the Arduino, they hear and read strange names such as Uno, Duemilanove, Diecimila, LilyPad, or Seeeduino. The problem is that there is no such thing as "the Arduino."

A couple of years ago, the Arduino team designed a microcontroller board and released it under an open-source license. You could buy fully assembled boards in a few electronics shops, but people interested in electronics could also download its schematic[1] and build it themselves.

Over the years, the Arduino team improved the board's design and released several new versions. They usually had Italian names, such as Uno, Duemilanove, or Diecimila; you can find online a list of all boards ever created by the Arduino team.[2]

Here's a small selection of Arduinos. They may differ in their appearance, but they have a lot in common, and you can program them all with the same tools and libraries.

Although they're the same in principle, they differ in some details. The Arduino Due[3] has many more IO pins than most of the other Arduinos and uses a powerful 32-bit ARM core microcontroller, while the Arduino Nano[4] was designed to be used on a breadboard, so it doesn't have any sockets. From my experience, beginners should start with one of the "standard" boards—that is, with an Uno, for example.

1. http://arduino.cc/en/uploads/Main/arduino-uno-schematic.pdf
2. See http://arduino.cc/en/Main/Boards and http://arduino.cc/en/Main/Products.
3. http://arduino.cc/en/Main/ArduinoBoardDue
4. http://arduino.cc/en/Main/ArduinoBoardNano

The Arduino team didn't only constantly improve the hardware design, they also invented new designs for special purposes. For example, they created the Arduino LilyPad[5] to embed a microcontroller board into textiles. You can use it to build interactive T-shirts.

In addition to the official boards, you can find countless Arduino clones on the Web. Everybody is allowed to use and change the original board design, and many people created their very own version of Arduino-compatible boards. Among many others, you can find the Freeduino, Seeeduino, Boarduino, and the amazing Paperduino,[6] an Arduino clone without a printed circuit board. All of its parts are attached to an ordinary piece of paper.

Arduino is a registered trademark—only the official boards are named "Arduino"—so clones usually have names ending with "duino." You can use every clone that is fully compatible with the original Arduino to build all of the book's projects.

Exploring the Arduino Board

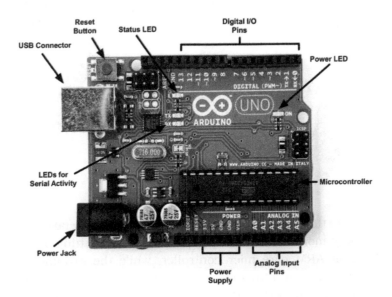

The photo shows an Arduino Uno board and its most important parts. I'll explain them one by one. Let's start with the USB connector. To connect an Arduino to your computer, you just need a USB cable. The type of the USB cable depends on the type of Arduino board you're using. The Arduino Uno

---

5. http://arduino.cc/en/Main/ArduinoBoardLilyPad
6. http://lab.guilhermemartins.net/2009/05/06/paperduino-prints/

comes with the big standard-B plug, while other boards, such as the Arduino Leonardo or the Arduino Due, have the small micro-B plugs.

You can use the USB connection for various purposes:

- Upload new software to the board. (You'll see how to do this in *Compiling and Uploading Programs*, on page 19.)

- Communicate with the Arduino board and your computer. (You'll learn that in *Using Serial Ports*, on page 28.)

- Supply the Arduino board with power.

As an electronic device, the Arduino needs power. One way to power it is to connect it to a computer's USB port, but that isn't a good solution in some cases. Some projects don't necessarily need a computer, and it would be overkill to use a whole computer just to power the Arduino. Also, the USB port delivers only 5 volts, and sometimes you need more.

In these situations, the best solution usually is an AC adapter supplying 9 volts. (The recommended range is 7V to 12V.)[7] You need an adapter with a 2.1mm barrel tip and a positive center. (You don't need to understand what that means; just ask for it in your local electronics store.) Plug it into the Arduino's power jack, and it will start immediately, even if it

Figure 1—A typical AC adapter.

isn't connected to a computer. By the way, even if you connect the Arduino to a USB port, it will use the external power supply if available.

Please note that older versions of the Arduino board (Arduino NG and Diecimila) don't switch automatically between an external power supply and a USB supply. They come with a power selection jumper labeled *PWR_SEL*, and you manually have to set it to EXT or USB, respectively. (See Figure 2, *Older Arduinos have a power source selection jumper*, on page 8.)

Now you know two ways to supply the Arduino with power. But the Arduino isn't greedy and happily shares its power with other devices. At the bottom of the board shown in *Exploring the Arduino Board*, on page 6, you can see

7. http://www.arduino.cc/playground/Learning/WhatAdapter

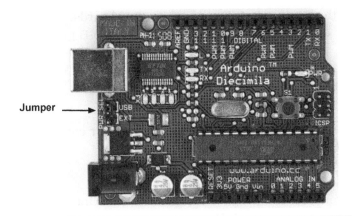

Figure 2—Older Arduinos have a power source selection jumper.

several sockets (sometimes I'll also call them *pins*, because internally they are connected to pins in the microcontroller) related to power supply:

- Using the pins labeled *3V3* and *5V*, you can power external devices connected to the Arduino with 3.3 volts or 5 volts.

- Two ground pins labeled *GND* allow your external devices to share a common ground with the Arduino.

- Some projects need to be portable, so they'll use a portable power supply, such as batteries. You connect an external power source, such as a battery pack, to the *Vin* and *GND* sockets.

If you connect an AC adapter to the Arduino's power jack, you can access the adapter's voltage through the *Vin* pin.

On the lower right of the board, you see six analog input pins named A0–A5. You can use them to connect analog sensors to the Arduino. They take sensor data and convert it into a number between 0 and 1023. In Chapter 5, *Sensing the World Around Us*, on page 77, we'll use them to connect a temperature sensor to the Arduino.

At the board's top are 14 digital IO pins named D0–D13. Depending on your needs, you can use these pins for both digital input and digital output, so you can read the state of a pushbutton or switch to turn on and off an LED. (We'll do this in *Working with Buttons*, on page 48.) Six of them (D3, D5, D6, D9, D10, and D11) can also act as analog output pins. In this mode, they convert values from 0 to 255 into analog voltages.

Analog and Digital Signals

Nearly all physical processes are analog. Whenever you observe a natural phenomenon, such as electricity or sound, you're actually receiving an analog signal. One of the most important properties of these analog signals is that they are continuous. For every given point in time, you can measure the strength of the signal, and in principle you could register even the tiniest variation of the signal.

But although we live in an analog world, we are also living in the digital age. When the first computers were built a few decades ago, people quickly realized that it's much easier to work with real-world information when it's represented as numbers and not as an analog signal, such as voltage or volume. For example, it's much easier to manipulate sounds using a computer when the sound waves are stored as a sequence of numbers. Every number in this sequence could represent the signal's loudness at a certain point in time.

So instead of storing the complete analog signal (as is done on records), we measure the signal only at certain points in time (see the following figure). We call this process *sampling*, and the values we store are called *samples*. The frequency we use to determine new samples is called the *sampling rate*. For an audio CD, the sampling rate is 44.1 kHz: we gather 44,100 samples per second.

We also have to limit the samples to a certain range. On an audio CD, every sample uses 16 bits. In the following figure, the range is denoted by two dashed lines, and we had to cut off a peak at the beginning of the signal.

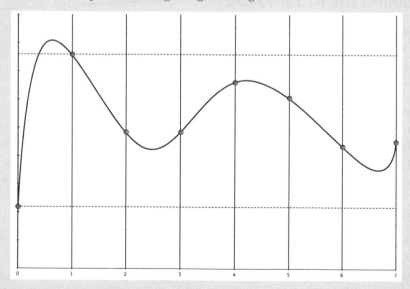

Although you can connect both analog and digital devices to the Arduino, you usually don't have to think much about it. The Arduino automatically performs the conversion from analog to digital for you.

All of these pins are connected to a microcontroller, which combines a CPU with some peripheral functions, such as IO channels. Many different types of microcontrollers are available, but the majority of Arduinos usually come with an ATmega328, an 8-bit microcontroller produced by a company named Atmel. Still there are Arduino models—for example, the Arduino Mega or the Arduino Due—that use more powerful microcontrollers.

Although modern computers load programs from a hard drive, microcontrollers usually have to be programmed. That means you have to load your software into the microcontroller via a cable, and once the program has been uploaded, it stays in the microcontroller until it gets overwritten with a new program. Whenever you supply power to the Arduino, the program currently stored in its microcontroller gets executed automatically. Sometimes you want the Arduino to start right from the beginning. With the reset button on the right side of the board, you can do that. If you press it, everything gets reinitialized, and the program stored in the microcontroller starts again. (We'll use it in *First Version of a Binary Die*, on page 45.)

On most Arduino boards you'll also find a couple of LEDs. You'll learn more about them in *Hello, World!*, on page 16.

Installing the Arduino IDE

To make it as easy as possible to get started with the Arduino, the developers have created a simple but useful integrated development environment (IDE). It runs on many different operating systems. Before you can create your first projects, you have to install it.

Important note: at the time of this writing, two different versions of the IDE are available (1.0.6 and 1.6.0).[8] Chances are good that the 1.0.x branch of the Arduino IDE will no longer be maintained in the future. So, you should use 1.6.x where possible and use 1.0.x only if you need to use libraries that don't work on 1.6.x yet. The following instructions refer to the 1.6.0 version.

Installing the Arduino IDE on Windows

The Arduino IDE runs on all the latest versions of Microsoft Windows, such as Windows 8.1 and Windows 7. The software comes in two flavors: as a Windows installer or as a self-contained zip archive. Check the Arduino's download page[9] for the latest version of either one.

---

8. There's even one more for the Arduino Galileo at https://communities.intel.com/docs/DOC-22226.
9. http://arduino.cc/en/Main/Software

If you have administrative privileges on your machine, use the installer because it installs not only the IDE, but also all the drivers you need. In this case you usually don't need anything else and can use the IDE right away.

If you don't have administrative privileges, download the zip archive and extract it to a location of your choice. Before you first start the IDE, you must install drivers for the Arduino's USB port. This process depends on the Arduino board you're using and on your flavor of Windows.

Installing the Drivers for Current Arduino Boards

To install drivers for recent boards, such as the Arduino Uno, plug the Arduino into a USB port first to start the automatic driver installation process. This process will likely fail, and you'll have to open the system Control Panel and start the Device Manager. (You can find it under System and Security.)[10] In the Ports (COM & LPT) section, you'll probably find an entry named Arduino Uno (COMxx).

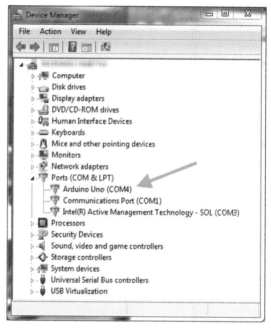

If you can't find that entry, search for Unknown Device in the Other Devices menu—Figure 3, *Sometimes the Arduino isn't recognized*, on page 12.

Right-click the entry belonging to the Arduino board and choose Update Driver Software. Select the Browse My Computer for Driver Software option. Go to the drivers folder of the archive you've extracted and select the arduino.inf file. (See Figure 4, *The content of the drivers folder*, on page 12.) In older versions of the IDE the file was named Arduino Uno.inf.

After you've installed the driver, you can start the Arduino IDE and work with the board. (If you're running Windows 8.x, you have to disable some protection mechanisms before you install the driver.)[11]

---

10. http://windows.microsoft.com/en-us/windows/open-device-manager#1TC=windows-7
11. https://learn.sparkfun.com/tutorials/installing-arduino-ide/windows

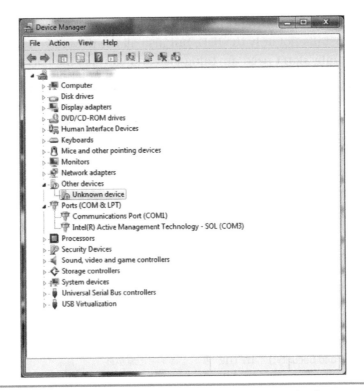

Figure 3—Sometimes the Arduino isn't recognized.

Figure 4—The content of the drivers folder

Installing the Drivers for Older Arduino Boards

Driver installation for older boards like the Duemilanove, Diecimila, or Nano is a bit different. Still, you have to plug in the board first.

On Windows Vista, driver installation usually happens automatically. Lean back and watch the hardware wizard's messages pass by until it says you can use the newly installed USB hardware.

Windows 8.x, Windows 7, and Windows XP may not find the drivers on Microsoft's update sites automatically. Sooner or later, the hardware wizard asks you for the path to the right drivers after you have told it to skip automatic driver installation from the Internet. Depending on your Arduino board, you have to point it to the right location in the Arduino installation directory—that is the drivers/FTDI USB Drivers directory.

After the drivers have been installed, you can start the Arduino executable from the archive's main directory by double-clicking it.

Please note that the USB drivers don't change as often as the Arduino IDE. Whenever you install a new version of the IDE, check whether you have to install new drivers, too. Usually it isn't necessary.

Installing the Arduino IDE on Mac OS X

The Arduino IDE is available as a zip file for Mac OS X.[12] The IDE depends on the Java Virtual Machine, and at the time of this writing it's available for Java 6 (recommended) and Java 7 (experimental). Download it, double-click it, and drag the Arduino icon to your Applications folder. If you hadn't installed Java already, Mac OS X will ask you for permission to install it.

If you're using an Arduino Uno or an Arduino Mega 2560, you are done and can start the IDE. Before you can use the IDE with an older Arduino, such as the Duemilanove, Diecimila, or Nano, you have to install drivers for the Arduino's serial port. You can find the latest version online.[13] Download the package for your platform (it usually has a name such as FTDIUSBSerialDriver_10_4_10_5_10_6.mpkg), double-click it, and follow the installation instructions on the screen.

When installing a new version of the Arduino IDE, you usually don't have to install the drivers again (only when more recent drivers are available).

---

12. http://arduino.cc/en/Main/Software
13. http://www.ftdichip.com/Drivers/VCP.htm

Installing the Arduino IDE on Linux

Installation procedures on Linux distributions are still not very homogeneous. The Arduino IDE works fine on nearly all modern Linux versions, but the installation process differs from distribution to distribution. Also, you often have to install additional software (the Java Virtual Machine, for example) that comes preinstalled with other operating systems.

It's best to check the official documentation[14] and look up the instructions for your preferred system.

Now that the drivers and IDE are installed, let's see what it has to offer.

Meeting the Arduino IDE

Compared to IDEs such as Eclipse, Xcode, or Microsoft Visual Studio, the Arduino IDE is simple. It mainly consists of an editor, a compiler, a loader, and a serial monitor. (See Figure 5, *The Arduino IDE is well organized*, on page 15 or, even better, start the IDE on your computer.)

It has no advanced features such as a debugger or code completion. You can change only a few preferences, and as a Java application it does not fully integrate into the Mac desktop. It's still usable, though, and even has decent support for project management.

The image that follows shows the IDE's toolbar, which gives you instant access to the functions you'll need most:

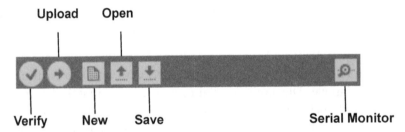

- With the Verify button, you can compile the program that's currently in the editor. So, in some respects, "Verify" is a misnomer, because clicking the button doesn't only verify the program syntactically, it also turns the program into a representation suitable for the Arduino board. You can invoke this function using the ⌘R keyboard shortcut on a Mac or Ctrl-R on all other systems.

---

14. http://www.arduino.cc/playground/Learning/Linux

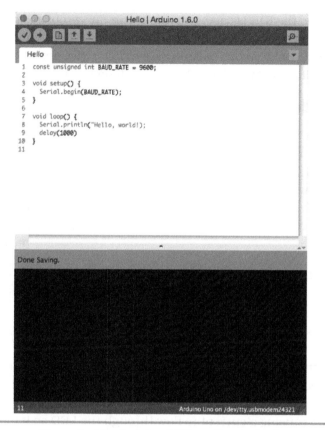

Figure 5—The Arduino IDE is well organized.

- When you click the Upload button (⌘U or Ctrl-U), the IDE compiles the current program and uploads it to the Arduino board you've chosen in the IDE's Tools > Serial Port menu. (You'll learn more about this in *Compiling and Uploading Programs*, on page 19.)

- The New button (⌘N or Ctrl-N) creates a new program by emptying the content of the current editor window. Before that happens, the IDE gives you the opportunity to store all unsaved changes.

- Open (⌘O or Ctrl-O) opens an existing program from the file system.

- Save (⌘S or Ctrl-S) saves the current program.

- The Arduino can communicate with a computer via a serial connection. Clicking the Serial Monitor button (⇧⌘M or Ctrl-Shift-M) opens a serial monitor window that allows you to watch the data sent by an Arduino and also to send data back.

Although using the IDE is easy, you might run into problems or want to look up something special. In such cases, take a look at the Help menu. It points to many useful resources at the Arduino's website that provide not only quick solutions to all typical problems, but also reference materials and tutorials.

Hello, World!

To get familiar with the IDE's most important features, we'll create a simple program that makes an light-emitting diode (LED) blink. An LED is a cheap and efficient light source, and the Arduino already comes with several LEDs. One LED shows whether the Arduino is currently powered, and two other LEDs blink when data is transmitted or received via a serial connection.

In our first little project, we'll make the Arduino's status LED blink. The status LED is connected to digital IO pin 13. Digital pins act as a kind of switch and can be in one of two states: HIGH or LOW. If set to HIGH, the output pin is set to 5 volts, causing a current to flow through the LED so it lights up. If set back to LOW, the current flow stops, and the LED turns off. You don't need to know exactly how electricity works at the moment, but if you're curious, take a look at *Current, Voltage, and Resistance*, on page 239.

Open the IDE and enter the following code in the editor:

```
Welcome/HelloWorld/HelloWorld.ino
const unsigned int LED_PIN = 13;
const unsigned int PAUSE = 500;

void setup() {
  pinMode(LED_PIN, OUTPUT);
}

void loop() {
  digitalWrite(LED_PIN, HIGH);
  delay(PAUSE);
  digitalWrite(LED_PIN, LOW);
  delay(PAUSE);
}
```

Let's see how this works and dissect the program's source code piece by piece. In the first two lines, we define two unsigned int constants using the const keyword. LED_PIN refers to the number of the digital IO pin we're using, and PAUSE defines the length of the blink period in milliseconds.

Every Arduino program needs a function named setup, and ours starts in line 4. A function definition always adheres to the following scheme:

```
<return value type> <function name> '(' <list of parameters> ')'
```

In our case the function's name is setup, and its return value type is void: it returns nothing. setup doesn't expect any arguments, so we left the parameter list empty. Before we continue with the dissection of our program, you should learn more about the Arduino's data types.

Arduino Data Types

Every piece of data you store in an Arduino program needs a type. Depending on your needs, you can choose from the following:

- boolean values take up one byte of memory and can be true or false.

- char variables take up one byte of memory and store numbers from -128 to 127. These numbers usually represent characters encoded in ASCII; that is, in the following example, c1 and c2 have the same value:

```
char c1 = 'A';
char c2 = 65;
```

Note that you have to use single quotes for char literals.

- byte variables use one byte and store values from 0 to 255.

- An int variable needs two bytes of memory; you can use it to store numbers from -32,768 to 32,767. Its unsigned equivalent unsigned int also consumes two bytes of memory but stores numbers from 0 to 65,535.

- For bigger numbers, use long. It consumes four bytes of memory and stores values from -2,147,483,648 to 2,147,483,647. The unsigned variant unsigned long also needs four bytes but ranges from 0 to 4,294,967,295.

- float and double are the same at the moment on most Arduino boards, and you can use these types for storing floating-point numbers. Both use four bytes of memory and are able to store values from -3.4028235E+38 to 3.4028235E+38. On the Arduino Due, double values are more accurate and occupy eight bytes of memory.

- You need void only for function declarations. It denotes that a function doesn't return a value.

- Arrays store collections of values having the same type:

```
int values[2];          // A two-element array
values[0] = 42;         // Set the first element
values[1] = -42;        // Set the second element
int more_values[] = { 42, -42 };
int first = more_values[0]; // first == 42
```

In the preceding example, the arrays values and more_values contain the same elements. We have used only two different ways of initializing an array. Note that the array index starts at 0, and keep in mind that uninitialized array elements contain unreliable values.

- A string is an array of char values. The Arduino environment supports the creation of strings with some syntactic sugar—all these declarations create strings with the same contents.

```
char string1[8] = { 'A', 'r', 'd', 'u', 'i', 'n', 'o', '\0' };
char string2[]  = "Arduino";
char string3[8] = "Arduino";
char string4[]  = { 65, 114, 100, 117, 105, 110, 111, 0 };
```

Strings should always be terminated by a zero byte. When you use double quotes to create a string, the zero byte will be added automatically. That's why you have to add one byte to the size of the corresponding array.

In *Emailing Directly from an Arduino*, on page 189, you'll learn how to use the Arduino's String class. It makes working with strings safer and more convenient.

Arduino Functions

Arduino calls setup once when it boots, and we use it in our "HelloWorld" example in *Hello, World!*, on page 16, for initializing the Arduino board and all the hardware we have connected to it. We use the pinMode method to turn pin 13 into an output pin. This ensures the pin can provide enough current to light up an LED. The default state of a pin is INPUT, and both INPUT and OUTPUT are predefined constants.[15]

Another mandatory function named loop begins in line 8. It contains the main logic of a program, and the Arduino calls it in an infinite loop. Our program's main logic has to turn on the LED connected to pin 13 first. To do this, we use digitalWrite and pass it the number of our pin and the constant HIGH. This

---

15. See http://arduino.cc/en/Tutorial/DigitalPins for the official documentation.

means the pin will output 5 volts until further notice, and the LED connected to the pin will light up.

The program then calls delay and waits for 500 milliseconds doing nothing. During this pause, pin 13 remains in HIGH state, and the LED continues to burn. The LED is eventually turned off when we set the pin's state back to LOW using digitalWrite again. We wait another 500 milliseconds, and then the loop function ends. The Arduino starts it again, and the LED blinks.

In the next section, you'll learn how to bring the program to life and transfer it to the Arduino.

Compiling and Uploading Programs

Before you compile and upload a program to the Arduino, you have to configure two things in the IDE: the type of Arduino you're using and the serial port your Arduino is connected to. Since Arduino 1.6.0, the IDE tries to identify all Arduino boards that are connected to your computer automatically. This feature works quite well, but it also fails sometimes. So, you need to learn how to determine the type of your Arduino board and the name of the serial port it is connected to.

Identifying the Arduino type is easy, because it is printed on the board. Popular types are Uno, Duemilanove, Diecimila, Nano, Mega, Mini, NG, BT, LilyPad, Pro, or Pro Mini. In some cases, you also have to check what microcontroller your Arduino uses—most have an ATmega328. You can find the microcontroller type printed on the microcontroller itself. When you have identified the exact type of your Arduino, choose it from the Tools > Board menu.

Now you have to choose the serial port your Arduino is connected to from the Tools > Serial Port menu. On Mac OS X, the name of the serial port usually starts with /dev/tty.usbserial or /dev/tty.usbmodem. (On my MacBook Pro, it's /dev/tty.usbmodem24321.) On Linux systems, it should be /dev/ttyUSB0, /dev/ttyUSB1, or something similar, depending on the number of USB ports your computer has.

On Windows systems, you have to use the Device Manager to find out the right serial port. In the Device Manager, look for USB Serial Port below the Ports (COM & LPT) menu entry. (See *Installing the Drivers for Current Arduino Boards*, on page 11) Usually the port is named COM1, COM2, or something similar.

After you have chosen the right serial port, click the Verify button, and you should see the following output in the IDE's message area (the Arduino IDE calls programs *sketches*):

```
Build options changed, rebuilding all

Sketch uses 1,030 bytes (3%) of program storage space. Maximum is 32,256 bytes.
Global variables use 9 bytes (0%) of dynamic memory, leaving 2,039 bytes for
  local variables. Maximum is 2,048 bytes.
```

This means the IDE has successfully compiled the source code into 1,030 bytes of machine code that we can upload to the Arduino. If you see an error message instead, check whether you have typed in the program correctly. (When in doubt, download the code from the book's website.)[16] Depending on the Arduino board you're using, the byte maximum may differ. On an Arduino Duemilanove, it's usually 14336, for example. Also, the size of the sketch might be slightly different depending on the version of the Arduino IDE.

Now click the Upload button, and after a few seconds, you should see the following output in the message area:

```
Sketch uses 1,030 bytes (3%) of program storage space. Maximum is 32,256 bytes.
Global variables use 9 bytes (0%) of dynamic memory, leaving 2,039 bytes for
  local variables. Maximum is 2,048 bytes.
```

This is exactly the same message we got after compiling the program, and it tells us that the 1,030 bytes of machine code were transferred successfully to the Arduino. In case of any errors, check whether you have selected the correct Arduino type and the correct serial port in the Tools menu.

During the upload process, the TX and RX LEDs will flicker for a few seconds. This is normal, and it happens whenever the Arduino and your computer communicate via the serial port. When the Arduino sends information, it turns on the TX LED. When it gets some bits, it turns on the RX LED. Because the communication is pretty fast, the LEDs start to flicker, and you cannot identify the transmission of a single byte. (If you can, you're probably an alien.)

As soon as the code has been transmitted completely, the Arduino executes it. In our case, this means the status LED starts to blink. It turns on for half a second, then it turns off for half a second, and so on.

---

16. http://www.pragprog.com/titles/msard2

The figure shows the activity on pin 13 while the program is running.

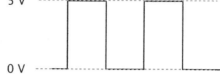

The pin starts in LOW state and doesn't output any current. We use digitalWrite to set it to HIGH and let it output 5 volts for 500 milliseconds. Finally, we set it back to LOW for 500 milliseconds and repeat the whole process.

That's it! You've created your first physical computing project. You've written some code, and it makes the world brighter. Your very own digital version of "fiat lux."[17]

Admittedly, the status LED doesn't look spectacular. In Chapter 3, *Building Binary Dice*, on page 39, we'll attach "real" LEDs to the Arduino.

You'll need the theory and skills you've learned in this chapter for nearly every Arduino project. In the next chapter, you'll see how to gain more control over LEDs, and you'll learn how to benefit from more advanced features of the Arduino IDE.

What If It Doesn't Work?

Choosing the wrong serial port or Arduino type is the most common mistake when doing the first experiments with an Arduino. If you get an error message such as "Serial port already in use" when uploading a sketch, check whether you have chosen the right serial port from the Tools > Serial Port menu. If you get messages such as "Problem uploading to board" or "Programmer is not responding," check whether you have chosen the right Arduino board from the Tools > Board menu.

Your Arduino programs, like all programs, will contain bugs. The compiler will detect typos and syntax errors. Figure 6, *The Arduino IDE explains syntax errors nicely*, on page 22 shows a typical error message. Instead of pinMode, we called pinMod, and because the compiler didn't find a function with that name, it stopped with an error message. The Arduino IDE highlights the line, showing the error with a yellow background, and prints a helpful error message.

Other bugs might be more subtle, and sometimes you have to carefully study your code and use some plain old debugging techniques. (In *Debug It! Find,*

---

17. http://en.wikipedia.org/wiki/Fiat_lux

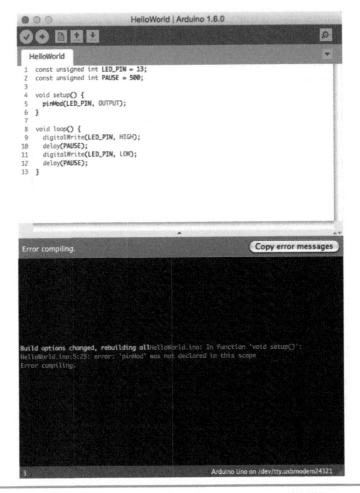

Figure 6—The Arduino IDE explains syntax errors nicely.

Repair, and Prevent Bugs in Your Code [But09], you can find plenty of useful advice on this topic.)

Exercises

- Try different blink patterns using more pauses and vary the pause length. (They don't necessarily all have to be the same.) Also, experiment with very short pauses that make the status LED blink at a high frequency. Can you explain the effect you're observing?

- Let the status LED output your name in Morse code.[18]

---

18. http://en.wikipedia.org/wiki/Morse_code

CHAPTER 2

Creating Bigger Projects with the Arduino

For simple applications, what you learned about the Arduino IDE in the preceding chapter is sufficient. But soon your projects will get more ambitious, and then it will be handy to split them into separate files that you can manage as a whole. So in this chapter, you'll learn how to stay in control of bigger projects with the Arduino IDE.

Usually, bigger projects need not only more software, but also more hardware—you will rarely use the Arduino board in isolation. You will use many more sensors than you might imagine, and you'll have to transmit the data they measure back to your computer. To exchange data with the Arduino, you'll use its serial port. This chapter explains everything you need to know about serial communication. To make things more tangible, you'll learn how to turn your computer into a very expensive light switch that lets you control an LED using the keyboard.

What You Need

To try this chapter's examples, you need only a few things:

1. An Arduino board, such as the Uno, Duemilanove, or Diecimila
2. A USB cable to connect the Arduino to your computer
3. An LED (optional)
4. A software serial terminal such as PuTTY (for Windows users) or screen for Linux and Mac OS X users (optional)

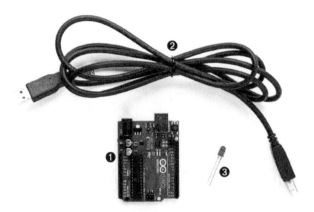

Managing Projects and Sketches

Modern software developers can choose from a variety of development tools that automate repetitive and boring tasks. That's also true for embedded systems like the Arduino. You can use integrated development environments (IDEs) to manage your programs, too. The most popular one has been created by the Arduino team.

The Arduino IDE manages all files belonging to your project. It also provides convenient access to all the tools you need to create the binaries that will run on your Arduino board. Conveniently, it does so unobtrusively.

Organizing all the files belonging to a project automatically is one of the most important features of an IDE. Under the hood, the Arduino IDE creates a directory for every new project, storing all the project's files in it. To add new files to a project, click the Tabs button on the right to open the Tabs pop-up menu, and then choose New Tab (Figure 7, *The Tabs menu in action*, on page 25). To add an existing file, use the Sketch > Add File menu item.

As you might have guessed from the names of the menu items, the Arduino IDE calls projects *sketches*. If you create a new sketch, the IDE gives it a name starting with sketch_. You can change the name whenever you like using the Save As command. If you do not save a sketch explicitly, the IDE stores it in a predefined folder you can look up in the Preferences menu. Whenever you get lost, you can check what folder the current sketch is in using the Sketch > Show Sketch Folder menu item.

Since Arduino 1.0, sketches have the extension ino. Older IDE versions used pde. Arduino 1.0 still supports pde files, but it will update them to ino when you save the sketch. (You can disable this behavior in the Preferences menu.)

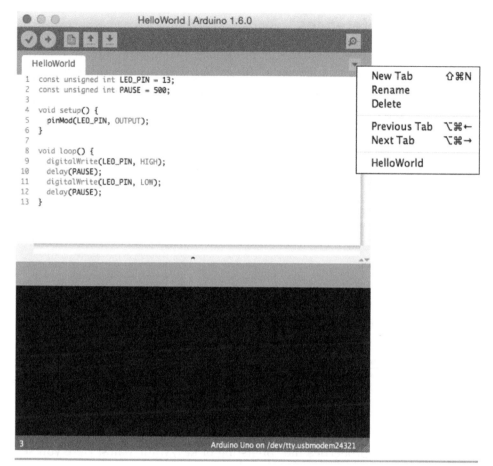

Figure 7—The Tabs menu in action

Not only can you create your own sketches using the IDE, but it also comes with many example sketches that you can use as a basis for your own experiments. Get to them via the File > Examples menu. Take some time to browse through them, even if you don't understand anything you see right now.

Note that many libraries come with examples, too. Whenever you install a new library (you'll learn how to do this later), you should have a look at the File > Examples menu again. It will probably contain new entries.

The Arduino IDE makes your life easier by choosing reasonable defaults for many settings. But it also allows you to change most of these settings, and you'll see how in the next section.

Changing Preferences

For your early projects, the IDE's defaults might be appropriate, but sooner or later you'll want to change some things. As you can see in the following figure, the IDE lets you change only a few preferences directly.

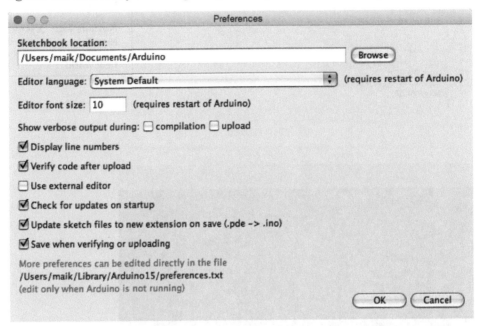

The dialog box refers to a file named preferences.txt containing more preferences. This file is a Java properties file consisting of key/value pairs. Here you see a few of them:

```
...
preproc.web_colors=true
editor.font=Monaco,plain,10
update.check=true
build.verbose=true
upload.verbose=true
...
```

Most of these properties control the user interface; that is, they change fonts, colors, and so on. But they can also change the application's behavior. You can enable more verbose output for operations such as compiling or uploading a sketch. Before Arduino 1.0, you had to edit preferences.txt and set both build.verbose and upload.verbose to true to achieve this. Today, you can change the verbose settings from the Preferences dialog box. Make sure that verbose output is enabled for compilation and upload. Also, it's helpful to enable the "Display line numbers" option.

Load the blinking LED sketch from Chapter 1, *Welcome to the Arduino*, on page 3, and compile it again. The output in the message panel should look like this:

Note that the IDE updates some of the Preferences values when it shuts down. So before you change any preferences directly in the preferences.txt file, you have to stop the Arduino IDE.

Now that you're familiar with the Arduino IDE, let's do some programming. We'll make the Arduino talk to the outside world.

The Arduino Programming Language

People sometimes get irritated when it comes to the language the Arduino gets programmed in. That's mainly because the typical sample sketches look as if they were written in a language that was exclusively designed for programming the Arduino. But that's not the case—it is plain old C++ (which implies that it supports C, too).

Most Arduino boards use an AVR microcontroller designed by a company named Atmel. (Atmel says that the name AVR doesn't stand for anything.) These microcontrollers are very popular, and many hardware projects use them. One reason for their popularity is the excellent tool chain that comes with them. Based on the GNU C++ compiler tools, it is optimized for generating code for AVR microcontrollers.

That means you feed C++ code to the compiler that is not translated into machine code for *your* computer, but for an AVR microcontroller. This technique is called *cross-compiling* and is the usual way to program embedded devices.

Using Serial Ports

Arduino makes many stand-alone applications—projects that do not involve any additional computers—possible. In such cases you need to connect the Arduino to a computer once to upload the software, and after that, it needs only a power supply. More often, people use the Arduino to enhance the capabilities of a computer using sensors or by giving access to additional hardware. Usually, you control external hardware via a serial port, so it is a good idea to learn how to communicate serially with the Arduino.

Although the standards for serial communication have changed over the past years (for example, we use USB today, and our computers no longer have RS232 connectors), the basic working principles remain the same. In the simplest case, we can connect two devices using only three wires: a common ground, a line for transmitting data (TX), and one for receiving data (RX).

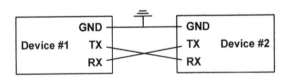

Serial communication might sound old-school, but it's still the preferred way for hardware devices to communicate. The S in USB stands for "serial"—and when was the last time you saw a parallel port? (Perhaps this is a good time to clean up the garage and throw out that old PC you wanted to turn into a media center someday....)

For uploading software, the Arduino has a serial port, and you can use it to connect the Arduino to other devices, too. (In *Compiling and Uploading Programs*, on page 19, you learned how to look up the serial port your Arduino is connected to.) In this section, you'll use the serial port to control Arduino's status LED using your computer's keyboard. The LED should be turned on when you press 1, and it should be turned off when you press 2. Here's all the code you need:

Welcome/LedSwitch/LedSwitch.ino
```
const unsigned int LED_PIN = 13;
const unsigned int BAUD_RATE = 9600;

void setup() {
  pinMode(LED_PIN, OUTPUT);
  Serial.begin(BAUD_RATE);
}

void loop() {
  if (Serial.available() > 0) {
    int command = Serial.read();
    if (command == '1') {
      digitalWrite(LED_PIN, HIGH);
      Serial.println("LED on");
    } else if (command == '2') {
      digitalWrite(LED_PIN, LOW);
      Serial.println("LED off");
    } else {
      Serial.print("Unknown command: ");
      Serial.println(command);
    }
  }
}
```

As in our previous examples, we define a constant for the pin the LED is connected to and set it to OUTPUT mode in the setup function. In line 6, we initialize the serial port using the begin function of the Serial class, passing a baud rate of 9600. (You can learn what a baud rate is in *Learning More About Serial Communication*, on page 253.) That's all we need to send and receive data via the serial port in our program.

So, let's read and interpret the data. The loop function starts by calling Serial's available method in line 10. available returns the number of bytes waiting on the serial port. If any data is available, we read it using Serial.read. read returns the first byte of incoming data if data is available and -1 otherwise.

If the byte we have read represents the character 1, we switch on the LED and send back the message "LED on" over the serial port. We use Serial.println, which adds a carriage return character (ASCII code 13) followed by a newline (ASCII code 10) to the text.

If we receive the character 2, we switch off the LED. If we receive an unsupported command, we send back a corresponding message and the command we didn't understand. Serial.print works exactly like Serial.println, but it doesn't add carriage return and newline characters to the message.

Let's see how the program works in practice. Compile it, upload it to your Arduino, and then switch to the serial monitor. At first glance, nothing happens. That's because we haven't sent a command to the Arduino yet. Make sure the drop-down menu at the bottom of the serial monitor is set to *No line ending*. Enter a 1 in the text box, and then click the Send button. Two things should happen now: the LED is switched on, and the message "LED on" appears in the serial monitor window (as shown in the following image). We are controlling an LED using our computer's keyboard!

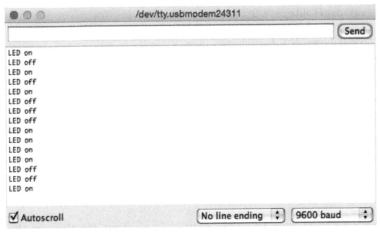

Play around with the commands 1 and 2, and also observe what happens when you send an unknown command. If you type in an uppercase *A*, the Arduino will send back the message "Unknown command: 65." The number 65 is the ASCII code of the letter *A*, and the Arduino outputs the data it got in its most basic form. That's the default behavior of Serial's print method, and you can change it by passing a format specifier to your function calls. To see the effect, replace line 20 with the following statements:

```
Serial.println(command, DEC);
Serial.println(command, HEX);
Serial.println(command, OCT);
Serial.println(command, BIN);
Serial.write(command);
Serial.println();
```

The output looks as follows when you send the character *A* again:

```
Unknown command: 65
41
101
1000001
A
```

Depending on the format specifier, Serial.println automatically converts a byte into another representation. DEC outputs a byte as a decimal number, HEX as a hexadecimal number, and so on. Note that such an operation usually changes the length of the data that get transmitted. The binary representation of the single byte 65 needs 7 bytes, because it contains seven characters. Also note that we have to use Serial.write instead of Serial.println to output a character representation of our command value. Former versions of the Arduino IDE had a BYTE modifier for this purpose, but it has been removed in Arduino 1.0.

Numbering Systems

It's an evolutionary accident that 10 is the basis for our numbering system. If we had only four fingers on each hand, it'd be probably eight, and we'd probably have invented computers a few centuries earlier.

For thousands of years, people have used denominational number systems, and we represent a number like 4711 as follows:

$$4\times10^3 + 7\times10^2 + 1\times10^1 + 1\times10^0$$

This makes arithmetic operations very convenient. But when working with computers that interpret only binary numbers, it's often good to use numbering systems based on the numbers 2 (binary), 8 (octal), or 16 (hexadecimal).

The decimal number 147 can be represented in octal and hexadecimal as:

$$2\times8^2 \quad + \quad 2\times8^1 \quad + \quad 3\times8^0 \quad = \quad 0223$$
$$9\times16^1 \quad + \quad 3\times16^0 \quad = \quad 0x93$$

In Arduino programs, you can define literals for all these numbering systems:

```
int decimal = 147;
int binary = B10010011;
int octal = 0223;
int hexadecimal = 0x93;
```

Binary numbers start with a B character, octal numbers with a 0, and hexadecimal numbers with 0x. Note that you can use binary literals only for numbers from 0 to 255.

Using Different Serial Terminals

For trivial applications, the IDE's serial monitor is sufficient, but you cannot easily combine it with other applications, and it lacks some features. That means you should have an alternative serial terminal to send data, and you can find plenty of them for every operating system.

Serial Terminals for Windows

PuTTY[1] is an excellent choice for Windows users. It is free, and it comes as an executable that doesn't even have to be installed. The following figure shows how to configure it for communication on a serial port.

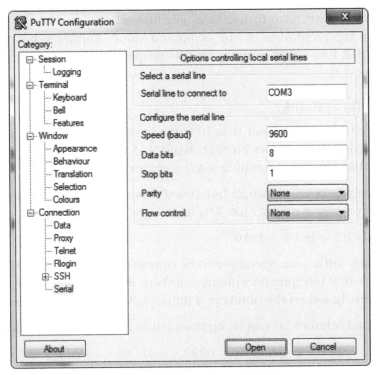

After you have configured PuTTY, you can open a serial connection to the Arduino. The following screenshot shows the corresponding dialog box. Click Open, and you'll see an empty terminal window.

---

1. http://www.chiark.greenend.org.uk/~sgtatham/putty/

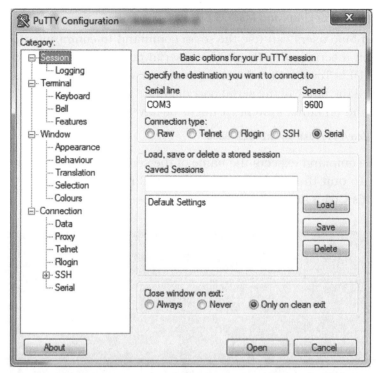

Now press 1 and 2 a few times to switch on and off the LED.

Serial Terminals for Linux and Mac OS X

Linux and Mac users can use the screen command to communicate with the Arduino on a serial port. Check which serial port the Arduino is connected to in the IDE's Tools > Board menu. Then run a command like this (with an older board the name of the serial port might be something like /dev/tty.usbserial-A9007LUY, and on Linux systems it might be /dev/ttyUSB1 or something similar):

```
$ screen /dev/tty.usbmodem24321 9600
```

The screen command expects the name of the serial port and the baud rate to be used. To quit the screen command, press Ctrl-a followed by k. (On some systems it's Ctrl-a followed by Ctrl-k.)

We can now communicate with the Arduino, and this has great implications: whatever is controlled by the Arduino can also be controlled by your computer, and vice versa. Switching LEDs on and off isn't too spectacular, but try to imagine what's possible now. You could move robots, automate your home, or create interactive games.

Here are some more important facts about serial communication:

• The Arduino Uno's serial receive buffer can hold up to 64 bytes. When sending large amounts of data at high speed, you have to synchronize sender and receiver to prevent data loss. Usually, the receiver sends an acknowledgment to the sender whenever it is ready to consume a new chunk of data.

- You can control many devices using serial communication, but the regular Arduino has only one serial port. If you need more, take a look at the Arduino Due, which has four serial ports.[2]

- A Universal Asynchronous Receiver/Transmitter (UART)[3] device supports serial communication on the Arduino. This device handles serial communication while the CPU takes care of other tasks. This greatly improves the system's overall performance. The UART uses digital pins 0 (RX) and 1 (TX), which means you cannot use them for other purposes when communicating on the serial port. If you need them, you can disable serial communication using Serial.end().

- With the SoftwareSerial[4] library, you can use any digital pin for serial communication. It has some limitations, but it is sufficient for most applications.

In this chapter, you saw how to communicate with the Arduino using the serial port, which opens the door to a whole new world of physical computing projects. (See *Learning More About Serial Communication*, on page 253, for more details about serial communication.) In the next chapters, you'll learn how to gather interesting facts about the real world using sensors, and you'll learn how to change the real world by moving objects. Serial communication is the basis for letting you control all of these actions using the Arduino and your PC.

What If It Doesn't Work?

If anything goes wrong with the examples in this chapter, you should take a look at *What If It Doesn't Work?*, on page 21, first. If you still run into problems, it may be because of some issues with serial communication. You might have set the wrong baud rate; in the following figure, you can see what happens in such a case.

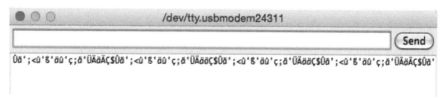

---

2.   http://arduino.cc/en/Main/arduinoBoardDue
3.   http://en.wikipedia.org/wiki/UART
4.   http://www.arduino.cc/en/Reference/SoftwareSerial

Make sure that the baud rate you've set in your call to Serial.begin matches the baud rate in the serial monitor.

Exercises

- Add new commands to the sample program. The command 3 could make the LED blink for a while.

- Try to make the commands more readable; that is, instead of 1, use the command "on", and instead of 2, use "off".

If you have problems solving these exercises, read Chapter 4, *Building a Morse Code Generator Library*, on page 61.

Part II

Eleven Arduino Projects

CHAPTER 3

Building Binary Dice

Things will really start to get interesting now that you've learned the basics of Arduino development. You now have the skills to create your first complex, stand-alone projects. After you've worked through this chapter, you'll know how to work with LEDs, buttons, breadboards, and resistors. Combining these parts with an Arduino gives you nearly endless opportunities for new and cool projects.

Our first project will be creating an electronic die. While regular dice display their results using one to six dots, ours will use LEDs instead. For our first experiments, a single LED was sufficient, but for the dice we need more than one. You need to connect several external LEDs to the Arduino. Because you cannot attach them all directly to the Arduino, you'll learn how to work with breadboards. Also, you need a button that rolls the dice, so you'll learn how to work with pushbuttons, too. To connect pushbuttons and LEDs to the Arduino, you need another important electronic part: the resistor. At the end of the chapter, you'll have many new tools in your toolbox.

What You Need

1. A half-size breadboard
2. Three LEDs (for the exercises you'll need additional LEDs)
3. Two 10kΩ resistors (see *Current, Voltage, and Resistance*, on page 239, to learn more about resistors)
4. Three 1kΩ resistors
5. Two pushbuttons
6. Some wires of different lengths
7. An Arduino board, such as the Uno, Duemilanove, or Diecimila
8. A USB cable to connect the Arduino to your computer

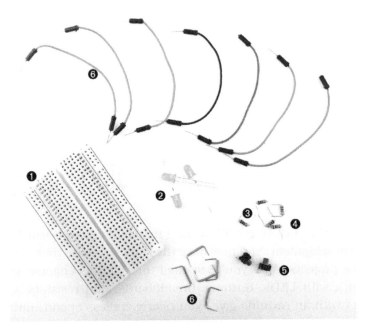

Working with Breadboards

Connecting parts directly to the Arduino is an option only in the simplest cases. Usually, you'll prototype your projects on a breadboard that you connect to the Arduino. A breadboard is like a circuit board, but you don't have to solder parts to it; instead, you simply plug them in.

All breadboards work the same way. They have a lot of sockets you can use for plugging in through-hole parts or wires. That alone wouldn't be a big deal, but the sockets are connected in a special way. Figure 9, *How sockets on a breadboard are connected*, on page 41 shows how.

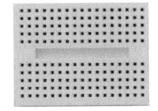

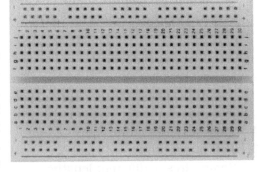

Figure 8— Breadboards come in various types and sizes—the picture shows two.

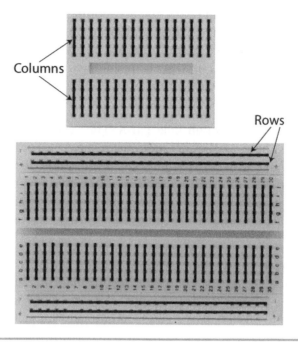

Figure 9—How sockets on a breadboard are connected

As you can see, most sockets are connected in columns. If one socket of a column is connected to a power supply, then automatically all the other sockets in this column are powered, too. On the bigger board in the photo, you can also see four rows of connected sockets. This is convenient for bigger circuits. Usually, you connect one row to your power supply and one to the ground. This way, you can distribute power and ground to any point on the board. Note that on some breadboards there are gaps between the sockets on a single row. On such breadboards you have to bridge the gaps using a wire if needed.

Now let's see how to put parts on a breadboard.

Using an LED on a Breadboard

Up to now, we used the status LED that is installed on the Arduino board. This LED is nice for testing purposes, but it's only sufficient for trivial electronics projects. Also, it's very small and not very bright, so it's a good idea to get some additional LEDs and learn how to connect them to the Arduino. It's really easy.

We won't use the same type of LEDs that are mounted on the Arduino board. They are surface-mounted devices (SMD) that are difficult to handle. At the beginning of your electronics career, you will rarely work with SMD parts, because for most of them you need special equipment and a lot of experience. They save costs as soon as you start mass production of an electronic device, but pure hobbyists won't need them often.

The LEDs we need are through-hole parts. They are named through-hole parts because they are mounted to a circuit board through holes. That's why they usually have one or more long wires. First you put the wires through holes in a printed circuit board. Then you usually bend, solder, and cut them to attach the part to the board. Where available, you can also plug them into sockets as you have them on the Arduino or on breadboards.

In this section you'll learn how to work with LEDs on a breadboard. Figure 10, *Connecting an LED on a breadboard to the Arduino*, on page 43 shows our circuit. It consists of an Arduino, a breadboard, an LED, three wires, and a 1kΩ resistor. (More on that part in a few minutes.) Connect the Arduino to the breadboard using two wires. Connect pin 12 with the ninth column of the breadboard, and connect the ground pin with the tenth column. This automatically connects all sockets in column 9 to pin 12 and all sockets in column 10 to the ground. This choice of columns was arbitrary; you could've used other columns instead.

Plug the LED's negative connector (the shorter one) into column 10 and its positive connector into column 9. When assembling an electronics project, parts fall into two categories: those you can mount any way you like and those that need a special direction. An LED has two connectors: an anode (positive) and a cathode (negative). It's easy to mix them up, and my science teacher taught me the following mnemonic: the *ca*thode is *ne*gative. It's also easy to remember what the negative connector of an LED is: it is shorter, minus, less than. If you are a more positive person, then think of the anode as being bigger, plus, more. You can alternatively identify an LED's connectors using its case. On the negative side the case is flat, while it's round on the positive side.

When you plug parts or wires into a breadboard, you have to press them firmly until they slip in. You might need more than one try, especially on new boards, and it's often useful to shorten the connectors with a wire cutter before plugging them into the breadboard. Make sure you can still identify the negative and positive connectors after you've shortened them. Shorten

Figure 10—Connecting an LED on a breadboard to the Arduino

the negative one a bit more. Also wear safety glasses to protect your eyes when you're cutting the connectors!

The things we've done up until now have been straightforward. That is, in principle we have only extended the Arduino's ground pin and its IO pin number 12. Why do we have to add a resistor, and what is a resistor? A resistor limits the amount of current that flows through an electric connection. In our case, it protects the LED from consuming too much power, because this would destroy the LED. You always have to use a resistor when powering an LED! In *Current, Voltage, and Resistance*, on page 239, you can learn more about resistors and their color bands. The following image shows a resistor in various stages: unprocessed, bent, and cut. (See *Learning How to Use a Wire Cutter*, on page 243, to learn how to use a wire cutter.)

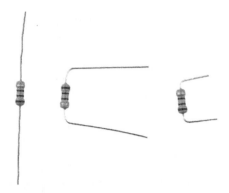

We don't want to fiddle around too much with the connectors, so we build the circuit as shown in the following figure. That is, we use both sides of the breadboard by connecting them with a short wire. Note that the resistor bridges the sides, too.

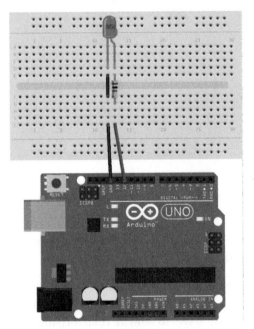

To make the LED blink, we can use the same sketch we used in *Meeting the Arduino IDE*, on page 14. We only have to set LED_PIN to 12 instead of 13:

BinaryDice/Blink/Blink.ino

```
const unsigned int LED_PIN = 12;
const unsigned int PAUSE = 500;

void setup() {
  pinMode(LED_PIN, OUTPUT);
}

void loop() {
  digitalWrite(LED_PIN, HIGH);
  delay(PAUSE);
  digitalWrite(LED_PIN, LOW);
  delay(PAUSE);
}
```

We've built a strong foundation for our project, and in the next section we'll build upon it.

First Version of a Binary Die

You're certainly familiar with a regular die displaying results in a range from one to six. To emulate such a die exactly with an electronic device, you'd need seven LEDs and some fairly complicated business logic. We'll take a shortcut and display the result of a die roll in binary.

For a binary die, we need only three LEDs to represent the current result. We turn the result into a binary number, and for every bit that is set, we light up a corresponding LED. The following diagram shows how the die results are mapped to LEDs. (A black triangle stands for a shining LED.)

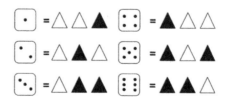

We already know how to control a single LED on a breadboard. Controlling three LEDs is similar and requires only more wires, LEDs, 1kΩ resistors, and pins. Figure 11, *A first working version of our binary die*, on page 46 shows the first working version of a binary die.

The most important difference is the common ground. When you need ground for a single LED, you can connect it to the LED directly. But we need ground for three LEDs now, so we'll use the breadboard's rows for the first time. Connect the row marked with a hyphen (-) to the Arduino's ground pin, and

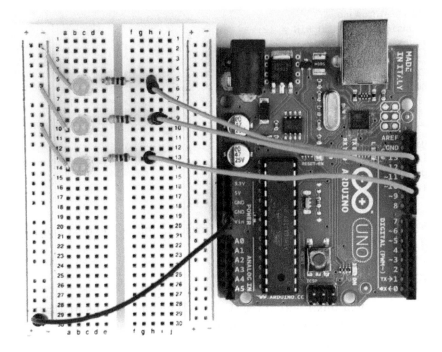

Figure 11—A first working version of our binary die

all sockets in this row will work as ground pins, too. Then you can connect this row's sockets to the LEDs using short wires.

Everything else in this circuit should look familiar, because we only had to clone the basic LED circuit from the previous section three times. Note that we have connected the three LEDs to pins 10, 11, and 12. The only thing missing is some software:

BinaryDice/BinaryDice/BinaryDice.ino

```
Line 1  const unsigned int LED_BIT0 = 12;
     -  const unsigned int LED_BIT1 = 11;
     -  const unsigned int LED_BIT2 = 10;
     -
     5  void setup() {
     -    pinMode(LED_BIT0, OUTPUT);
     -    pinMode(LED_BIT1, OUTPUT);
     -    pinMode(LED_BIT2, OUTPUT);
     -
    10    randomSeed(analogRead(A0));
     -    long result = random(1, 7);
     -    output_result(result);
     -  }
```

```
15  void loop() {
 -  }
 -
 -  void output_result(const long result) {
 -    digitalWrite(LED_BIT0, result & B001);
20    digitalWrite(LED_BIT1, result & B010);
 -    digitalWrite(LED_BIT2, result & B100);
 -  }
```

This is all the code we need to implement the first version of a binary die. As usual, we define some constants for the output pins the LEDs are connected to. In the setup function, we set all the pins into OUTPUT mode. For the die, we need random numbers in the range from one to six. The random function returns random numbers in a specified range using a pseudorandom number generator. In line 10, we initialize the generator with some noise we read from analog input pin A0. (See *Generating Random Numbers*, on page 48, to learn why we have to do that.) You might wonder where the constant A0 is from. The Arduino IDE defines constants for all analog pins named A0, A1, and so on. Then we actually generate a new random number between one and six and output it using the output_result function. (The seven in the call to random is correct, because it expects the upper limit plus one.)

The function output_result takes a number and outputs its lower three bits by switching on or off our three LEDs accordingly. Here we use the & operator and binary literals. The & operator takes two numbers and combines them bitwise. When two corresponding bits are 1, the result of the & operator is 1, too. Otherwise, it is 0. The B prefix allows you to put binary numbers directly into your source code. For example, B11 is the same as 3.

You might have noticed that the loop function was left empty, and you might wonder how such a die works. It's pretty simple: whenever you restart the Arduino, it outputs a new number, and to roll the die again, you have to press the reset button.

Compile the code, upload it to the Arduino, and play with your binary die. You have mastered your first advanced electronics project! Enjoy it for a moment!

Whenever you want to see a new result, you have to reset the Arduino. That's probably the most pragmatic user interface you can build, and for a first prototype, this is okay. But it's more elegant to control the dice with your own button. That's what we'll do in the next section.

Generating Random Numbers

Some computing problems are surprisingly difficult, and creating good random numbers is one of them. After all, one of the most important properties of a computer is deterministic behavior. Still, we often need—at least seemingly—random behavior for a variety of purposes, ranging from games to cryptographic algorithms.

The most popular approach (used in Arduino's random() function) is to create pseudo-random numbers.[a] They seem to be random, but they actually are the result of a formula. Different kinds of algorithms exist, but usually each new pseudorandom number is calculated from its predecessors. This implies that you need an initialization value to create the first random number of the sequence. This initialization value is called a *random seed*, and to create different sequences of pseudorandom numbers, you have to use different random seeds.

Creating pseudorandom numbers is cheap, but if you know the algorithm and the random seed, you can easily predict them. So, you shouldn't use them for cryptographic purposes.

In the real world, you can find countless random processes, and with the Arduino, it's easy to measure them to create real random numbers. Often it's sufficient to read some random noise from analog pin 0 and pass it as the random seed to the random-Seed() function. You can also use this noise to create real random numbers; there is even a library for that purpose.[b]

If you need strong random numbers, the Arduino is a perfect device for creating them. You can find many projects that observe natural processes solely to create random numbers. One of them watches an hourglass using the Arduino.[c]

a.   http://en.wikipedia.org/wiki/Pseudo-random_numbers
b.   http://code.google.com/p/tinkerit/wiki/TrueRandom
c.   http://www.circuitlake.com/usb-hourglass-sand-timer.html

Working with Buttons

In this section you'll learn how pushbuttons work in principle and how you can use them with an Arduino. We'll start small and build a circuit that uses a pushbutton to control a single LED.

What exactly is a pushbutton? The following figure shows three views of a typical pushbutton. It has four connectors that fit perfectly on a breadboard (at least after you have straightened them with a pair of pliers). Two opposite pins connect when the button is pushed; otherwise, they are disconnected.

The following picture shows a simple circuit using a pushbutton. Connect pin 7 (chosen completely arbitrarily) to the pushbutton, and connect the pushbutton via a 10kΩ resistor to ground. Then connect the 5-volt power supply to the other pin of the button. Make sure the pushbutton's orientation is right. Its connected pins have to bridge the gap of the breadboard.

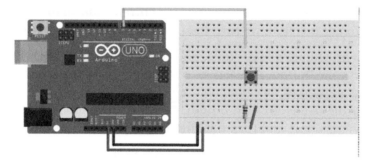

All in all, this approach seems straightforward, but why do we need a resistor again? The problem is that we expect the pushbutton to return a default value (LOW) in case it isn't pressed. But when the button isn't pressed, it would be directly connected to ground and would flicker because of static and interference. Only a little bit of current flows through the resistor, and this helps prevent random fluctuations in the voltage at the input pin.

When the button is pressed, there will still be 5 volts at the Arduino's digital pin, but when the button isn't pressed, it will cleanly read the connection to ground. We call this a *pull-down resistor*; a *pull-up resistor* works exactly the other way around. That is, you have to connect the Arduino's signal pin to power through the pushbutton and connect the other pin of the pushbutton to ground using a resistor.

Now that we've eliminated all this ugly unstable real-world behavior, we can return to the stable and comforting world of software development. The following program checks whether a pushbutton is pressed and lights an LED accordingly:

BinaryDice/SimpleButton/SimpleButton.ino
```
const unsigned int BUTTON_PIN = 7;
const unsigned int LED_PIN    = 13;

void setup() {
  pinMode(LED_PIN, OUTPUT);
  pinMode(BUTTON_PIN, INPUT);
}
void loop() {
  const int BUTTON_STATE = digitalRead(BUTTON_PIN);

  if (BUTTON_STATE == HIGH)
    digitalWrite(LED_PIN, HIGH);
  else
    digitalWrite(LED_PIN, LOW);
}
```

We connect the button to pin 7 and the LED to pin 13 and initialize those pins in the setup function. In loop, we read the current state of the pin connected to the button. If it is HIGH, we turn the LED on. Otherwise, we turn it off.

Upload the program to the Arduino, and you'll see that the LED is on as long as you press the button. As soon as you release the button, the LED turns off. This is pretty cool, because now we nearly have everything we need to control our die using our own button. But before we proceed, we'll slightly enhance our example and turn the button into a real light switch.

To build a light switch, we start with the simplest possible solution. Do not change the current circuit, and upload the following program to your Arduino:

BinaryDice/UnreliableSwitch/UnreliableSwitch.ino
```
Line 1  const unsigned int BUTTON_PIN = 7;
   -    const unsigned int LED_PIN    = 13;
   -
   -    void setup() {
   5      pinMode(LED_PIN, OUTPUT);
   -      pinMode(BUTTON_PIN, INPUT);
   -    }
   -    int led_state = LOW;
   -    void loop() {
   10     const int CURRENT_BUTTON_STATE = digitalRead(BUTTON_PIN);
   -      if (CURRENT_BUTTON_STATE == HIGH) {
   -        if (led_state == LOW)
   -          led_state = HIGH;
   -        else
   15         led_state = LOW;
   -        digitalWrite(LED_PIN, led_state);
   -      }
   -    }
```

We begin with the usual pin constants, and in setup we set the modes of the pins we use. In line 8, we define a global variable named led_state to store the current state of our LED. It will be LOW when the LED is off and HIGH otherwise. In loop, we check the button's current state. When we press the button, its state switches to HIGH, and we toggle the content of led_state. That is, if led_state was HIGH, we set it to LOW, and vice versa. At the end, we set the physical LED's state to our current software state accordingly.

Our solution is really simple, but unfortunately, it doesn't work. Play around with it, and you'll quickly notice some annoying behavior. If you press the button, the LED sometimes will turn on and then off immediately. Also, if you release it, the LED will often remain in a more or less arbitrary state; that is, sometimes it will be on and sometimes off.

The problem is that the Arduino executes the loop method over and over again. Although the Arduino's CPU is comparatively slow, this would happen quite often—regardless of whether we are currently pressing the button. But if you press it and keep it pressed, its state will constantly be HIGH, and you'd constantly toggle the LED's state (because this happens so fast, it seems like the LED is constantly on). When you release the button, the LED is in a more or less arbitrary state.

To improve the situation, we have to store not only the LED's current state, but also the pushbutton's previous state:

BinaryDice/MoreReliableSwitch/MoreReliableSwitch.ino

```
const unsigned int BUTTON_PIN = 7;
const unsigned int LED_PIN    = 13;

void setup() {
  pinMode(LED_PIN, OUTPUT);
  pinMode(BUTTON_PIN, INPUT);
}
int old_button_state = LOW;
int led_state = LOW;

void loop() {
  const int CURRENT_BUTTON_STATE = digitalRead(BUTTON_PIN);
  if (CURRENT_BUTTON_STATE != old_button_state && CURRENT_BUTTON_STATE == HIGH)  {
    if (led_state == LOW)
      led_state = HIGH;
    else
      led_state = LOW;
    digitalWrite(LED_PIN, led_state);
  }
  old_button_state = CURRENT_BUTTON_STATE;
}
```

After initializing the button and LED pins, we declare two variables: old_button_state stores the previous state of our pushbutton, and led_state stores the LED's current state. Both can be either HIGH or LOW.

In the loop function, we still have to read the current button state, but now we not only check whether it is HIGH, but we also check whether it has changed since the last time we read it. Only when both conditions are met do we toggle the LED's state. So, we no longer turn the LED on and off over and over again as long as the button is pressed. At the end of our program, we have to store the button's current state in old_button_state.

Upload the new version, and you'll see that this solution works much better than our old one. But you will still find some cases when the button doesn't behave fully as expected. Problems mainly occur in the moment you release the button.

These problems occur because the mechanical buttons bounce for a few milliseconds when you press them. In the following figure, you can see a typical signal produced by a mechanical button. Right after you have pressed the button, it doesn't emit a clear signal. To overcome this effect, you have to *debounce* the button. It's usually sufficient to wait a short period of time until the button's signal stabilizes. Debouncing ensures that the input pin reacts only once to a push of the button:

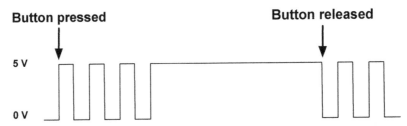

In addition to debouncing, we still have to store the current state of the LED in a variable. Here's how to do that:

BinaryDice/DebounceButton/DebounceButton.ino
```
const unsigned int BUTTON_PIN = 7;
const unsigned int LED_PIN    = 13;
void setup() {
  pinMode(LED_PIN, OUTPUT);
  pinMode(BUTTON_PIN, INPUT);
}

int old_button_state = LOW;
int led_state = LOW;

void loop() {
```

```
 -     const int CURRENT_BUTTON_STATE = digitalRead(BUTTON_PIN);
 -     if (CURRENT_BUTTON_STATE != old_button_state &&
 -         CURRENT_BUTTON_STATE == HIGH)
15     {
 -       if (led_state == LOW)
 -         led_state = HIGH;
 -       else
 -         led_state = LOW;
20       digitalWrite(LED_PIN, led_state);
 -       delay(50);
 -     }
 -     old_button_state = CURRENT_BUTTON_STATE;
 - }
```

This final version of our LED switch differs from the previous one in only a single line: to debounce the button, we wait for 50 milliseconds in line 21 before we enter the main loop again. For the moment this solution is sufficient, but you'll learn about an even better one in a few minutes.

That's everything you need to know about pushbuttons for now. In the next section, we'll use two buttons to turn our binary die into a real game.

Adding Your Own Button

Now that you know how to work with pushbuttons, you no longer have to abuse the Arduino's reset button to control the die. You can add your own pushbutton instead. As Figure 12, *Our binary die with its own start button*, on page 54, we need to change our current circuit only slightly. Actually, we don't have to change the existing parts at all; we only need to add some things. First, we plug a button into the breadboard and connect it to pin 7. Then we connect the button to the ground via a 10kΩ resistor and use a small piece of wire to connect it to the 5-volt pin.

That's all the hardware we need. Here's the corresponding software:

BinaryDice/DiceWithButton/DiceWithButton.ino
```
const unsigned int LED_BIT0 = 12;
const unsigned int LED_BIT1 = 11;
const unsigned int LED_BIT2 = 10;
const unsigned int BUTTON_PIN = 7;

void setup() {
  pinMode(LED_BIT0, OUTPUT);
  pinMode(LED_BIT1, OUTPUT);
  pinMode(LED_BIT2, OUTPUT);
  pinMode(BUTTON_PIN, INPUT);
  randomSeed(analogRead(A0));
}
```

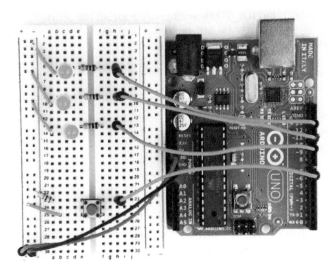

Figure 12—Our binary die with its own start button

```
int current_value = 0;
int old_value = 0;
void loop() {
  current_value = digitalRead(BUTTON_PIN);
  if (current_value != old_value && current_value == HIGH) {
    output_result(random(1, 7));
    delay(50);
  }
  old_value = current_value;
}
void output_result(const long result) {
  digitalWrite(LED_BIT0, result & B001);
  digitalWrite(LED_BIT1, result & B010);
  digitalWrite(LED_BIT2, result & B100);
}
```

That's a perfect merge of the original code and the code needed to control a debounced button. As usual, we initialize all pins we use: three output pins for the LEDs and one input pin for the button. We also initialize the random seed, and in the loop function we wait for new button presses. Whenever the button gets pressed, we roll the die and output the result using the LEDs. We've replaced the reset button with our own!

Now that you know how easy it is to add a pushbutton, we'll add another one in the next section to turn our simple die into a game.

Building a Dice Game

Turning our rudimentary die into a full-blown game requires adding another pushbutton. With the first one we can still roll the die, and with the second one we can program a guess. When we roll the die again and the current result equals our guess, the three LEDs on the die will blink. Otherwise, they will remain dark.

To enter a guess, press the guess button the correct number of times. If you think the next result will be a 3, press the guess button three times and then press the start button.

To add another button to the circuit, do exactly the same thing as you did for the first one. Figure 13, *Our binary die now has a guess button*, on page 56 shows that we have added yet another button circuit to the breadboard. This time we've connected it to pin 5.

Now we need some code to control the new button. You might be tempted to copy it from the previous program—after all, we copied the hardware design, right? In the real world, some redundancy is totally acceptable, because you actually need two physical buttons, even if they are the same in principle. In the world of software, redundancy is a no-go, though, because it quickly leads to maintenance hell. You should always make sure that every important piece of information is represented only once in your program. Instead of copying numbers, you should use constants. Instead of copying code, you should use functions or classes. This way your code will become more compact and more readable. As a bonus, it will be much easier to change your code, because when you copy code you have to remember all the places you've copied it to when you have to make a change. If you've isolated the code in a single place, you have to change it only once.

So, we won't copy our debounce logic, but we'll use the Bounce2 library[1] that was written for this purpose. Download the library[2] and unpack its contents into ~/Documents/Arduino/libraries (on a Mac) or My Documents\Arduino\libraries (on a Windows machine). Usually that's all you have to do, but it never hurts to read the installation instructions and documentation on the web page.

Now that's all done, our dice game is complete. Here's the code of the final version:

---

1.   https://github.com/thomasfredericks/Bounce-Arduino-Wiring
2.   https://github.com/thomasfredericks/Bounce-Arduino-Wiring/archive/master.zip

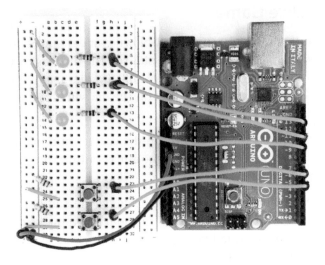

Figure 13—Our binary die now has a guess button.

BinaryDice/DiceGame/DiceGame.ino
```
Line 1  #include <Bounce2.h>
     -  const unsigned int LED_BIT0 = 12;
     -  const unsigned int LED_BIT1 = 11;
     -  const unsigned int LED_BIT2 = 10;
     5  const unsigned int GUESS_BUTTON_PIN = 5;
     -  const unsigned int START_BUTTON_PIN = 7;
     -  const unsigned int BAUD_RATE = 9600;
     -  const unsigned int DEBOUNCE_DELAY = 20;
     -
    10  int guess = 0;
     -  Bounce start_button;
     -  Bounce guess_button;
     -
     -  void setup() {
    15    pinMode(LED_BIT0, OUTPUT);
     -    pinMode(LED_BIT1, OUTPUT);
     -    pinMode(LED_BIT2, OUTPUT);
     -    pinMode(START_BUTTON_PIN, INPUT);
     -    pinMode(GUESS_BUTTON_PIN, INPUT);
    20    start_button.attach(START_BUTTON_PIN);
     -    start_button.interval(DEBOUNCE_DELAY);
     -    guess_button.attach(GUESS_BUTTON_PIN);
     -    guess_button.interval(DEBOUNCE_DELAY);
     -    randomSeed(analogRead(A0));
    25    Serial.begin(BAUD_RATE);
     -  }
     -
```

```
    -   void loop() {
    -     handle_guess_button();
   30     handle_start_button();
    -   }
    -
    -   void handle_guess_button() {
    -     if (guess_button.update()) {
   35       if (guess_button.read() == HIGH) {
    -         guess = (guess % 6) + 1;
    -         output_result(guess);
    -         Serial.print("Guess: ");
    -         Serial.println(guess);
   40       }
    -     }
    -   }
    -
    -   void handle_start_button() {
   45     if (start_button.update()) {
    -       if (start_button.read() == HIGH) {
    -         const int result = random(1, 7);
    -         output_result(result);
    -         Serial.print("Result: ");
   50         Serial.println(result);
    -         if (guess > 0) {
    -           if (result == guess) {
    -             Serial.println("You win!");
    -             hooray();
   55           } else {
    -             Serial.println("You lose!");
    -           }
    -         }
    -         delay(2000);
   60         guess = 0;
    -       }
    -     }
    -   }
    -   void output_result(const long result) {
   65     digitalWrite(LED_BIT0, result & B001);
    -     digitalWrite(LED_BIT1, result & B010);
    -     digitalWrite(LED_BIT2, result & B100);
    -   }
    -
   70  void hooray() {
    -     for (unsigned int i = 0; i < 3; i++) {
    -       output_result(7);
    -       delay(500);
    -       output_result(0);
   75       delay(500);
    -     }
    -   }
```

Admittedly that's a lot of code, but you know most of it already, and the new parts are fairly easy. In the first line, we include the Bounce2 library we'll use later to debounce our two buttons. Then we define constants for the pins we use, and we define the variable guess that will hold the player's current guess.

The Bounce2 library declares a class named Bounce, and you have to create a Bounce object for every button you want to debounce. That's what happens in lines 11 and 12.

In the setup method, we initialize all our pins and set the random seed. We also initialize the serial port, because we'll output some debug messages. In lines 20 to 23, we initialize the two Bounce objects. The attach method connects a Bounce object to a certain pin. With the interval method you can set a button's debounce delay in milliseconds.

Our loop function has been reduced to two function calls. One is responsible for dealing with guess button pushes, and the other one handles pushes of the start button. In handle_guess_button, we use the Bounce class for the first time. To determine the current state of our guess_button object, we have to call its update method. Afterward, we read its current status using the read method.

If the button was pressed, its state is set to HIGH, and we increment the guess variable. To make sure that the guess is always in the range between 1 and 6, we use the modulus operator (%) in line 36. This operator divides two values and returns the remainder. For 6, it returns values between 0 and 5, because when you divide a number by 6, the remainder is always between 0 and 5. Add 1 to the result, and you get values between 1 and 6. Finally, we output the current guess using the three LEDs, and we also print it to the serial port.

The handling of the start button in handle_start_button works exactly the same as the handling of the guess button. When the start button is pressed, we calculate a new result and output it on the serial port. Then we check whether the user has entered a guess (guess is greater than zero in this case) and whether the user has guessed the correct result. In either case, we print a message to the serial port, and if the user guessed right, we also call the hooray method. hooray lets all three LEDs blink several times.

At the end of the method, we wait for two seconds until the game starts again, and we reset the current guess to zero.

After you've uploaded the software to the Arduino, start the IDE's serial monitor. It will print the current value of the guess variable whenever you press the guess button. Press the start button, and the new result appears. In the following figure, you can see a typical output of our binary die.

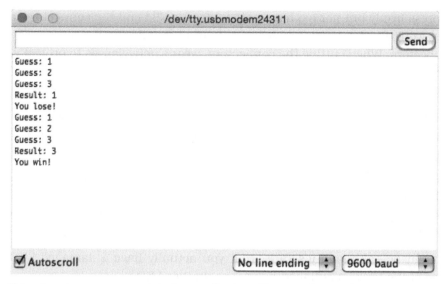

In this chapter, you completed your first really complex Arduino project. You needed a breadboard, LEDs, buttons, resistors, and wires, and you wrote a nontrivial piece of software to make all the hardware come to life.

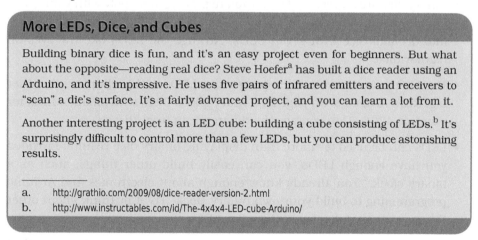

More LEDs, Dice, and Cubes

Building binary dice is fun, and it's an easy project even for beginners. But what about the opposite—reading real dice? Steve Hoefer[a] has built a dice reader using an Arduino, and it's impressive. He uses five pairs of infrared emitters and receivers to "scan" a die's surface. It's a fairly advanced project, and you can learn a lot from it.

Another interesting project is an LED cube: building a cube consisting of LEDs.[b] It's surprisingly difficult to control more than a few LEDs, but you can produce astonishing results.

---

a. http://grathio.com/2009/08/dice-reader-version-2.html
b. http://www.instructables.com/id/The-4x4x4-LED-cube-Arduino/

In the next chapter, we'll write an even more sophisticated program for generating Morse code. You'll also learn how to create your own Arduino libraries that you can easily share with the rest of the world.

What If It Doesn't Work?

Don't panic! A lot of things will probably go wrong when you work with breadboards for the first time. The biggest problem usually is that you didn't connect parts correctly. It takes some time to find the right technique for plugging LEDs, wires, resistors, and buttons into the breadboard. You have to press firmly but not too hard—otherwise, you'll bend the connectors, and they won't fit. It's usually easier to plug in parts after you've shortened the connectors. When cutting the connectors, wear safety glasses to protect your eyes!

While fiddling around with the parts, don't forget that some of them—LEDs, for example—need a certain direction. Pushbuttons are candidates for potential problems, too. Take a close look at the pushbuttons on page 48 and make sure that you've mounted them in the right direction.

Even simple things, such as ordinary wires, can lead to problems, especially if they aren't the right length. If a wire is too short and might potentially slip out of its socket, replace it immediately. Wires are too cheap to waste your valuable time with unnecessary and annoying debugging sessions.

It might be—although it's rare—that you actually have a damaged LED. If none of the tricks mentioned helps, try another LED.

Exercises

- Binary dice are all very well when you're playing Monopoly with your geeky friends, but most people prefer more familiar dice. Try turning binary dice into decimal dice with seven LEDs. Arrange the LEDs like the eyes on regular dice.

- The 1kΩ resistors we used to protect our LEDs in this chapter are rather big. Read *Resistors*, on page 241, and replace them with smaller ones, for example 470Ω. Can you see the difference in brightness?

- LEDs can be used for more than displaying binary dice results. Provided you have enough LEDs, you can easily build other things, such as a binary clock.[3] You already know enough about electronics and Arduino programming to build your own binary clock. Try it or think about other things you could display using a few LEDs.

---

3. http://www.instructables.com/id/My-Arduino-Binary-Clock/

CHAPTER 4

Building a Morse Code Generator Library

You now know enough about the Arduino development environment and about blinking LEDs to start a bigger project. In this chapter, we'll develop a Morse code generator that reads text from the serial port and outputs it as light signals using an LED.

By building this project, you'll deepen your understanding of serial communication between the Arduino and your computer. You'll also learn a lot about the typical Arduino development process: how to use existing libraries and how to structure bigger projects into your own libraries. At the end, you'll be able to create a library that is ready for publishing on the Internet.

What You Need

1. An Arduino board such as the Uno, Duemilanove, or Diecimila
2. A USB cable to connect the Arduino to your computer
3. A speaker or a buzzer (optional)

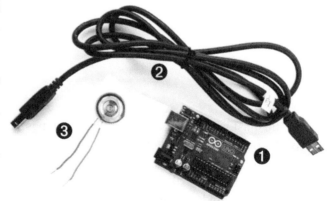

Learning the Basics of Morse Code

Morse code was invented to turn text into sounds.[1] In principle, it works like a character set encoding, such as ASCII. But while ASCII encodes characters as numbers, in Morse code they're sequences of dots and dashes (also called *dits* and *dahs*). Dits are shorter in length than dahs. An *A* is encoded as · − and − − · · is *Z*.

Morse code also specifies a timing scheme that defines the length of the dits and dahs. It specifies how long the pauses between symbols and words have to be. The base unit of Morse code is the length of a dit, and a dah is as long as three dits. You insert a pause of one dit between two symbols, and you separate two letters by three dits. You insert a pause of seven dits between two words.

To transmit a message encoded in Morse code, you need a way to emit signals of different lengths. The classic approach is to use sounds, but we will use an LED that is turned on and off for varying periods of time. Sailors still transmit Morse code using blinking lights.

Let's implement a Morse code generator!

Building a Morse Code Generator

The main part of our library will be a C++ class named Telegraph. In this section, we'll define its interface, but we will start with a new sketch that looks as follows:

TelegraphLibrary/TelegraphLibrary.ino
```
void setup() {
}

void loop() {
}
```

This is the most minimalistic Arduino program possible. It doesn't do anything except define all mandatory functions, even if they are empty. We do this so we can compile our work in progress from time to time and check whether there are any syntactical errors. Save the sketch as TelegraphLibrary, and the IDE will create a folder named TelegraphLibrary and a file named TelegraphLibrary.ino in it. All the files and directories we need for our library will be stored in the TelegraphLibrary folder.

---

1. http://en.wikipedia.org/wiki/Morse_Code

Now open a new tab, and when asked for a filename, enter telegraph.h. Yes, we will create a good old C header file. (To be precise, it will even be a C++ header file.)

TelegraphLibrary/telegraph.h
```
#ifndef __TELEGRAPH_H__
#define __TELEGRAPH_H__

class Telegraph {
public:
  Telegraph(const int output_pin, const int dit_length);
  void send_message(const char* message);

private:
  void dit();
  void dah();
  void output_code(const char* code);
  void output_symbol(const int length);

  int _output_pin;
  int _dit_length;
  int _dah_length;
};

#endif
```

Ah, obviously object-oriented programming is not only for the big CPUs anymore! This is an interface description of a Telegraph class that you could use in your next enterprise project (provided that you need to transmit some information as Morse code, that is).

We start with the classic double-include prevention mechanism; that is, the body of the header file defines a preprocessor macro named _TELEGRAPH_H_. We wrap the body (that contains this definition) in an #ifndef so that the body is only compiled if the macro has not been defined. That way, you can include the header as many times as you want, and the body will be compiled only once.

The interface of the Telegraph class consists of a public part that users of the class have access to and a private part that only members of the class can use. In the public part, you find two things: a constructor that creates new Telegraph objects and a method named send_message that sends a message by emitting it as Morse code. In your applications, you can use the class as follows:

```
Telegraph telegraph(13, 200);
telegraph.send_message("Hello, world!");
```

In the first line, we create a new Telegraph object that communicates on pin 13 and emits dits that are 200 milliseconds long. Then we emit the message "Hello, world!" as Morse code. This way, we are able to send whatever message we want, and we can change easily the pin and the length of a dit.

Now that we have defined the interface, we will implement it.

Fleshing Out the Morse Code Generator's Interface

Declaring interfaces is important, but it's as important to implement them. Create a new tab and enter the filename telegraph.cpp.

This is the right place to explain why we've used TelegraphLibrary and not Telegraph as the sketch' name, even though it'd be a more natural choice. The reason is that the Arduino IDE turns every sketch (ending with .ino) into a C++ file (ending with .cpp). For a sketch named Telegraph.ino it generates a C++ file named Telegraph.cpp. In a case-insensitive file system, this conflicts with a file named telegraph.cpp, and it leads to some strange error messages.

Enter the following code now in the newly created tab:

TelegraphLibrary/telegraph.cpp
```
#include <ctype.h>
#include <Arduino.h>
#include "telegraph.h"

const char* LETTERS[] = {
  ".-",    "-...",  "-.-.",  "-..",   ".",     // A-E
  "..-.",  "--.",   "....",  "..",    ".---",  // F-J
  "-.-",   ".-..",  "--",    "-.",    "---",   // K-O
  ".--.",  "--.-",  ".-.",   "...",   "-",     // P-T
  "..-",   "...-",  ".--",   "-..-",  "-.--",  // U-Y
  "--.."                                       // Z
};

const char* DIGITS[] = {
  "-----", ".----", "..---", "...--", // 0-3
  "....-", ".....", "-....", "--...", // 4-7
  "---..", "----."                    // 8-9
};
```

Like most C++ programs, ours imports some libraries first. Because we need functions such as toupper later, we include ctype.h, and we have to include telegraph.h to make our class declaration and its corresponding function declarations available. But what is Arduino.h good for?

Until now we haven't thought about where constants such as HIGH, LOW, or OUTPUT came from. They are defined in several header files that come with the

Arduino IDE, and you can find them in the hardware/arduino/cores/arduino directory of the IDE. Have a look at Arduino.h (in older Arduino versions this file was named WProgram.h). It contains all the constants we have used so far and many more. It also declares many useful macros and the Arduino's most basic functions.

When you edit regular sketches, you don't have to worry about including any standard header files, because the IDE does it automatically behind the scenes. As soon as you create more complex projects that contain "real" C++ code, you have to manage everything yourself. You have to explicitly import all the libraries you need, even for basic stuff such as the Arduino constants.

After importing all necessary header files, we define two string arrays named LETTERS and DIGITS. They contain the Morse code for all letters and digits, and we'll use them later to translate regular text into Morse code. Before we do that, we define the constructor that is responsible for creating and initializing new Telegraph objects:

TelegraphLibrary/telegraph.cpp
```
Telegraph::Telegraph(const int output_pin, const int dit_length) {
  _output_pin = output_pin;
  _dit_length = dit_length;
  _dah_length = dit_length * 3;
  pinMode(_output_pin, OUTPUT);
}
```

The constructor expects two arguments: the number of the pin the Morse code should be sent to and the length of a dit measured in milliseconds. Then it stores these values in corresponding instance variables, calculates the correct length of a dah, and turns the communication pin into an output pin.

You've probably noticed that all private instance variables start with an underscore. I like that convention personally, but it isn't enforced by C++ or the Arduino IDE.

Outputting Morse Code Symbols

After everything has been initialized, we can start to output Morse code symbols. We use several small helper methods to make our code as readable as possible:

TelegraphLibrary/telegraph.cpp
```
void Telegraph::output_code(const char* code) {
  const unsigned int code_length = strlen(code);

  for (unsigned int i = 0; i < code_length; i++) {
    if (code[i] == '.')
```

```
      dit();
    else
      dah();
    if (i != code_length - 1)
      delay(_dit_length);
  }
}

void Telegraph::dit() {
  Serial.print(".");
  output_symbol(_dit_length);
}

void Telegraph::dah() {
  Serial.print("-");
  output_symbol(_dah_length);
}
void Telegraph::output_symbol(const int length) {
  digitalWrite(_output_pin, HIGH);
  delay(length);
  digitalWrite(_output_pin, LOW);
}
```

The function output_code takes a Morse code sequence consisting of dots and dashes and turns it into calls to dit and dah. The dit and dah methods then print a dot or a dash to the serial port and delegate the rest of the work to output_symbol, passing it the length of the Morse code symbol to be emitted. output_symbol sets the output pin to HIGH for the length of the symbol, and then it sets it back to LOW. Everything works exactly as described in the Morse code timing scheme, and only the implementation of send_message is missing:

TelegraphLibrary/telegraph.cpp
```
Line 1  void Telegraph::send_message(const char* message) {
   -      for (unsigned int i = 0; i < strlen(message); i++) {
   -        const char current_char = toupper(message[i]);
   -        if (isalpha(current_char)) {
   5          output_code(LETTERS[current_char - 'A']);
   -          delay(_dah_length);
   -        } else if (isdigit(current_char)) {
   -          output_code(DIGITS[current_char - '0']);
   -          delay(_dah_length);
  10        } else if (current_char == ' ') {
   -          Serial.print(" ");
   -          delay(_dit_length * 7);
   -        }
   -      }
  15      Serial.println();
   -    }
```

send_message outputs a message character by character in a loop. In line 3, we turn the current character into uppercase, because lowercase characters are not defined in Morse code (that's why you can't implement a chat client using Morse code). Then we check whether the current character is a letter using C's isalpha function. If it is, we use the character to determine its Morse code representation that is stored in the LETTERS array. To do that, we use an old trick: in the ASCII table, all letters (and digits) appear in the correct order—that is, A=65, B=66, and so on. To transform the current character into an index for the LETTERS array, we have to subtract 65 (or 'A') from its ASCII code. When we have determined the correct Morse code, we pass it to output_symbol and delay the program for the length of a dah afterward.

The algorithm works exactly the same for outputting digits; we only have to index the DIGITS array instead of the LETTERS array, and we have to subtract the ASCII value of the character '0'.

In line 10, we check whether we received a blank character. If yes, we print a blank character to the serial port and wait for seven dits. All other characters are ignored: we only process letters, digits, and blanks. At the end of the method, we send a newline character to the serial port to mark the end of the message.

Installing and Using the Telegraph Class

Our Telegraph class is complete, and we should now create some example sketches that actually use it. This is important for two reasons: we can test our library code, and for users of our class it's good documentation for how to use it.

The Arduino IDE looks for libraries in two places: in its global libraries folder relative to its installation directory and in the user's local sketchbook directory. During development, it's best to use the local sketchbook directory. You can find its location in the IDE's Preferences (see Figure 14, *Find the sketchbook location in the Preferences*, on page 68). Create a new directory named libraries in the sketchbook directory.

To make the Telegraph class available, create a Telegraph subfolder in the libraries folder. Then copy telegraph.h and telegraph.cpp to the new libraries/Telegraph folder. (Do not copy TelegraphLibrary.ino.) Restart the IDE.

Let's start with the mother of all programs: "Hello, world!" Create a new sketch named HelloWorld and enter the following code:

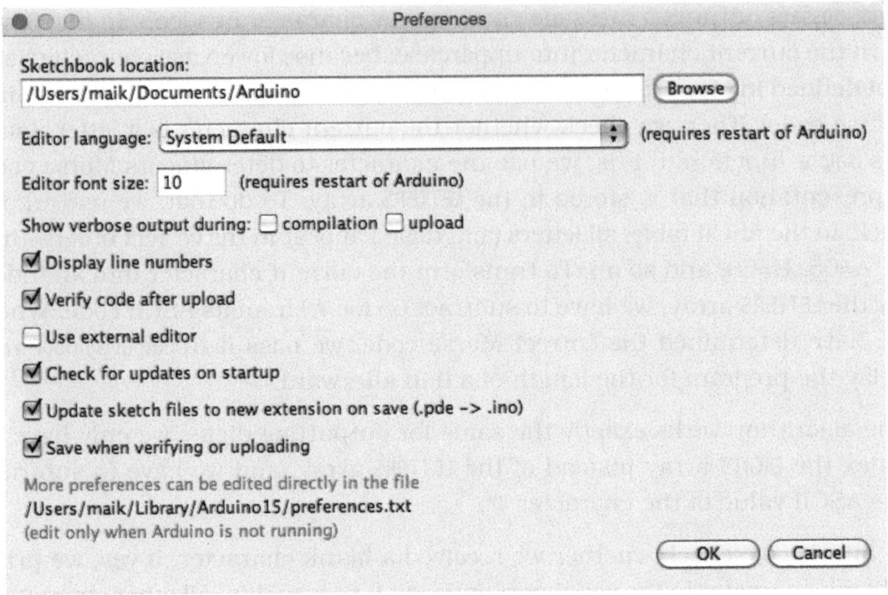

Figure 14—Find the sketchbook location in the Preferences.

TelegraphLibrary/examples/HelloWorld/HelloWorld.ino
```
#include "telegraph.h"
const unsigned int BAUD_RATE  = 9600;
const unsigned int OUTPUT_PIN = 13;
const unsigned int DIT_LENGTH = 200;

Telegraph telegraph(OUTPUT_PIN, DIT_LENGTH);

void setup() {
  Serial.begin(BAUD_RATE);
}
void loop() {
  telegraph.send_message("Hello, world!");
  delay(5000);
}
```

This sketch emits the string "Hello, world!" as Morse code every five seconds. To achieve this, we include the definition of our Telegraph class, and we define constants for the pin our LED is connected to and for the length of our dits. Then we create a global Telegraph object and an empty setup function. In loop, we then invoke send_message on our Telegraph instance every five seconds.

When you compile this sketch, the Arduino IDE automatically compiles the telegraph library, too. If you forgot to copy the library files to the libraries/Telegraph folder, you'll get an error message such as "Telegraph does not name a type."

If you've copied the files but made any syntactical errors, you'll also be notified now. If you have to correct some errors, make sure you change your original source code files. After you've fixed the errors, copy the files to the libraries folder again, and don't forget to restart the IDE.

Turning a static string into Morse code is nice, but wouldn't it be great if our program could work for arbitrary strings? So, let's add a more sophisticated example. This time, we'll write code that reads messages from the serial port and feeds them into a Telegraph instance.

Create a new sketch named MorseCodeGenerator and enter the following code:

TelegraphLibrary/examples/MorseCodeGenerator/MorseCodeGenerator.ino
```
#include "telegraph.h"

const unsigned int OUTPUT_PIN = 13;
const unsigned int DIT_LENGTH = 200;
const unsigned int MAX_MESSAGE_LEN = 128;
const unsigned int BAUD_RATE = 9600;
const char NEWLINE = '\n';

char message_text[MAX_MESSAGE_LEN];
int index = 0;

Telegraph telegraph(OUTPUT_PIN, DIT_LENGTH);

void setup() {
  Serial.begin(BAUD_RATE);
}

void loop() {
  if (Serial.available() > 0) {
    int current_char = Serial.read();
    if (current_char == NEWLINE || index == MAX_MESSAGE_LEN - 1) {
      message_text[index] = 0;
      index = 0;
      telegraph.send_message(message_text);
    } else {
      message_text[index++] = current_char;
    }
  }
}
```

Again, we include the header file of the Telegraph class, and as usual we define some constants: OUTPUT_PIN defines the pin our LED is connected to, and DIT_LENGTH contains the length of a dit measured in milliseconds. NEWLINE is set to the ASCII code of the newline character. We need it to determine the end of the message to be emitted as Morse code. Finally, we set MAX_MESSAGE_LEN to the maximum length of the messages we are able to send.

Next we define three global variables: message_text is a character buffer that gets filled with the data we receive on the serial port. index keeps track of our current position in the buffer, and telegraph is the Telegraph object we'll use to convert a message into "blinkenlights."[2]

setup initializes the serial port, and in loop we check whether new data has arrived, calling Serial.available. We read the next byte if new data is available, and we check whether it is a newline character or whether it is the last byte that fits into our character buffer. In both cases, we set the last byte of message_text to 0, because strings in C/C++ are null-terminated. We also reset index so we can read the next message, and finally we send the message using our telegraph. In all other cases, we add the latest byte to the current message text and move on.

You should compile and upload the program now. Open the serial monitor and choose "Newline" from the line endings drop-down menu at the bottom of the window. With this option set, the serial monitor will automatically append a newline character to every line it sends to the Arduino. Enter a message such as your name, click the Send button, and see how the Arduino turns it into light. In the following figure, you can see what happens when you enter my name.

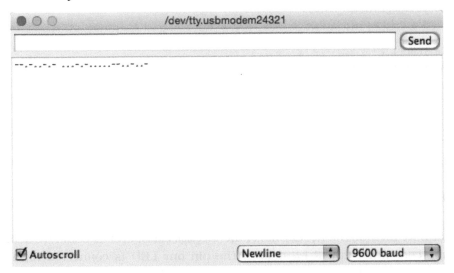

Because we've encapsulated the whole Morse code logic in the Telegraph class, our main program is short and concise. Creating software for embedded devices doesn't mean we can't benefit from the advantages of object-oriented programming.

Still, we have some minor things to do to turn our project into a first-class library. Read more about it in the next section.

Publishing Your Own Library

One of the nice features of the Arduino IDE is its syntax coloring. Class names, function names, variables, and so on all have different colors in the editor. This makes it much easier to read source code, and it's possible to add syntax coloring for libraries. You only have to add a file named keywords.txt to your project:

TelegraphLibrary/keywords.txt
```
# Syntax-coloring for the telegraph library

Telegraph       KEYWORD1
send_message    KEYWORD2
```

Blank lines and lines starting with a # character will be ignored. The remaining lines contain the name of one of the library's members and the member's type. Separate them with a tab character. Classes have the type KEYWORD1, while functions have the type KEYWORD2. For constants, use LITERAL1.

To enable syntax coloring for the telegraph library, copy keywords.txt to the libraries/Telegraph folder and restart the IDE. Now the name of the Telegraph class will be orange, and send_message will be brown.

Before you finally publish your library, you should add a few more things:

- Store all example sketches in a folder named examples and copy it to the libraries/Telegraph folder. Every example sketch should get its own subdirectory within that folder.

- Choose a license for your project and copy its terms into a file named LICENSE.[3] You might think this is over the top for many libraries, but it will give your potential audience confidence.

- Add installation instructions and documentation. Usually, users expect to find documentation in a file named README, and they will look for installation instructions in a file named INSTALL. You should try to install

---

3. At http://www.opensource.org/, you can find a lot of background information and many standard licenses.

your library on as many operating systems as possible and provide installation instructions for all of them.

• Publish your project on GitHub,[4] Google Code,[5] or any other popular sites for hosting open-source projects. This way, other people can contribute easily to your project.

After you've done all this, your libraries/Telegraph folder should look like this:

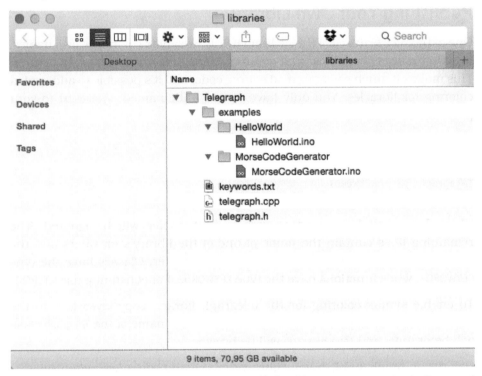

Finally, create a zip archive containing all the files in your project. On most operating systems, it's sufficient to right-click the directory in the Explorer, Finder, or whatever you are using and turn the directory into a zip archive. On Linux systems and Macs, you can also use one of the following command-line statements to create an archive:

```
maik> zip -r Telegraph Telegraph
maik> tar cfvz Telegraph.tar.gz Telegraph
```

4.   http://github.com
5.   https://code.google.com/

The first command creates a file named Telegraph.zip, and the second one creates Telegraph.tar.gz. Both formats are widespread, and it's best to offer them both for download.

Although you have to perform a lot of manual file operations, it's still easy to create an Arduino library. So, there's no excuse: whenever you think you've built something cool, make it publicly available.

Note that the structure for library projects has slightly changed in the Arduino IDE 1.5.x and later.[6] The biggest change is that all library source files (telegraph.h and telegraph.cpp, in our case) now have to be stored in a separate folder named src. The new specification is backwards compatible—that is, old libraries will still work in the new IDE.

Until now, our projects have communicated with the outside world using LEDs (output) and pushbuttons (input). In the next chapter, you'll learn how to work with more sophisticated input devices, such as ultrasonic sensors. You'll also learn how to visualize data that an Arduino sends to programs running on your computer.

What If It Doesn't Work?

The Arduino IDE has a strong opinion on naming files and directories, and it was built for creating sketches, not libraries. So, you need to perform a few manual file operations to get everything into the right place. In the figure on the preceding page, you can see the final directory layout. If you have more than one version of the Arduino IDE installed, make sure you're using the correct libraries folder.

Remember that you have to restart the IDE often. Whenever you change one of the files belonging to your library, restart the IDE.

If syntax coloring doesn't work, make sure your keywords file is actually named keywords.txt. Double-check whether you have separated all objects and type specifiers by a tab character. Restart your IDE!

Exercises

- Morse code not only supports letters and digits, but it also defines symbols such as commas. Improve the Telegraph class so that it understands all characters of the Morse code.

---

6. https://github.com/arduino/Arduino/wiki/Arduino-IDE-1.5:-Library-specification

- Blinking LEDs are great, but when we think of Morse code, we usually think of beeping sounds, so replace the LED with a piezo speaker, which is cheap and easy to use. The following figure shows how you connect it to an Arduino. Piezo speakers have a ground pin and a signal pin, so connect the speaker's ground to the Arduino's ground, and connect the signal pin to Arduino pin 13.

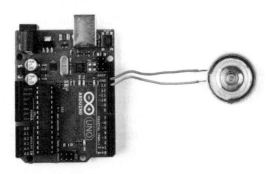

Then replace the output_symbol method with the following code:

```
void Telegraph::output_symbol(const int length) {
  const int frequency = 131;
  tone(_output_pin, frequency, length);
```

This sends a square wave to the speaker, and it plays a tone having a frequency of 131 Hertz. (Look at the example under File > Examples > 02.Digital > toneMelody that comes with the Arduino IDE to learn more about playing notes with a piezo speaker.)

- The Arduino IDE offers an alternative way to handle serial communication. Have a look at *Serial Communication Using Various Languages*, on page 255, and rewrite the Morse code library so that it uses the new serialEvent function. Also, use String objects instead of character arrays.

- Improve the library's design to make it easier to support different output devices. You could pass some kind of OutputDevice object to the Telegraph constructor. Then derive a LedDevice and a SpeakerDevice from OutputDevice. It could look as follows:

```
class OutputDevice {
  public:
  virtual void output_symbol(const int length);
};

class Led : public OutputDevice {
```

```
  public:
  void output_symbol(const int length) {
    // ...
  }
};

class Speaker : public OutputDevice {
  public:
  void output_symbol(const int length) {
    // ...
  }
};
```

You can then use these classes as follows:

```
Led led;
Speaker speaker;
OutputDevice* led_device = &led;
OutputDevice* speaker_device = &speaker;

led_device->output_symbol(200);
speaker_device->output_symbol(200);
```

The rest is up to you.

- Try to learn Morse code. Let someone else type some messages into the serial terminal and try to recognize what that person sent. This isn't necessary for learning Arduino development, but it's a lot of fun!

CHAPTER 5

Sensing the World Around Us

Instead of communicating via mouse or keyboard as with regular computers, you need to connect special sensors to the Arduino so that it can sense changes around it. You can attach sensors that measure the current temperature, the acceleration, or the distance to the nearest object.

Sensors make up an important part of physical computing, and the Arduino makes using various sensor types a breeze. In this chapter, we will use both digital and analog sensors to capture some real-world state, and all we need is a couple of wires and some small programs.

We'll take a close look at two sensor types: an ultrasonic sensor that measures distances and a temperature sensor that measures, well, temperatures. With the ultrasonic sensor, we'll build a digital metering rule to help us measure distances remotely.

Although ultrasonic sensors deliver quite accurate results, we can still improve their precision with some easy tricks. Interestingly, the temperature sensor will help us with this, and at the end of the chapter, we will have created a fairly accurate digital distance meter. We'll also build a nice graphical application that visualizes the data we get from the sensors.

But the Arduino doesn't only make using sensors easy. It also encourages good design for both your circuits and your software. For example, although we end up using two sensors, they are completely independent. All the programs we develop in this chapter will run without changes on the final circuit.

What You Need

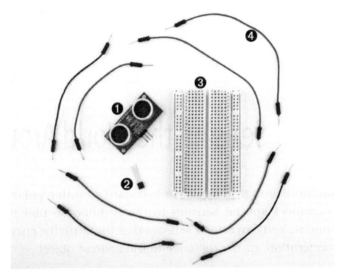

1. A Parallax PING))) sensor
2. A TMP36 temperature sensor from Analog Devices
3. A breadboard
4. Some wires
5. An Arduino board, such as the Uno, Duemilanove, or Diecimila
6. A USB cable to connect the Arduino to your computer

Measuring Distances with an Ultrasonic Sensor

Measuring distances automatically and continuously comes in handy in many situations. Think of a robot that autonomously tries to find its way or of an automatic burglar alarm that rings a bell or calls the police whenever someone is too near your house or the *Mona Lisa*. All this is possible with Arduino. But before you can create that burglar alarm or robot, you need to understand some key concepts.

Many different types of sensors for measuring distances are available, and the Arduino plays well with most of them. Some sensors use ultrasound, while others use infrared light or even laser. But in principle all sensors work the same way: they emit a signal, wait for the echo to return, and measure the time the whole process took. Because we know how fast sound and light travel through the air, we can then convert the measured time into a distance.

In our first project, we'll build a device that measures the distance to the nearest object and outputs it on the serial port. For this project, we use the

Parallax PING))) ultrasonic sensor[1] because it's easy to use, comes with excellent documentation, and has a nice feature set. It can detect objects in a range between 2 centimeters and 3 meters, and we use it directly with a breadboard, so we don't have to solder. It's also a perfect example of a sensor that provides information via variable-width pulses. (More on that in a few paragraphs.) With the PING))) sensor, we can easily build a sonar or a robot that automatically finds its way through a maze without touching a wall.

As mentioned earlier, ultrasonic sensors usually don't return the distance to the nearest object. Instead, they return the time the sound needed to travel to the object and back to the sensor. The PING))) is no exception, and its innards are fairly complex. Fortunately, they are hidden behind three simple pins: power, ground, and signal.

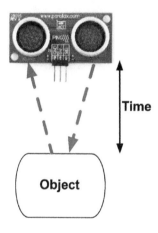

This makes it easy to connect the sensor to the Arduino. First, connect Arduino's ground and 5V power supply to the corresponding PING))) pins. Then connect the PING)))'s sensor pin to one of the Arduino's digital IO pins. (We're using pin 7 for no particular reason.) For a diagram and for a photo of our circuit, see Figure 15, *PING))) basic circuit*, on page 80 and Figure 16, *Photo of PING)))* *basic circuit*, on page 81.

To bring the circuit to life, we need some code that communicates with the PING))) sensor:

InputDevices/Ultrasonic/Simple/Simple.ino

```
Line 1  const unsigned int PING_SENSOR_IO_PIN = 7;
     -  const unsigned int BAUD_RATE = 9600;
     -
     -  void setup() {
     5    Serial.begin(BAUD_RATE);
     -  }
     -
     -  void loop() {
     -    pinMode(PING_SENSOR_IO_PIN, OUTPUT);
    10    digitalWrite(PING_SENSOR_IO_PIN, LOW);
     -    delayMicroseconds(2);
     -
     -    digitalWrite(PING_SENSOR_IO_PIN, HIGH);
     -    delayMicroseconds(5);
```

---

1. http://www.parallax.com/product/28015

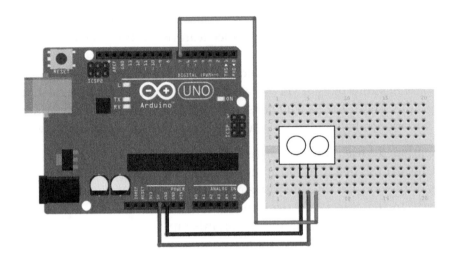

Figure 15—PING))) basic circuit

```
15    digitalWrite(PING_SENSOR_IO_PIN, LOW);

      pinMode(PING_SENSOR_IO_PIN, INPUT);
      const unsigned long duration = pulseIn(PING_SENSOR_IO_PIN, HIGH);
      if (duration == 0) {
20      Serial.println("Warning: We did not get a pulse from sensor.");
      } else {
        Serial.print("Distance to nearest object: ");
        Serial.print(microseconds_to_cm(duration));
        Serial.println(" cm");
25    }

      delay(100);
    }

30  unsigned long microseconds_to_cm(const unsigned long microseconds) {
      return microseconds / 29 / 2;
    }
```

First we define a constant for the IO pin the PING))) sensor is connected to. If you want to connect your sensor to another digital IO pin, you have to change the program's first line. In the setup method, we set the serial port's baud rate to 9600, because we'd like to see some sensor data on the serial monitor.

Figure 16—Photo of PING))) basic circuit

The real action happens in loop, where we actually implement the PING))) protocol. According to the data sheet,[2] we can control the sensor using pulses, and it returns results as variable-width pulses, too.

In lines 9 to 11, we set the sensor's signal pin to LOW for 2 microseconds to bring it to a proper state. This will ensure clean HIGH pulses that are needed in the next steps. (In the world of electronics, you should always be prepared for jitters in the power supply.)

Finally, it's time to tell the sensor to do some work. In lines 13 to 15, we set the sensor's signal pin to HIGH for 5 microseconds to start a new measurement. Afterward, we set the pin to LOW again, because the sensor will respond with a HIGH pulse of variable length on the same pin.

---

2. http://www.parallax.com/downloads/ping-ultrasonic-distance-sensor-product-guide

With a digital pin, you have only a few options to transmit information. You can set the pin to HIGH or LOW, and you can control how long it remains in a particular state. For many purposes, this is absolutely sufficient, and in our case it is, too. When the PING))) sensor sends out its 40-kHz chirp, it sets the signal pin to HIGH and then sets it back to LOW when it receives the echo. That is, the signal pin remains in a HIGH state for exactly the time it takes the sound to travel to an object and back to the sensor. Loosely speaking, we are using a digital pin for measuring an analog signal. In the following figure, you can see a diagram showing typical activity on a digital pin connected to a PING))) sensor.

We could measure the duration the pin remains in HIGH state manually, but the pulseIn method already does all the dirty work for us. So, we use it in line 18 after we have set the signal pin into input mode again. pulseIn accepts three parameters:

- *pin*: Number of the pin to read the pulse from.

- *type*: Type of the pulse that should be read. It can be HIGH or LOW.

- *timeout*: Timeout measured in microseconds. If no pulse could be detected within the timeout period, pulseIn returns 0. This parameter is optional and defaults to one second.

Note that in the whole process, only one pin is used to communicate with the PING))). Sooner or later, you'll realize that IO pins are a scarce resource on the Arduino, so it's really a nice feature that the PING))) uses only one digital pin. When you can choose between different parts performing the same task, try to use as few pins as possible.

We have only one thing left to do: convert the duration we have measured into a length. Sound travels at 343 meters per second, which means it needs 29.155 microseconds per centimeter. So, we have to divide the duration by 29 and then by 2, because the sound has to travel the distance twice. It travels to the object and then back to the PING))) sensor. The microseconds_to_cm method performs the calculation.

According to the specification of the PING))) sensor, you have to wait at least 200 microseconds between two measurements. For high-speed measurements, we could calculate the length of a pause more accurately by actually measuring the time the code takes. But in our case this is pointless, because all the statements that are executed during two measurements in the loop method take far more than 200 microseconds. And outputting data to the serial connection is fairly expensive. Despite this, we have added a small delay of 100 microseconds to slow down the output.

You might wonder why we use the const keyword so often. To program the Arduino you use C/C++, and in these languages it's considered a good practice to declare constant values as const (see *Effective C++: 50 Specific Ways to Improve Your Programs and Designs [Mey97]*). Not only will using const make your program more concise and prevent logical errors early, but it will also help the compiler to decrease your program's size.

Although most Arduino programs are comparatively small, software development for the Arduino is still software development, and it should be done according to all the best practices we know. So, whenever you define a constant value in your program, declare it as such (using const, not using #define). This is true for other programming languages as well, so we will use final in our Java programs, too.

Now it's time to play around with the sensor and get familiar with its strengths and weaknesses. Compile the program, upload it to your Arduino board, and open the serial monitor (don't forget to set the baud rate to 9600). You should see something like this:

```
Distance to nearest object: 42 cm
Distance to nearest object: 33 cm
Distance to nearest object: 27 cm
Distance to nearest object: 27 cm
Distance to nearest object: 29 cm
Distance to nearest object: 36 cm
```

In addition to the output in the terminal, you will see that the LED on the PING))) sensor is turned on whenever the sensor starts a new measurement.

Test the sensor's capabilities by trying to detect big things or very small things. Try to detect objects from different angles, and try to detect objects that are below or above the sensor. You should also do some experiments with objects that don't have a flat surface. Try to detect stuffed animals, and you will see that they are not detected as well as solid objects. (That's probably why bats don't hunt bears—they can't see them.)

With only three wires and a few lines of code, we have built a first version of a digital metering rule. At the moment, it outputs only centimeter distances in whole numbers, but we'll increase its accuracy tremendously in the next section by changing our software and adding more hardware.

Increasing Precision Using Floating-Point Numbers

According to the specification, the PING))) sensor is accurate for objects that are between 2 centimeters and 3 meters away. (By the way, the reason for this is the length of the pulse that is generated. Its minimum length is 115 microseconds, and the maximum length is 18.5 milliseconds.) With our current approach, we don't fully benefit from its precision because all calculations are performed using integer values. We can only measure distances with an accuracy of a centimeter. To enter the millimeter range, we have to use floating-point numbers.

Normally it's a good idea to use integer operations, because compared to regular computers the Arduino's memory and CPU capacities are severely limited and calculations containing floating-point numbers are often expensive. But sometimes it's useful to enjoy the luxury of highly accurate floating-point numbers, and the Arduino supports them well. We'll use them to improve our project now:

InputDevices/Ultrasonic/Float/Float.ino

```
Line 1  const unsigned int PING_SENSOR_IO_PIN = 7;
     -  const unsigned int BAUD_RATE = 9600;
     -  const float MICROSECONDS_PER_CM = 29.155;
     -  const float MOUNTING_GAP = 0.2;
     5  const float SENSOR_OFFSET = MOUNTING_GAP * MICROSECONDS_PER_CM * 2;
     -
     -  void setup() {
     -    Serial.begin(BAUD_RATE);
     -  }
    10  void loop() {
     -    const unsigned long duration = measure_distance();
     -    if (duration == 0)
     -      Serial.println("Warning: We did not get a pulse from sensor.");
     -    else
    15      output_distance(duration);
     -  }
     -
     -  const float microseconds_to_cm(const unsigned long microseconds) {
     -    const float net_distance = max(0, microseconds - SENSOR_OFFSET);
    20    return net_distance / MICROSECONDS_PER_CM / 2;
     -  }
     -
     -
```

```
   const unsigned long measure_distance() {
25   pinMode(PING_SENSOR_IO_PIN, OUTPUT);
     digitalWrite(PING_SENSOR_IO_PIN, LOW);
     delayMicroseconds(2);
     digitalWrite(PING_SENSOR_IO_PIN, HIGH);
     delayMicroseconds(5);
30   digitalWrite(PING_SENSOR_IO_PIN, LOW);
     pinMode(PING_SENSOR_IO_PIN, INPUT);
     return pulseIn(PING_SENSOR_IO_PIN, HIGH);
   }

35 void output_distance(const unsigned long duration) {
     Serial.print("Distance to nearest object: ");
     Serial.print(microseconds_to_cm(duration));
     Serial.println(" cm");
   }
```

This program doesn't differ much from our first version. First, we use the more accurate value 29.155 for the number of microseconds it takes sound to travel 1 centimeter. In addition, the distance calculation now takes a potential gap between the sensor and the case into account. If you plug the sensor into a breadboard, usually a small gap between the sensor and the breadboard's edge exists. This gap is defined in line 5, and it will be used in the distance calculation later on. The gap is measured in centimeters, and it gets multiplied by two because the sound travels out and back.

The loop method looks much cleaner now, because the program's main functionality has been moved to separate functions. The whole sensor control logic lives in the measure_distance method, and output_distance takes care of outputting values to the serial port. The big changes happened in the microseconds_to_cm function. It returns a float value now, and it subtracts the sensor gap from the measured duration. To make sure we don't get negative values, we use the max function.

Compile and upload the program, and you should see something like the following in your serial monitor window:

```
Distance to nearest object: 17.26 cm
Distance to nearest object: 17.93 cm
Distance to nearest object: 17.79 cm
Distance to nearest object: 18.17 cm
Distance to nearest object: 18.65 cm
Distance to nearest object: 18.85 cm
```

This not only looks more accurate than our previous version, it actually *is* more accurate. If you have worked with floating-point numbers in any programming language before, you might ask yourself why the Arduino rounds them automatically to two decimal digits. The secret lies in the print method of the Serial class. In recent versions of the Arduino platform, it works for all possible data types, and when it receives a float variable, it rounds it to two decimal digits before it gets output. You can specify the number of decimal digits. For example, Serial.println(3.141592, 4); prints 3.1416.

Only the output is affected by this; internally it is still a float variable. By the way, on most Arduinos, float and double values are the same at the moment. Only on the Arduino Due is double more accurate than float.

So, what does it actually cost to use float variables? Their memory consumption is 4 bytes—that is, they consume as much memory as long variables. On the other hand, floating-point calculations are fairly expensive and should be avoided in time-critical parts of your software. The biggest costs are the additional library functions that have to be linked to your program for float support. Serial.print(3.14) might look harmless, but it increases your program's size tremendously.

Comment line 37 out and recompile the program to see the effect. It will no longer work properly, but we can see how this statement affects the program size. With my current setup, it needs 3,002 bytes without float support for Serial.print and 5,070 bytes otherwise. That's a difference of 2,068 bytes!

In some cases, you can still get the best of both worlds: float support without paying the memory tax. You can save a lot of space by converting the float values to integers before sending them over a serial connection. To transfer values with a precision of two digits, multiply them by 100, and don't forget to divide them by 100 on the receiving side. We'll use this trick (including rounding) later.

Increasing Precision Using a Temperature Sensor

Support for floating-point numbers is an improvement, but it mainly increases the precision of our program's output. We could've achieved a similar effect using some integer math tricks. But now we'll add an even better improvement that cannot be imitated using software: a temperature sensor.

When I told you that sound travels through air at 343 m/s, I wasn't totally accurate, because the speed of sound isn't constant—among other things, it depends on the air's temperature. If you don't take temperature into account, the error can grow up to a quite significant 12 percent. We calculate the actual speed of sound C with a simple formula:

C = 331.5 + (0.6 * t)

To use it, we only have to determine the current temperature t in Celsius. We will use the TMP36 voltage output temperature sensor from Analog Devices.[3] It's cheap and easy to use.

To connect the TMP36 to the Arduino, connect the Arduino's ground and power to the corresponding pins of the TMP36. Then connect the sensor's signal pin to the pin A0—that is, the analog pin number 0:

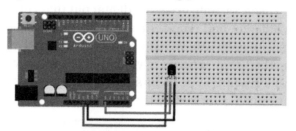

As you might've guessed from its vendor's name, the TMP36 is an analog device: it changes the voltage on its signal pin corresponding to the current temperature. The higher the temperature, the higher the voltage. For us, it's an excellent opportunity to learn how to use the Arduino's analog IO pins. So, let's see some code that uses the sensor:

InputDevices/Temperature/SensorTest/SensorTest.ino

```
const unsigned int TEMP_SENSOR_PIN = A0;
const float SUPPLY_VOLTAGE = 5.0;
const unsigned int BAUD_RATE = 9600;

void setup() {
  Serial.begin(BAUD_RATE);
}

void loop() {
  const float tempC = get_temperature();
  const float tempF = (tempC * 9.0 / 5.0) + 32.0;
  Serial.print(tempC);
  Serial.print(" C, ");
  Serial.print(tempF);
  Serial.println(" F");
  delay(1000);
}

const float get_temperature() {
  const int sensor_voltage = analogRead(TEMP_SENSOR_PIN);
  const float voltage = sensor_voltage * SUPPLY_VOLTAGE / 1024;
  return (voltage * 1000 - 500) / 10;
}
```

---

3. http://tinyurl.com/msard-analog

In the first two lines, we define constants for the analog pin the sensor is connected to and for the Arduino's supply voltage. Then we have a pretty normal setup method followed by a loop method that outputs the current temperature every second. The whole sensor logic has been encapsulated in the get_temperature method. It returns the temperature in degrees Celsius, and we convert it to a Fahrenheit value, too.

For the PING))) sensor, we only needed a digital pin that could be HIGH or LOW. Analog pins are different and represent a voltage ranging from 0V to the current power supply (usually 5V). We can read the Arduino's analog pins using the analogRead method that returns a value between 0 and 1023, because analog pins have a resolution of 10 bits ($1024 = 2^{10}$). We use it in line 20 to read the current voltage supplied by the TMP36.

How to Encode Sensor Data

Encoding sensor data is a problem that has to be solved often in Arduino projects, because all the nice data we collect usually has to be interpreted by applications running on regular computers.

When defining a data format, you have to take several things into account. Among others, the format shouldn't waste the Arduino's precious memory. In our case, we could've used XML for encoding the sensor data:

```
<sensor-data>
  <temperature>30.05</temperature>
  <distance>51.19</distance>
</sensor-data>
```

Obviously this isn't a good choice, because now we're wasting a multiple of the actual data's memory for creating the file format's structure. In addition, the receiving application has to use an XML parser to interpret the data.

But you shouldn't go to the other extreme, either. That is, you should use binary formats only if absolutely necessary or if the receiving application expects binary data anyway.

All in all, the simplest data formats, such as character-separated values (CSV), are often the best choice.

There's one problem left, though: we have to turn the value returned by analogRead into an actual voltage value, so we must know the Arduino's current power supply. It usually is 5V, but there are Arduino models (such as the Arduino Pro, for example) that use only 3.3V. You have to adjust the constant SUPPLY_VOLTAGE accordingly.

We can turn the analog pin's output into a voltage value by dividing it by 1024 and by multiplying it by the supply voltage, which we do in line 21.

We now have to convert the voltage the sensor delivers into degrees Celsius. In the sensor's data sheet, we find the following formula:

T = ((sensor output in mV) - 500) / 10

We have to subtract 500 millivolts because the sensor always outputs a positive voltage. This way, we can represent negative temperatures, too. The sensor's resolution is 10 millivolts, so we have to divide by 10. A voltage value of 750 millivolts corresponds to a temperature of (750 - 500) / 10 = 25°C. See it implemented in line 22.

Compile the program, upload it to the Arduino, and you'll see something like the following in your serial monitor:

```
20.80 C, 69.44 F
20.80 C, 69.44 F
20.31 C, 68.56 F
20.80 C, 69.44 F
20.80 C, 69.44 F
```

As you can see, the sensor needs some time to calibrate, but its results get stable fairly quickly. By the way, you'll always need to insert a short delay between two calls to analogRead, because the Arduino's internal analog system needs some time (0.0001 seconds on the Uno) between two readings. We use a delay of a whole second to make the output easier to read and because we don't expect the temperature to change rapidly. Otherwise, a delay of a single millisecond would be enough.

Now we have two separate circuits: one for measuring distances and one for measuring temperatures. See them combined to a single circuit in Figure 17, *The TMP36 and the PING))) sensors working together*, on page 90 and Figure 18, *Photo of final circuit*, on page 90.

Use the following program to bring the circuit to life:

InputDevices/Ultrasonic/PreciseSensor/PreciseSensor.ino
```
Line 1  const unsigned int TEMP_SENSOR_PIN = A0;
   -    const float SUPPLY_VOLTAGE = 5.0;
   -    const unsigned int PING_SENSOR_IO_PIN = 7;
   -    const float SENSOR_GAP = 0.2;
   5    const unsigned int BAUD_RATE = 9600;
   -    float current_temperature = 0.0;
   -    unsigned long last_measurement = millis();
   -
   -
```

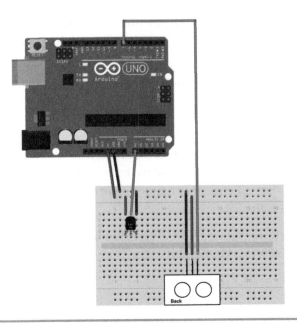

Figure 17—The TMP36 and the PING))) sensors working together

Figure 18—Photo of final circuit

```
10  void setup() {
 -    Serial.begin(BAUD_RATE);
 -  }
 -
 -  void loop() {
15    unsigned long current_millis = millis();
 -    if (abs(current_millis - last_measurement) >= 1000) {
 -      current_temperature = get_temperature();
 -      last_measurement = current_millis;
 -    }
20    Serial.print(scaled_value(current_temperature));
 -    Serial.print(",");
 -    const unsigned long duration = measure_distance();
 -    Serial.println(scaled_value(microseconds_to_cm(duration)));
 -  }
25
 -  long scaled_value(const float value) {
 -    float round_offset = value < 0 ? -0.5 : 0.5;
 -    return (long)(value * 100 + round_offset);
 -  }
30
 -  const float get_temperature() {
 -    const int sensor_voltage = analogRead(TEMP_SENSOR_PIN);
 -    const float voltage = sensor_voltage * SUPPLY_VOLTAGE / 1024;
 -    return (voltage * 1000 - 500) / 10;
35  }
 -
 -  const float microseconds_per_cm() {
 -    return 1 / ((331.5 + (0.6 * current_temperature)) / 10000);
 -  }
40
 -  const float sensor_offset() {
 -    return SENSOR_GAP * microseconds_per_cm() * 2;
 -  }
 -
45  const float microseconds_to_cm(const unsigned long microseconds) {
 -    const float net_distance = max(0, microseconds - sensor_offset());
 -    return net_distance / microseconds_per_cm() / 2;
 -  }
 -
50  const unsigned long measure_distance() {
 -    pinMode(PING_SENSOR_IO_PIN, OUTPUT);
 -    digitalWrite(PING_SENSOR_IO_PIN, LOW);
 -    delayMicroseconds(2);
 -    digitalWrite(PING_SENSOR_IO_PIN, HIGH);
55    delayMicroseconds(5);
 -    digitalWrite(PING_SENSOR_IO_PIN, LOW);
 -    pinMode(PING_SENSOR_IO_PIN, INPUT);
 -    return pulseIn(PING_SENSOR_IO_PIN, HIGH);
 -  }
```

The code is nearly a perfect merge of the programs we used to get the PING)))
and the TMP36 sensors working. Only a few things were changed:

- The constant MICROSECONDS_PER_CM has been replaced by the microsec-
  onds_per_cm function, which determines the microseconds sound needs to
  travel 1 centimeter dynamically, depending on the current temperature.

- Because the current temperature usually won't change often or rapidly,
  we don't measure it permanently, but only once a second. We use millis in
  line 7 to determine the number of milliseconds that have passed since
  the Arduino started. From lines 15 to 19, we check whether more than a
  second has passed since the last measurement. If yes, we measure the
  current temperature again.

- We no longer transfer the sensor data as floating-point numbers on the
  serial port, but instead use scaled integer values. This is done by the
  scaled_value function, which rounds a float value to two decimal digits and
  converts it into a long value by multiplying it by 100. On the receiving
  side, you have to divide it by 100 again.

If you upload the program to your Arduino and play around with your hand
in front of the sensor, you'll see an output similar to the following:

```
2129,1016
2129,1027
2129,1071
2129,1063
2129,1063
2129,1063
```

The output is a comma-separated list of values where the first value represents
the current temperature in degree Celsius, and the second is the distance to
the nearest object measured in centimeters. Both values have to be divided
by 100 to get the actual sensor data.

Our little project now has two sensors. One is connected to a digital pin, while
the other uses an analog one. In the next section, you'll learn how to transfer
sensor data back to a PC and use it to create applications based on the current
state of the real world.

Creating Your Own Dashboard

Instead of printing our digital and analog sensor data to a serial port, we'll
simulate a small part of a modern car's dashboard in this section. Most cars
today show the current temperature, and many also have a parking-distance
control system that warns you if you get too close to another object.

Save the Climate Using Sonar Sensors

Researchers from Northwestern University and University of Michigan have created a sonar system that uses only a computer's microphone and speakers to detect whether the computer is currently used.[a] If it's not being used, the computer automatically powers off its screen, saving the environment.

Instead of using a microphone and speakers, you can also use a PING))) sensor. With the lessons you've learned in this chapter, you can build such a system yourself with ease. Try it!

---

a. http://blog.makezine.com/2009/10/15/using-sonar-to-save-power/

In my car, the parking-distance control consists of a couple of orange and red LEDs. If nothing's near the car, all LEDs are off. As soon as the distance between the car and a potential obstacle gets too small, the first orange LED lights up. The shorter the distance, the more LEDs that light up. If the distance reaches a critical limit, all LEDs are on, and the car plays an annoying beep tone.

Here's the application we're going to build. It shows the current temperature, and you can also see that the first red light is already on, indicating that there's something very close to the distance sensor.

We'll implement the application as a Google Chrome app. (Now is a good time to read Appendix 4, *Controlling the Arduino with a Browser*, on page 267, if you haven't done so already.) The application's manifest.json file contains no surprises:

InputDevices/Dashboard/manifest.json
```
{
  "manifest_version": 2,
  "name": "Dashboard Demo",
  "version": "1",
  "permissions": [ "serial" ],
  "app": {
    "background": {
      "scripts": ["background.js"]
    }
  },
  "minimum_chrome_version": "33"
}
```

It defines all meta information needed, and it declares that the Chrome App needs to access the serial port. The background.js file isn't very exciting, either:

InputDevices/Dashboard/background.js
```
chrome.app.runtime.onLaunched.addListener(function() {
  chrome.app.window.create('main.html', {
    id: 'main',
    bounds: { width: 600, height: 300 }
  });
});
```

It opens a new window and displays the main.html file:

InputDevices/Dashboard/main.html
```
Line 1   <!DOCTYPE html>
    -    <html lang="en">
    -      <head>
    -        <meta charset="utf-8"/>
    5        <link rel="stylesheet" type="text/css" href="css/dashboard.css"/>
    -        <title>Dashboard Demo</title>
    -      </head>
    -      <body>
    -        <div id="dashboard">
   10          <div id="distance-display">
    -            <p>
    -              <span id="d1">&#x25cf;</span>
    -              <span id="d2">&#x25cf;</span>
    -              <span id="d3">&#x25cf;</span>
   15              <span id="d4">&#x25cf;</span>
    -              <span id="d5">&#x25cf;</span>
    -              <span id="d6">&#x25cf;</span>
    -              <span id="d7">&#x25cf;</span>
    -              <span id="d8">&#x25cf;</span>
   20            </p>
    -          </div>
    -          <div id="temperature-display">
    -            <p><span id="temperature"></span> &#x2103;</p>
    -          </div>
   25        </div>
    -        <script src="js/serial_device.js"></script>
    -        <script src="js/dashboard.js"></script>
    -      </body>
    -    </html>
```

To create the dashboard's user interface, we need only some basic HTML. We define the whole parking-distance control display in lines 12 to 19. We represent each LED by a <span> element containing the Unicode character (&#x25cf) for a filled circle. Each <span> element gets a unique ID, so we can refer to the individual LEDs later on.

The temperature display is even simpler. It consists of a single <span> element. We've added the Unicode character for a degrees Celsius symbol (&#x2103) to make it look more professional. Let's add a little bit of CSS to make the dashboard even more appealing:

InputDevices/Dashboard/css/dashboard.css

```css
body {
  font-size: 50px;
  background: black;
  color: white;
}

#distance-display,
#temperature-display {
  text-align: center;
}
```

The stylesheet increases the font size and sets the background color to black and the text color to white. Also, it centers both the LED display and the temperature display.

Now it's time to bring the dashboard to life using some JavaScript:

InputDevices/Dashboard/js/dashboard.js

```javascript
Line 1  var arduino = new SerialDevice("/dev/tty.usbmodem24321", 9600);

        arduino.onConnect.addListener(function() {
          console.log("Connected to: " + arduino.path);
    5   });

        arduino.onReadLine.addListener(function(line) {
          console.log("Read line: " + line);
          var attr = line.split(",");
   10     if (attr.length == 2) {
            var temperature = Math.round(parseInt(attr[0]) / 100.0 * 10) / 10;
            var distance = parseInt(attr[1]) / 100.0;
            updateUI(temperature, distance);
          }
   15   });

        var lights = {
          d1: [35.0, "orange"],
          d2: [30.0, "orange"],
   20     d3: [25.0, "orange"],
          d4: [20.0, "orange"],
          d5: [15.0, "orange"],
          d6: [10.0, "orange"],
          d7: [7.0, "red"],
   25     d8: [5.0, "red"]
        };
```

```
   function updateUI(temperature, distance) {
     document.getElementById("temperature").innerText = temperature;
30   for (var i = 1; i < 9; i++) {
       var index = "d" + i;
       if (distance <= lights[index][0])
         document.getElementById(index).style.color = lights[index][1];
       else
35       document.getElementById(index).style.color = "white";
     }
   }

   arduino.connect();
```

To read the sensor data from the Arduino, we use the SerialDevice class we've defined in *Writing a SerialDevice Class*, on page 274. We create a new instance named arduino in the first line. Make sure you're using the right serial port path.

Then we define an onConnect handler that prints a message to the browser's JavaScript console as soon as the application has connected to an Arduino. In principle, you don't need the onConnect handler. In this case, it's mostly useful for debugging purposes.

Things get more interesting in the onReadLine handler. In line 9, we split the data we've received from the Arduino. We make sure that we've actually received two values. In this case we turn both values into numbers using parseInt, and we also divide them by 100 because the Arduino sends values that have been multiplied by 100 before. In line 11, we use a popular Java-Script trick to round the temperature value to one decimal digit. After we've turned both the distance and the temperature into proper numbers, we pass them to updateUI.

updateUI sets the new temperature value first in line 29. To do this, it looks up the HTML element having the ID temperature using the getElementById function. Then it sets the element's innerText property to the current temperature.

Updating the artificial LED display is a bit more complex, but not too difficult. We've defined a data structure named lights that maps the IDs of our display's <span> elements to arrays having two elements each. For example, it maps the ID d1 to an array containing the values 35.0 and "orange". That means that the color of the element having the ID d1 will be set to orange when the distance to the next object is less than or equal 35.0 centimeters.

Using the lights data structure, it's easy to implement the LED display. In line 30, we start a loop iterating over all LEDs. We determine the current LED's

ID in line 31. Then we check whether the current distance is less than or equal to the threshold value that belongs to the current LED. If yes, we change the LED's color accordingly. Otherwise, we set its color to white.

Some Fun with Sensors

With an ultrasonic sensor, you can easily detect whether someone is nearby. This automatically brings a lot of useful applications to mind. You could open a door automatically as soon as someone is close enough, for example.

Alternatively, you can use advanced technology for pure fun. What about some Halloween gimmicks, such as a pumpkin that shoots silly string whenever you cross an invisible line?[a] It could be a nice gag for your next party, and you can build it using the PING))) sensor.

---

a.   http://www.instructables.com/id/Arduino-controlled-Silly-String-shooter/

Connect the Arduino to your computer and upload the sketch we developed in the previous section. Start the Chrome App and move your hand back and forth in front of the PING))) sensor. The display on the screen will look exactly like the display in a typical car.

Sensors are an exciting topic, and in this chapter you've learned the basics of working with both analog and digital sensors. In the next chapter, we'll build on that foundation and connect the Arduino to an accelerometer to create a motion-sensing game controller.

What If It Doesn't Work?

See *What If It Doesn't Work?*, on page 59, and make sure that you've connected all parts properly to the breadboard. Take special care with the PING))) and the TMP36 sensors, because you haven't worked with them before. Make sure you've connected the right pins to the right connectors of the sensors.

In case of any errors with the software—no matter whether it's JavaScript or Arduino code—download the code from the book's website and see whether it works.

If you have problems with serial communication, double-check whether you've used the right serial port and the right Arduino type. Remember to adjust the path to your Arduino's serial port in the first line of dashboard.js. Also check whether the baud rate in the JavaScript code matches the baud rate you've used in the Arduino code.

Make sure that the serial port isn't blocked by another application, such as a serial monitor window you forgot to close.

Exercises

- Build an automatic burglar alarm that shows a stop sign whenever someone is too close to your computer.[4] Make the application as smart as possible. It should have a small activation delay to prevent it from showing a stop sign immediately when it's started.

- The speed of sound depends not only on the temperature, but also on humidity and atmospheric pressure. Do some research to find the right formula and the right sensors. Use your research results to make the circuit for measuring distances even more precise.

- Use an alternative technology for measuring distances—for example, an infrared sensor. Try to find an appropriate sensor, read its data sheet, and build a basic circuit so you can print the distance to the nearest object to the serial port.

---

4. You can find a stop sign here: http://en.wikipedia.org/wiki/File:Stop_sign_MUTCD.svg.

CHAPTER 6

Building a Motion-Sensing Game Controller

It's astonishing how quickly we get used to new technologies. A decade ago, not many people would've imagined that we would use devices someday to follow our movements. Today, it's absolutely normal for us to physically turn our smartphones when we want to change from portrait to landscape view. Even small children intuitively know how to use motion-sensing controllers for video game consoles, such as Nintendo's Wii. You can build your own motion-sensing devices using an Arduino, and in this chapter you'll learn how.

We'll work with one of the most widespread motion-sensing devices: the *accelerometer*. Accelerometers detect movement in all directions—they notice if you move them up or down (Z-axis), forward or backward (Y-axis), and to the left or to the right (X-axis). Many popular gadgets, such as the iPhone and the Nintendo Wii controllers, contain accelerometers, so accelerometers are produced in large quantities. That's why they're cheap.

Both fun and serious projects can benefit from accelerometers. When working with your computer, you certainly think of devices, such as game controllers or other input control devices, that you connect via USB. But you can also use them when exercising or to control a real-life marble maze. They are also the right tool for measuring acceleration indirectly, such as in a car.

You will learn how to interpret accelerometer data correctly and how to get the most accurate results. Then you'll use an accelerometer to build a motion-sensing game controller, and in the next chapter you'll implement a game that uses it.

What You Need

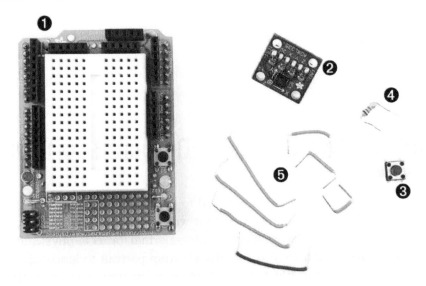

1. An Arduino Proto Shield (optional)
2. An ADXL335 accelerometer
3. A pushbutton
4. A 10kΩ resistor
5. Some wires
6. A half-size breadboard (if you're not using a Proto Shield)
7. An Arduino board, such as the Uno, Duemilanove, or Diecimila
8. A USB cable to connect the Arduino to your computer
9. A 6-pin 0.1-inch standard header

Wiring Up the Accelerometer

There are many different accelerometers, differing mainly in the number of spatial axes they support (usually two or three). I'll use the ADXL335 from Analog Devices—it's easy to use and widely available.[1] Analog Devices offers many more accelerometers, named ADXL345, ADXL377, or ADXL326, for example. They all work the same, and they differ only in accuracy and price.

In this section, we'll connect the ADXL335 to the Arduino and create a small demo program showing the raw data the sensor delivers. At that point, we will have a quick look at the sensor's specification and interpret the data.

---

1. http://www.analog.com/en/sensors/inertial-sensors/adxl335/products/product.html

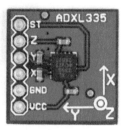

This picture shows a breakout board containing an ADXL335 sensor on the right. The sensor is the small black integrated circuit (IC), and the rest is just a carrier to allow connections. On the top, you see a 6-pin 0.1-inch standard header. The sensor has six connectors, labeled GND, Z, Y, X, VCC, and ST. To use the sensor on a breadboard, solder the standard header to the connectors. This not only makes it easier to attach the sensor to a breadboard, but it also stabilizes the sensor so it doesn't move accidentally. You can see the result on the left side of the photo. (Note that the breakout board on the left isn't the same as on the right, but it's very similar.) Don't worry if you've never soldered before. In *Learning How to Solder*, on page 243, you can learn how to do it.

You can ignore the connector labeled ST, and the meaning of the remaining connectors should be obvious. To power the sensor, connect GND to the Arduino's ground pin and VCC to the Arduino's 3.3V power supply. X, Y, and Z will then deliver acceleration data for the x-, y-, and z-axes.

Note that not all breakout boards have the same connectors. Usually, they have six or seven connectors. Some breakout boards can cope with 5V, while others only work with 3.3V. Some boards have an input pin named VIN that you have to connect to one of the Arduino's power supply pins (5V or 3.3V).

Like the TMP36 temperature sensor we used in *Increasing Precision Using a Temperature Sensor*, on page 86, the ADXL335 is an analog device: it delivers results as voltages that have to be converted into acceleration values. So, the X, Y, and Z connectors have to be connected to three analog pins on the Arduino. We connect Z to analog pin 0, Y to analog pin 1, and X to analog pin 2. (See the following image and double-check the pin labels on the breakout board you're using!) Naturally, you'll move around the accelerometer a lot, so it's best to use long wires.

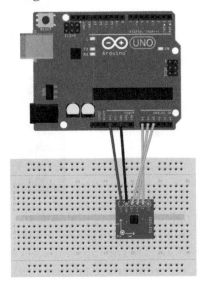

Now that we've connected the ADXL335 to the Arduino, let's use it.

Bringing Your Accelerometer to Life

A pragmatic strategy to get familiar with a new device is to hook it up and see what data it delivers. The following program reads input values for all three axes and outputs them to the serial port:

MotionSensor/SensorTest/SensorTest.ino

```
const unsigned int X_AXIS_PIN = A2;
const unsigned int Y_AXIS_PIN = A1;
const unsigned int Z_AXIS_PIN = A0;
const unsigned int BAUD_RATE = 9600;

void setup() {
  Serial.begin(BAUD_RATE);
}

void loop() {
  Serial.print(analogRead(X_AXIS_PIN));
  Serial.print(" ");
  Serial.print(analogRead(Y_AXIS_PIN));
  Serial.print(" ");
  Serial.println(analogRead(Z_AXIS_PIN));
  delay(100);
}
```

Our test program is as simple as it can be. We define constants for the three analog pins and initialize the serial port in the setup function. Note that we didn't set the analog pins to INPUT explicitly, because that's the default anyway.

In the loop function, we constantly output the values we read from the analog pins to the serial port. Open the serial monitor and move the sensor around —tilt it around the different axes. You should see output like this:

```
344 331 390
364 276 352
388 286 287
398 314 286
376 332 289
370 336 301
```

These values represent the data we get for the x-, y-, and z-axes. When you move the sensor only around the x-axis, for example, you can see that the first value changes accordingly. In the next section, we'll take a closer look at these values.

Finding and Polishing Edge Values

The physical world often is far from perfect. That's especially true for the data many sensors emit, and accelerometers are no exception. They vary slightly in the minimum and maximum values they generate, and they often jitter. They might change their output values even though you haven't moved them, or they might not change their output values correctly. In this section, we'll determine the sensor's minimum and maximum values, and we'll flatten the jitter.

Finding the edge values of the sensor is easy, but it cannot be easily automated. You have to constantly read the sensor's output while moving it. Here's a program that does the job:

MotionSensor/SensorValues/SensorValues.ino
```
const unsigned int X_AXIS_PIN = A2;
const unsigned int Y_AXIS_PIN = A1;
const unsigned int Z_AXIS_PIN = A0;
const unsigned int BAUD_RATE = 9600;

int min_x, min_y, min_z;
int max_x, max_y, max_z;

void setup() {
  Serial.begin(BAUD_RATE);
  min_x = min_y = min_z = 1000;
  max_x = max_y = max_z = -1000;
}
```

```
void loop() {
  const int x = analogRead(X_AXIS_PIN);
  const int y = analogRead(Y_AXIS_PIN);
  const int z = analogRead(Z_AXIS_PIN);

  min_x = min(x, min_x); max_x = max(x, max_x);
  min_y = min(y, min_y); max_y = max(y, max_y);
  min_z = min(z, min_z); max_z = max(z, max_z);

  Serial.print("x(");
  Serial.print(min_x);
  Serial.print("/");
  Serial.print(max_x);
  Serial.print("), y(");
  Serial.print(min_y);
  Serial.print("/");
  Serial.print(max_y);
  Serial.print("), z(");
  Serial.print(min_z);
  Serial.print("/");
  Serial.print(max_z);
  Serial.println(")");
}
```

We declare variables for the minimum and maximum values of all three axes, and we initialize them with numbers that are definitely out of the sensor's range (-1000 and 1000). In the loop function, we permanently measure the acceleration of all three axes and adjust the minimum and maximum values accordingly.

Compile and upload the sketch, then move the breadboard with the sensor in all directions, and then tilt it around all axes. Move it slowly, move it fast, tilt it slowly, and tilt it fast. Be careful when moving and rotating the breadboard that you don't accidentally loosen a connection.

After a short while, the minimum and maximum values will stabilize, and you should get output like this:

```
x(247/649), y(253/647), z(278/658)
```

Write down these values, because we'll need them later, and you'll probably need them when you do your own sensor experiments.

Now let's see how to get rid of the jitter. In principle, it's simple. Instead of returning the acceleration data immediately, we collect the last readings and return their average. This way, small changes will be ironed out. The code looks as follows:

MotionSensor/Buffering/Buffering.ino

```
Line 1  const unsigned int X_AXIS_PIN = 2;
     -  const unsigned int Y_AXIS_PIN = 1;
     -  const unsigned int Z_AXIS_PIN = 0;
     -  const unsigned int NUM_AXES = 3;
     5  const unsigned int PINS[NUM_AXES] = {
     -    X_AXIS_PIN, Y_AXIS_PIN, Z_AXIS_PIN
     -  };
     -  const unsigned int BUFFER_SIZE = 16;
     -  const unsigned int BAUD_RATE = 9600;
    10  int buffer[NUM_AXES][BUFFER_SIZE];
     -  int buffer_pos[NUM_AXES] = { 0 };
     -
     -  void setup() {
     -    Serial.begin(BAUD_RATE);
    15  }
     -
     -  int get_axis(const int axis) {
     -    delay(1);
     -    buffer[axis][buffer_pos[axis]] = analogRead(PINS[axis]);
    20    buffer_pos[axis] = (buffer_pos[axis] + 1) % BUFFER_SIZE;
     -    long sum = 0;
     -    for (unsigned int i = 0; i < BUFFER_SIZE; i++)
     -      sum += buffer[axis][i];
     -    return round(sum / BUFFER_SIZE);
    25  }
     -
     -  int get_x() { return get_axis(0); }
     -  int get_y() { return get_axis(1); }
     -  int get_z() { return get_axis(2); }
    30  void loop() {
     -    Serial.print(get_x());
     -    Serial.print(" ");
     -    Serial.print(get_y());
     -    Serial.print(" ");
    35    Serial.println(get_z());
     -  }
```

As usual, we define some constants for the pins we use first. This time, we also define a constant named NUM_AXES that contains the number of axes we are measuring. We also have an array named PINS that contains a list of the pins we use. This will help us keep our code more generic later.

In line 10, we declare buffers for all axes. They will be filled with the sensor data we measure, so we can calculate average values when we need them. We have to store our current position in each buffer, so in line 11, we define an array of buffer positions.

setup only initializes the serial port; the real action takes place in get_axis.

It starts with a small delay to give the Arduino some time to switch between analog pins; otherwise, you might get bad data. Then it reads the acceleration for the axis we have passed and stores it at the current buffer position belonging to the axis. It increases the buffer position and sets it back to zero when the end of the buffer has been reached. Finally, we return the average value of the data we have gathered so far for the current axis.

That's the whole trick, and the data structure we've just built is named circular buffer.[2] To see its effect, leave the sensor untouched on your desk and run the program with different buffer sizes. If you don't touch the sensor, you wouldn't expect the program's output to change. But if you set BUFFER_SIZE to 1, you will quickly see small changes. They will disappear as soon as the buffer is big enough.

The acceleration data we measure now is accurate enough that we can finally build a game controller that won't annoy users with unexpected movements.

Building Your Own Game Controller

To build a full-blown game controller, we only need to add a button to our breadboard. Figure 19, *Game controller with accelerometer and pushbutton,* on page 107 shows you how to do it. (Please double-check the pin labels on your breakout board!)

That's how it looks inside a typical modern game controller. We won't build a fancy housing for the controller, but we still should think about ergonomics for a moment. Our current breadboard solution is rather fragile (see the following figure), and you cannot really wave around the board when it's connected to the Arduino. Sooner or later you'll disconnect some wires, and the controller will stop working.

To solve this problem, you could try to attach the breadboard to the Arduino using some rubber bands. That works, but it doesn't look very pretty, and it's still hard to handle.

A much better solution is to use an Arduino Proto Shield—a pluggable breadboard that lets you quickly build circuit prototypes. The breadboard is surrounded by the Arduino's pins, so you no longer need long wires. Shields are a great way to enhance an Arduino's capabilities, and you can get shields for many different purposes, such as adding Ethernet, sound, displays, and so on. The figure on page 108 shows a bare Proto Shield and a shield containing our motion sensor.

---

2.   http://en.wikipedia.org/wiki/Circular_buffer

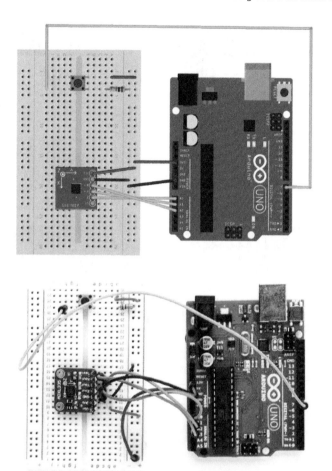

Figure 19—Game controller with accelerometer and pushbutton

Now that the hardware is complete, we need a final version of the game controller software. It supports the button we've added, and it performs the anti-jittering we created in *Finding and Polishing Edge Values*, on page 103:

MotionSensor/Controller/Controller.ino
```
#include <Bounce2.h>
const unsigned int BUTTON_PIN = 7;
const unsigned int X_AXIS_PIN = A2;
const unsigned int Y_AXIS_PIN = A1;
const unsigned int Z_AXIS_PIN = A0;
const unsigned int NUM_AXES = 3;
const unsigned int PINS[NUM_AXES] = {
  X_AXIS_PIN, Y_AXIS_PIN, Z_AXIS_PIN
};
```

Figure 20—An empty Proto Shield (left), and one holding our game controller (right)

```
const unsigned int BUFFER_SIZE = 16;
const unsigned int BAUD_RATE = 38400;
int buffer[NUM_AXES][BUFFER_SIZE];
int buffer_pos[NUM_AXES] = { 0 };
boolean button_pressed = false;

Bounce button;

void setup() {
  Serial.begin(BAUD_RATE);
  pinMode(BUTTON_PIN, INPUT);
  button.attach(BUTTON_PIN);
  button.interval(20);
}

int get_axis(const int axis) {
  delay(1);
  buffer[axis][buffer_pos[axis]] = analogRead(PINS[axis]);
  buffer_pos[axis] = (buffer_pos[axis] + 1) % BUFFER_SIZE;

  long sum = 0;
  for (unsigned int i = 0; i < BUFFER_SIZE; i++)
    sum += buffer[axis][i];
  return round(sum / BUFFER_SIZE);
}
int get_x() { return get_axis(0); }
int get_y() { return get_axis(1); }
int get_z() { return get_axis(2); }
```

```
void loop() {
  Serial.print(get_x());
  Serial.print(" ");
  Serial.print(get_y());
  Serial.print(" ");
  Serial.print(get_z());
  Serial.print(" ");
  if (button.update()) {
    button_pressed = button.read() == HIGH;
  }
  Serial.println(button_pressed == HIGH ? "1" : "0");
  delay(10);
}
```

As in *Building a Dice Game*, on page 55, we use the Bounce class to debounce the button. The rest of the code is pretty much standard, and the only thing worth mentioning is that we use a 38,400 baud rate to transfer the controller data sufficiently fast.

Compile and upload the code, open the serial terminal, and play around with the controller. Move it, press the button sometimes, and it should output something like the following:

```
324 365 396 0
325 364 397 0
325 364 397 1
325 364 397 0
325 365 397 0
325 365 397 1
326 364 397 0
```

A homemade game controller is nice, and you can use it for many projects. For example, you could use it to control devices such as a robot, a marble maze, or something similar. Its original purpose is to control games, so we'll build one in the next chapter.

More Projects

If you keep your eyes open, you'll quickly find many more applications for accelerometers than you might imagine. Here's a small collection of both commercial and free products:

- It's a lot of fun to create a marble maze computer game and control it using the game controller we built in this chapter. How much more fun will it be to build a real marble maze?[3]

- In this chapter, we have measured only direct acceleration; that is, we usually have the accelerometer in our hand and move it. But you can also build many interesting projects that measure indirect acceleration, such as when you are driving a car.[4]

What If It Doesn't Work?

All advice from *What If It Doesn't Work?*, on page 97, also applies to the project in this section. In addition, you should check whether you've soldered the pin header correctly to the breakout board. Use a magnifying glass and study every single solder joint carefully. Did you use enough solder? Did you use too much and connect two joints?

Exercises

- To get a better feeling for the data the accelerometer emits, you should write a few more sketches that focus on a particular axis. Write a sketch that outputs only the current value for the X-axis, for example. Turn an LED on when the X-axis value is above a predefined threshold value. Otherwise, turn it off.

---

3. http://www.electronicsinfoline.com/New/Everything_Else/marble-maze-that-is-remote-controlled-using-an-accelerometer.html

4. http://www.dimensionengineering.com/appnotes/Gmeter/Gmeter.htm

CHAPTER 7

Writing a Game for the
Motion-Sensing Game Controller

To test our game controller, we'll program a simple Breakout[1] clone in Java-Script. The player's goal is to destroy all bricks in the upper half of the screen using a ball. It'll look something like the following figure.

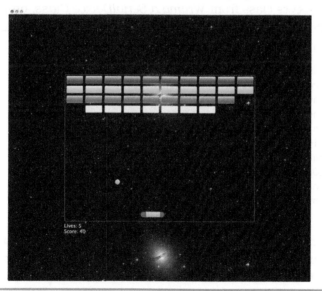

Figure 21—Our Breakout clone
Background image credit: ESA/Hubble, NASA, Digitized SkySurvey, MPG/ESO.
Acknowledgment: Davide de Martin

1.　http://en.wikipedia.org/wiki/Breakout_%28arcade_game%29

To control the ball with the paddle at the bottom of the screen, you can tilt the controller around the x-axis to move the paddle horizontally. The game runs in a web browser, and it communicates with the Arduino via a serial port. It reads the game controller's state several times per second to determine the controller's current x-axis position.

Although this isn't a book about game programming, it won't hurt to take a look at the game's innards, especially because game programming with JavaScript is really pure fun! Also, JavaScript is very popular. It's available on nearly every computer, because all modern web browsers come with JavaScript interpreters.

We'll implement the game as a Google Chrome app, so make sure you've read Appendix 4, *Controlling the Arduino with a Browser*, on page 267. The Chrome app implements the game's logic, and it talks to our game controller via serial port. It reads the current controller state and turns it into movements of our paddle on the screen.

Writing a GameController Class

With the SerialDevice class from *Writing a SerialDevice Class*, on page 274, it's easy to create a GameController class that provides even more convenient access to our motion-sensing Arduino. Here's its constructor function:

```
BrowserGame/GameController/js/game_controller.js
var GameController = function(path, threshold) {
  this.arduino = new SerialDevice(path);
  this.threshold = threshold || 325;
  this.moveLeft = false;
  this.moveRight = false;
  this.buttonPressed = false;
  this.boundOnReadLine = this.onReadLine.bind(this);
  this.arduino.onReadLine.addListener(this.boundOnReadLine);
  this.arduino.connect();
}
```

This function defines several properties. First, it creates a property named arduino and initializes it with a new SerialDevice object. The next property defines a threshold for the game controller's x-axis. To check whether a user has tilted the game controller to the left or to the right, we need to know the controller's resting point. Instead of looking for the exact resting point, we'll add some tolerance, and that's the value we'll store in threshold.

The following three properties are all Boolean flags representing the controller's current state. If moveLeft is true, the user has moved the controller to the left.

Eventually, we add our own onReadLine listener to the SerialDevice object and use our usual bind trick.

The onReadLine listener interprets the data we get from the Arduino:

BrowserGame/GameController/js/game_controller.js
```
GameController.prototype.onReadLine = function(line) {
  const TOLERANCE = 5;
  var attr = line.trim().split(' ');
  if (attr.length == 4) {
    this.moveRight = false;
    this.moveLeft = false;
    var x = parseInt(attr[0]);
    if (x <= this.threshold - TOLERANCE) {
      this.moveLeft = true;
    } else if (x >= this.threshold + TOLERANCE) {
      this.moveRight = true;
    }

    this.buttonPressed = (attr[3] == '1');
  }
  var message = 'moveLeft(' + this.moveLeft + '), ' +
    'moveRight (' + this.moveRight + '), ' +
    'buttonPressed(' + this.buttonPressed + ')';
  console.log(message);
  document.getElementById('output').innerText = message;
}
```

The method splits the line it receives at each blank character. Then it makes sure that the line contains exactly four attributes. If yes, it checks whether the current X position is to the left or to the right of the controller's tipping point. Note that we use the threshold value here to make the movement detection smoother.

Finally, the method checks whether the controller's button is currently pressed. Also, it writes the controller's current state to the console.

By the way, if you'd like to control the game using a Nunchuk later on (see Chapter 9, *Tinkering with the Wii Nunchuk*, on page 145), you only have to adjust the GameController class.

In Figure 22, *The game controller communicates with a Chrome app*, on page 114, you can see the output of a sample Chrome app that outputs the game controller's state to the JavaScript console.

We can now conveniently combine Chrome apps with our motion-sensing controller. In the next section, you'll learn how to create a more advanced application using these techniques.

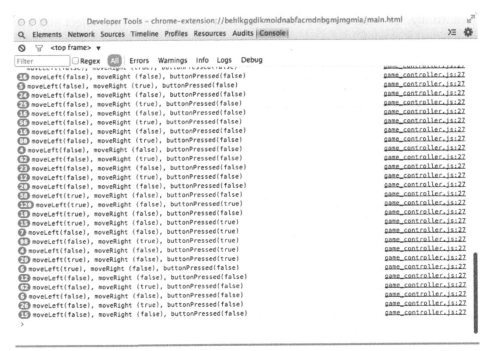

Figure 22—The game controller communicates with a Chrome app.

Creating the Game

At this point you know enough about Chrome apps and controlling a motion-sensing game controller to create an entertaining video game. Writing a video game isn't directly related to programming the Arduino. Still, it'll show you some techniques you can use in other projects, and it'll give you a much better understanding of how the integration of hardware and software works.

Before you dive into the code, download it from the book's website[2] and play the game. Doing so will help you find your way through the code much easier.

When programming a browser game, you usually start with its HTML code. In our case it looks like this:

BrowserGame/Arduinoid/main.html
```html
<!DOCTYPE html>
<html lang="en">
  <head>
    <meta charset="utf-8"/>
    <link rel="stylesheet" type="text/css" href="css/arduinoid.css"/>
    <title>Arduinoid</title>
```

---

2. http://www.pragprog.com/titles/msard2

```
    </head>
    <body>
      <div id="game">
        <div id="playfield">
          <div id="paddle"></div>
          <div id="ball"></div>
          <div id="winner" class="message">
            <p>You win!</p>
          </div>
          <div id="game_over" class="message">
            <p>Game Over</p>
          </div>
        </div>
        <div id="stats">
          <div>Lives: <span id="lives"/></div>
          <div>Score: <span id="score"/></div>
        </div>
      </div>
      <audio src="sound/awake10_megaWall.mp3" autoplay loop/>
      <script src="js/jquery-1.11.1.min.js"></script>
      <script src="js/serial_device.js"></script>
      <script src="js/game_controller.js"></script>
      <script src="js/arduinoid.js"></script>
    </body>
</html>
```

There's nothing special about this HTML document. At the top we associate the document with a style sheet named arduinoid.css. We'll specify all things related to layout in this file.

Next, we define a couple of <div> elements. The main element has its id attribute set to game, and it contains all the other elements. Most elements are fairly self-explanatory. The playfield element is where the action happens. It hosts a paddle and a ball. These elements represent the game's main objects—that is, the player's paddle and the ball.

The winner and game_over elements contain messages we'll display in case the player has won or lost the game. They'll be invisible when the game starts.

In the stats element, you can find the game's most important statistical information: the number of lives left and the current score.

After that, we add a cool chiptune[3] created by Alex Smith[4] to the game using the audio element. The autoplay attribute starts the song immediately, and the loop attribute makes it loop forever. It's a great song, so that doesn't hurt.

---

3. http://opengameart.org/content/awake-megawall-10
4. http://cynicmusic.com/

Finally, we import all the JavaScript code we need. The jQuery[5] library is a very popular tool for creating dynamic web applications. It makes it very easy to manipulate HTML elements, and it'll make our life much easier.

You already know the serial_device.js and game_controller.js files. The arduinoid.js file is more interesting because it contains the actual game logic. It starts with the definition of a few data structures holding the game's most important status information:

BrowserGame/Arduinoid/js/arduinoid.js

```javascript
const MAX_LIVES = 5;

var GameStates = {
  RUNNING: 'running',
  PAUSED: 'paused',
  LOST: 'lost',
  WON: 'won'
}

var Game = {
  lives: MAX_LIVES,
  score: 0,
  state: GameStates.PAUSED,

  paddle: {
    speed: 15,
    width: $("#paddle").width(),
    height: $("#paddle").height()
  },

  playfield: {
    width: $("#playfield").width(),
    height: $("#playfield").height(),
    rows: 4,
    columns: 10
  },

  ball: {
    diameter: $("#ball").width(),
    vx: 5 + Math.random() * 5,
    vy: -10
  },

  controller: new GameController('/dev/tty.usbmodem24321')
}
```

First of all, it defines a constant named MAX_LIVES that contains the maximum number of lives in the game. This is the place to go for cheaters. The GameStates map defines the game's possible states. This is a very common pattern in game programming, and you'll see later how easy it is to write the game's main loop when you identify the game states properly.

The Game object defines all of the game's properties, such as the current score, the number of lives left, and the game's current state. It also contains all information about the game's object, such as the ball's current velocity in all directions or the paddle's speed. Of course, it also defines a GameController object, and you have to adjust the path to the Arduino's serial port.

Most of the Game objects are constants at the beginning; we set only the ball's velocity in the X direction to a random value. This way, the ball won't always go into the same direction each time you start a new round.

Note that we use jQuery functions for the first time when we determine the width and height of the game objects. Look at the following piece of code:

```
width: $("#paddle").width()
```

It looks cryptic at first, but it should be obvious that it somehow determines the paddle's width. Therefore, it uses jQuery's most important method. Its name is $ (yes, you can actually define a JavaScript function named $), and it's a versatile method you can use for various purposes.

The $ function expects a single argument you can use to specify a certain element in your current HTML page. To identify the element, you can use the usual CSS selectors. In our case, we'd like to get the element with the ID paddle, and in CSS you can look up elements specified by an ID by inserting the # character before the ID.

After we've retrieved the element we're looking for, we use jQuery's width method to read its width. jQuery offers many more methods for accessing all possible CSS attributes. Using these methods for getting and setting CSS attributes is much easier than using JavaScript's native functions for looking up and manipulating elements on the current HTML page.

Now that we've set up the game's data structures, we can implement the game's main logic. We start by defining a few methods for initializing and resetting the game.

```
BrowserGame/Arduinoid/js/arduinoid.js
```

```
Line 1  function initGame() {
   -      Game.state = GameStates.PAUSED;
   -      Game.lives = MAX_LIVES;
```

```
  -       Game.score = 0;
  5       resetMovingObjects();
  -       updateStatistics();
  -       drawPlayfield();
  -     }
  -
 10   function resetMovingObjects() {
  -       $("#paddle").css("left", (Game.playfield.width - Game.paddle.width) / 2);
  -       $("#ball").css("left", (Game.playfield.width - Game.ball.diameter) / 2);
  -       $("#ball").css("top", parseInt($("#paddle").css("top")) - Game.paddle.height);
  -     }
 15
  -   function updateStatistics() {
  -       $('#lives').text(Game.lives);
  -       $('#score').text(Game.score);
  -     }
 20
  -   function drawPlayfield() {
  -       var colors = ['blue', 'green', 'red', 'yellow'];
  -       var $playfield = $('#playfield');
  -       $playfield.children('.row').remove();
 25
  -       for (var row = 0; row < Game.playfield.rows; row++) {
  -         var $row = $('<div class="row"></div>');
  -         $row.appendTo($playfield);
  -         for (var col = 0; col < Game.playfield.columns; col++) {
 30         var $block = $("<div class='block'></div>");
  -           $block.css("background", 'url("img/' + colors[row] + '.png")');
  -           $block.appendTo($row);
  -         }
  -       }
 35   }
```

initGame pretty much deserves its name, because it actually initializes the game. It sets a few properties of the Game object to their default values directly. Then it calls several functions for initializing specific game objects. resetMovingObjects sets the positions of the ball and the paddle to their default values. The paddle appears at the middle of the playfield's bottom. The ball then sits on top of the paddle.

updateStatistics copies the current number of lives and the current score to the HTML page. It uses jQuery's text method to set the text of the elements specified by the IDs lives and score. In the initGame function, the game's default values will be copied, of course, but we'll call this function later on, when the game is running.

The drawPlayfield function draws the bricks that the player has to hit with the ball. It creates four <div> elements with their class attribute set to row. Within each row element, it creates ten <div> elements of class block. To achieve this, it first removes all row elements that might exist already in line 24. Again, we use jQuery to our advantage. The children method returns all children of the playfield element having the class row. The remove method removes all of these elements from the HTML page.

Note that variable names can contain the $ character, too, in JavaScript. We use it for naming variables such as $playfield that refer to jQuery objects, which is a helpful convention.

With two nested for loops, we create the bricks afterwards. Here we use the omnipotent $ function again to create all the <div> elements we need. If you pass a string containing HTML code to the $ method, it actually creates the element. In line 27 we create a new row, and in the following line we insert the newly created row into the current HTML page.

In the following for loop, we do the same for the actual blocks. Here we not only create the <div> elements, but we also set their background property to an image depending on the block's row. The images are gradient images that make the blocks more colorful.

Now that the game has been initialized, we can implement the game loop that gets called for each frame.

BrowserGame/Arduinoid/js/arduinoid.js
```javascript
function gameLoop() {
  switch (Game.state) {
    case GameStates.PAUSED:
      if (Game.controller.buttonPressed) {
        Game.state = GameStates.RUNNING;
      }
      break;
    case GameStates.RUNNING:
      movePaddle();
      moveBall();
      checkCollisions();
      updateStatistics();
      break;
    case GameStates.WON:
      handleMessageState("winner");
      break;
    case GameStates.LOST:
      handleMessageState("game_over");
      break;
    default:
      break;
  }
}
```

```
function handleMessageState(message) {
  $("#" + message).show();
  if (Game.controller.buttonPressed) {
    $("#" + message).hide();
    initGame();
  }
}
```

The gameLoop function is surprisingly simple, because it only checks the game's current state and then delegates its work accordingly. If the game is paused currently, it checks whether the player has pressed the game controller's button. If yes, it changes the game's state to GameStates.RUNNING.

If the game is running already, gameLoop moves all game objects, checks for potential collisions, and updates the game's statistics. If the game was won or lost, it calls handleMessageState to display a corresponding message.

handleMessageState displays a message by manipulating an HTML element's content. It also checks whether the game controller's button was pressed. If yes, it hides the message and initializes the game so the player can start a new round. After a player has won or lost a game, he or she can start a new game by pressing the button on the game controller.

Moving the objects on the screen is the most important part in many video games. Thanks to jQuery, it's not that difficult.

BrowserGame/Arduinoid/js/arduinoid.js

```
Line 1  function moveBall() {
   -      var ball_pos = $("#ball").position();
   -      var ball_x = ball_pos.left;
   -      var ball_y = ball_pos.top;
   5      var next_x_pos = ball_x + Game.ball.vx;
   -      var next_y_pos = ball_y + Game.ball.vy;
   -
   -      if (next_x_pos <= 0) {
   -        Game.ball.vx *= -1;
  10        next_x_pos = 1;
   -      } else if (next_x_pos >= Game.playfield.width - Game.ball.diameter) {
   -        Game.ball.vx *= -1;
   -        next_x_pos = Game.playfield.width - Game.ball.diameter - 1;
   -      }
  15
   -      var paddle_y = $("#paddle").position().top;
   -      if (next_y_pos <= 0) {
   -        Game.ball.vy *= -1;
   -        next_y_pos = 1;
  20      } else if (next_y_pos + Game.ball.diameter >= paddle_y) {
   -        var paddle_x = $("#paddle").position().left;
```

```
         if (next_x_pos >= paddle_x &&
             next_x_pos <= paddle_x + Game.paddle.width)
         {
25         Game.ball.vy *= -1;
           next_y_pos = paddle_y - Game.ball.diameter;
         }
       }

30     $("#ball").css({ "left" : next_x_pos, "top" : next_y_pos });
     }

     function movePaddle() {
       if (Game.controller.moveLeft) {
35       var paddle_x = $("#paddle").position().left;
         if (paddle_x - Game.paddle.speed >= 0) {
           $("#paddle").css("left", paddle_x - Game.paddle.speed);
         } else {
           $("#paddle").css("left", 0);
40       }
       }

       if (Game.controller.moveRight) {
         var paddle_x = $("#paddle").position().left;
45       var next_pos = paddle_x + Game.paddle.width + Game.paddle.speed;
         if (next_pos < Game.playfield.width) {
           $("#paddle").css("left", paddle_x + Game.paddle.speed);
         }
       }
50   }
```

The most useful jQuery method when moving objects is position. It returns an object that contains an HTML element's current left and top attributes. In CSS, these attributes specify an object's x- and y-coordinates on the screen. In lines 2 to 4 of the moveBall function, we use the position function to determine the ball's current screen coordinates. In the following two lines, we calculate the ball's new position by adding the current velocities for both directions.

After that, we check whether the ball's new position would be out of the screen. If yes, we clip the coordinates to the screen's boundaries. In lines 8 to 14, we make sure that the ball's x-coordinate is greater than zero and less than the playfield's width. If the ball hits the left or right boundary of the playfield, we multiply vx by -1, so it changes its direction.

Nearly the same happens in lines 16 to 28 for the ball's y-coordinate. Whenever the ball hits the top of the playfield, we multiply vy by -1. The playfield has no bottom boundary, but we have to check whether the ball would hit the paddle. If it does, we invert vy, too.

Eventually, we set the ball's position to the new values in line 30.

Moving the paddle is similar, but it depends on the current state of the game controller. If the player wants the paddle to move left, we subtract the paddle's current speed from the paddle's x-coordinate. We also make sure that the paddle doesn't leave the screen. Movement to the right works nearly the same. We only have to add the paddle's current speed.

A difficult problem in video games is collision detection. You've probably played a game or two and yelled "No, that thing didn't hit me!" or "I'm sure I killed that alien first!" In most cases inexact collision detection is the cause of your frustration.

Even for our simple game, exact collision detections aren't easy. The blocks have rounded corners, so checking whether the ball overlaps one of the corners or has actually touched the block isn't trivial. For a good game experience this isn't necessary, so I've simplified the collision detection.

BrowserGame/Arduinoid/js/arduinoid.js

```
Line 1  function checkCollisions() {
   -      if (ballDropped()) {
   -        Game.lives = Game.lives - 1;
   -        if (Game.lives == 0) {
   5          Game.state = GameStates.LOST;
   -        } else {
   -          Game.state = GameStates.PAUSED;
   -          resetMovingObjects();
   -        }
   10     }
   -      if (!checkBlockCollision()) {
   -        Game.state = GameStates.WON;
   -      }
   -    }
   15
   -    function ballDropped() {
   -      var ball_y = $("#ball").position().top;
   -      var paddle_y = $("#paddle").position().top;
   -      return ball_y + Game.ball.diameter > paddle_y + Game.paddle.height;
   20   }
   -
   -    function inXRange(ball_left, block_left, block_width) {
   -      return (ball_left + Game.ball.diameter >= block_left) &&
   -             (ball_left <= block_left + block_width);
   25   }
   -
   -    function inYRange(ball_top, block_top, block_height) {
   -      return (ball_top + Game.ball.diameter >= block_top) &&
   -             (ball_top <= block_top + block_height);
   30   }
```

```
   function checkBlockCollision() {
     var block_width = $(".block").first().width();
     var block_height = $(".block").first().height();
35   var ball_left = $("#ball").position().left;
     var ball_top = $("#ball").position().top;
     var blocks_left = false;
     $(".block").each(function() {
       if ($(this).css("visibility") == "visible") {
40         blocks_left = true;
         var block_top = $(this).position().top;
         var block_left = $(this).position().left;
         var in_x = inXRange(ball_left, block_left, block_width);
         var in_y = inYRange(ball_top, block_top, block_height);
45         if (in_x && in_y) {
           Game.score += 10;
           $(this).css("visibility", "hidden");
           if (in_x) {
             Game.ball.vy *= -1;
50           }
           if (in_y) {
             Game.ball.vx *= -1;
           }
         }
55       }
     });
     return blocks_left;
   }
```

The checkCollisions function first checks whether the player has dropped the ball. In this case we decrease the number of lives. Then we check whether the player has lost all of his lives. If yes, we set the game's state to GameStates.LOST. Otherwise, we pause the game and set the ball and paddle positions to their defaults.

ballDropped compares the y-coordinate of the ball's bottom with the y-coordinate of the paddle's bottom. If the ball's bottom is greater, the ball has been dropped.

Next we define two helper functions named inXRange and inYRange. They check whether the ball overlaps with a block horizontally or vertically. We use these functions in checkBlockCollision to see whether any visible block has been hit by the ball.

Therefore, we need a few more jQuery methods. In line 33, we select all elements belonging to the class block using $(".block"). If you pass a selector to the $ function that selects more than one element, the function automatically returns a list of objects. We select the first object using the first method; then we read its width. In the next line we do the same to determine the block's height. Because all blocks have the same width and height, we have to do this only once. After that we determine the ball's current position.

In line 38, we use the each method to loop over all blocks in the HTML document. each expects a callback function that gets called for each block. Note that the function doesn't get any arguments, because you can find the current block in $(this).

In the loop function, we check whether the current block is visible, because if it's not, we don't have to check it for a collision. We use our helper functions inXRange and inYRange to see whether the current block has been hit by the ball. In that case we make it invisible, and depending on the way the ball has hit the block, we invert the ball's velocities.

Finally, we have to make sure that the gameLoop function is called every 30 milliseconds to make the game run smoothly:

BrowserGame/Arduinoid/js/arduinoid.js
```
$(function() {
  initGame();
  setInterval(gameLoop, 30);
});
```

We use yet another variant of jQuery's $ function. This time we pass it an anonymous function that gets called as soon as the HTML page has been loaded completely. In this function, we initialize the game and make sure the gameLoop function is called every 30 milliseconds.

The game is complete, so play a few rounds and relax! You deserve it!

What If It Doesn't Work?

If you cannot make this chapter's code run, you should download the code from the book's website and try to run it. Make sure you're using the right serial port in the arduinoid.js and game_controller.js files in the code/BrowserGame/Arduinoid/js/ directory.

Exercises

- Create your own computer mouse using the ADXL335 accelerometer. It should work in free air, and it should emit the current acceleration around the x- and y-axes. It should also have a left button and a right button. Write a Chrome app (or perhaps code in a programming language of your choice?) to control a mouse pointer on the screen.

Creating Games and Game Controllers with the Arduino

If you're thinking about a proper case for the game controller you've built in the preceding chapter, you might have a look at the Lego/Arduino controller.[a] Its innards differ from the controller we've built, but its case is really cool.

You can use the Arduino to build more than your own cool game controllers. You can also use it to build some cool games. With the right extension shields, you can even turn an Arduino into a powerful gaming console. The most powerful extension shields are probably the Gameduino[b] and its successor, Gameduino 2.[c]

If you don't need color graphics and stereo sound, you can find even cheaper solutions, such as the Video Game Shield[d] or the Hackvision.[e] They generate a monochrome video signal, and you can learn how to do it yourself in Chapter 8, *Generating Video Signals with an Arduino*, on page 127.

While looking for a solution that doesn't need an external monitor, someone built a Super Mario Bros. clone with minimal hardware requirements.[f] It's a perfect example of the unbelievable creativity that the Arduino sets free.

---

a.   http://strangemeadowlarkprojects.blogspot.de/2014/05/a-legoarduino-game-controller.html

b.   http://excamera.com/sphinx/gameduino/

c.   http://excamera.com/sphinx/gameduino2/index.html#gameduino2

d.   http://www.wayneandlayne.com/projects/video-game-shield/

e.   http://nootropicdesign.com/store/index.php?main_page=index&cPath=2

f.   http://blog.makezine.com/archive/2010/03/super-mario-brothers-with-an-arduin.html

CHAPTER 8

Generating Video Signals with an Arduino

So far we've used several different technologies to communicate with the outside world. We've used LEDs to represent our binary die's results, for example, and we've used the serial port to send more elaborate messages. We've also turned data received on the serial port into shiny applications running in our browser.

For many projects this way of displaying information is sufficient, but in some cases you want a real display. You could use an LCD display, for example, and you'll find multicolor TFT touch displays you can attach to the Arduino, too. Another option is surprisingly cheap: you can connect the Arduino to your TV set and display information right on the screen.

In this chapter, not only will you learn how analog TV works in principle, you'll also learn how to generate a stable monochrome video signal using your Arduino. At the end of the chapter, you'll have a graphical thermometer that will run on the TV set in your living room.

What You Need

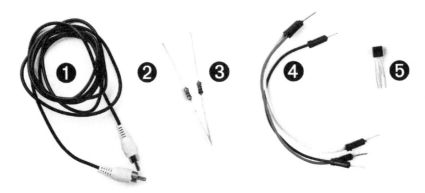

1. An RCA cable
2. A 470Ω resistor
3. A 1kΩ resistor
4. Some wires
5. A TMP36 temperature sensor from Analog Devices
6. An Arduino board, such as the Uno, Duemilanove, or Diecimila
7. A USB cable to connect the Arduino to your computer

How Analog Video Works

Before you create your own video signals, it helps to understand how analog TV systems work in general. If you're impatient, you can skip the theory and jump straight to *Connecting the Arduino to Your TV Set*, on page 131.

First of all, you should note that analog video is completely different from digital video in most regards. In this chapter, we'll only talk about analog video signals that you can feed to your TV set's composite input.

You might remember the good old days when TV sets were huge, heavy boxes with ridiculously tiny screens. These boxes had to be so big because they contained a small electron cannon that produced images by firing electrons to the screen. The cannon drew an image line by line—that is, it started at the top-left corner of the screen and drew the first line of the image. At the end of the line, it moved back to the left side and drew the second line. This technique is called *raster scan*. Figure 23, *How raster scan works*, on page 129 shows how it worked.

After the last line was drawn, the electron beam moved back to the top and drew the next image. Depending on the TV standard, this process happened

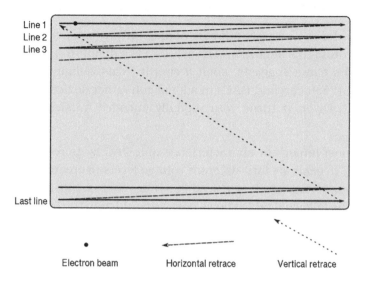

Figure 23—How raster scan works
(Image created by Ian Harvey)

50 to 60 times per second, and it was fast enough to create the illusion of motion. (Actually, most TV sets needed two passes to draw a single image using a mechanism called *interlacing*, but for our purposes that's irrelevant.)

Moving the electron beam across the screen isn't sufficient. You have to somehow encode the information you'd like to draw. Therefore, you have to change the electron beam's intensity while it traverses the screen. Due to a chemical reaction, the TV screen will glow in different colors when the electron cannon hits it with different intensities. For a monochrome signal, you need to generate the voltages explained in the following table.

Voltage:	0.0V	0.3V	0.6V	1.0V
Color:	SYNC	Black	Gray	White

A voltage of 0V represents the SYNC signal. It tells the TV set that a new line of the image begins. All the other voltages represent different colors. To draw a white dot, you have to set the voltage to 1V.

All we have to do is create a couple of different voltage levels. That doesn't sound too difficult, but unfortunately, the Arduino has only analog input pins. It cannot emit analog output signals. At least not directly, but in the next section you'll learn how to do it.

Building a Digital-to-Analog Converter (DAC)

The Arduino doesn't natively support analog output signals, so we need to find a way around this limitation. The solution is a digital-to-analog converter (DAC).[1] As the name suggests, such a circuit turns a digital input into an analog output. You can find DACs in a lot of consumer devices—for example, in your MP3 player. It turns your digitally encoded music into an analog sound wave.

One of the most important characteristics of a DAC is its resolution. In our case we need to generate four different voltage levels to create a video signal. To encode four voltage levels, we need two bits—that is, our DAC has a 2-bit resolution. The following table shows how we could map the four binary input values to their voltage levels.

Binary input:	00	01	10	11
Output voltage:	0.0V	0.3V	0.6V	1.0V

We can use two of the Arduino's digital pins to control the DAC's input value, but we still have to find a way to generate different voltages depending on the pins' values.

There are several ways to achieve this, but one of the easiest is by using a binary-weighted DAC. It has the following characteristics:

- You need a resistor for every input bit.
- All resistors have to be in parallel.
- Resistor value for bit #0 is R. For bit #1 it's 2R, for bit #3 it's 4R, and so on.

Let's say we use the Arduino's digital pins D7 and D9 to control the DAC's input value. In the following figure, you can see our DAC's circuit. You have to add the 470Ω and 1kΩ resistors yourself, but you get the 75Ω resistor for free, because it's part of your TV set's input connector.

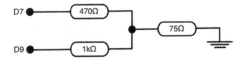

In principle, the binary-weighted DAC is a voltage divider[2]—that is, it turns an input voltage into a smaller voltage. The output voltage depends on the

1. http://en.wikipedia.org/wiki/Digital-to-analog_converter
2. http://en.wikipedia.org/wiki/Voltage_divider

resistor values—75Ω, 470Ω, and 1kΩ, in our case. If you set both input signals to 0V, the output voltage will be 0V, too. That's how we can create the SYNC signal.

Calculating the output voltage for the remaining three combinations of input values isn't rocket science, but the theory and formulas of voltage division are beyond the scope of this book. Just to give you a feeling, the following figure shows how to calculate the output voltage when you set D7 to 0V and D9 to 5V.

$$\frac{\dfrac{75 \cdot 470}{75 + 470}}{1000 + \dfrac{75 \cdot 470}{75 + 470}} \cdot 5V = 0.3V$$

The following table shows the corresponding output voltages for all possible combinations of pin values.

Pin D7	Pin D9	Output Voltage	Color
0V	0V	0.0V	SYNC
0V	5V	0.3V	Black
5V	0V	0.65V	Gray
5V	5V	0.95V	White

Now you should see why we've used a 470Ω and a 1kΩ resistor. The value 1000 is roughly 470 times 2, so the resistor values follow the rules of a binary-weighted DAC. Also, these two resistors (combined with the TV set's 75Ω resistor) produce the output voltages we need. Note that the output voltages don't exactly match the specification, but in practice the small differences are negligible.

Connecting the Arduino to Your TV Set

Even with a digital-to-analog converter in place, we still have a problem: the Arduino doesn't have an RCA jack—that is, you cannot plug an RCA cable into an Arduino. We could attach an RCA jack to a breadboard and connect it to the Arduino, but there's an easier solution. We'll modify an RCA cable and connect it directly to the Arduino.

First, you have to cut off one of the cable's connectors using a wire cutter. (See *Learning How to Use a Wire Cutter*, on page 243, to learn more about wire cutters.) Then remove about three centimeters of the cable's outer insulation.

Be careful, because the insulation isn't very thick. Use the wire cutter to cut it slightly and then remove it by pushing it slowly toward the cable's end. The cable should look like the following image.

As you can see, there's a mesh of wires below the outer insulation. Bring back the mesh into wire shape by rubbing it between your thumb and forefinger, so you can solder it to a solid-core wire later. The result should look like the following image.

The cable usually also contains an inner insulation made of plastic. Use the wire cutter again to remove the inner insulation. In my experience, it's best to put the insulation between the wire cutter's blades and then turn the cable slowly and carefully, increasing the pressure while turning the cable. Be very careful that you don't accidentally cut the signal wire! After you've cut through the whole insulation, you can easily remove it. You should now see the cable's signal wire, and your cable should look like the following image.

Finally, we have to connect the two resistors to the RCA cable's signal wire, and it's not sufficient to simply knot them together. You have to solder them. While you're at it, connect the RCA cable's ground wire to a piece of solid-core wire, so you can easily attach it to the Arduino. The following image shows what it should look like.

That's it! You've turned an RCA cable into a binary-weighted DAC that you can can connect to your Arduino to generate your own video signal. Plug the 470Ω resistor into port D7, the 1kΩ resistor into D9, and the ground wire into one of the Arduino's GND ports. You can see the final circuit in the following image.

Using the TVout Library

Okay, the hardware's done, but how do we bring it to life? We could try to write our own library to emit video signals, but I have to admit that I didn't tell you the whole truth. To generate a clean and stable video signal, you not only have to output different voltages, but you also have to make sure that you emit your signals according to a very accurate schedule. The timing has to be so accurate that you have to implement it in assembly language!

Don't worry! Of course there's a library for that. The TVout library[3] not only generates crystal-clear video signals, but also comes with a lot of utility functions for drawing geometric shapes. On top of that, it supports different fonts in several sizes.

Note that the TVout library doesn't support every Arduino board. For example, it won't work on the Arduino Leonardo or the Arduino Due. Check the TVout's website for a list of compatible hardware.

Download TVout,[4] unzip it, and copy the contents of the zip archive to the libraries folder of the Arduino IDE. Then restart your IDE.

The library comes with a few examples. The most important ones are DemoNTSC and DemoPAL. In principle, it's only one example that demonstrates all of the library's features, but it comes in two flavors: NTSC and PAL. This is necessary because there are different standards for analog TV. NTSC and PAL are two very popular ones. They don't differ much, and modern TV sets are usually capable of working with both. Still, your TV set might be pickier about its input. If you're living in the United States, you'll probably need the NTSC demo; in Europe, PAL is the way to go.

Compile and upload the sketch to your Arduino; then connect the Arduino to your TV set's composite input using the RCA cable. You should see an impressive demo showing TVout's capabilities. At the end it even shows the inevitable rotating 3D cube.

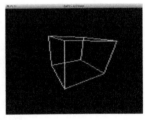

The library's standard example shows nearly all of TVout's functions in action, so it's a good idea to have a look at the code. Still, the best way to learn how to use the library is to write your own code. In the next section, you'll create a graphical thermometer that displays the current temperature on your TV screen.

Building a TV Thermometer

To build our TV thermometer, we'll use the TMP36 sensor again, so we'll combine the circuit we created in *Increasing Precision Using a Temperature Sensor*, on page 86, with the circuit we created for generating the video signal. You can see the result in Figure 24, *Circuit of the TV thermometer*, on page 135.

---

3.   https://code.google.com/p/arduino-tvout/
4.   https://arduino-tvout.googlecode.com/files/TVoutBeta1.zip

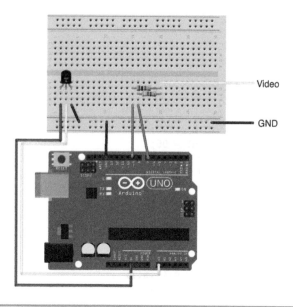

Figure 24—Circuit of the TV thermometer

Don't get confused by what the circuit for the video signal looks like in the circuit diagram. That's how you would build the circuit on a breadboard. Of course, you can still connect the modified RCA cable directly to the Arduino. Then connect the circuit for the TMP36 sensor.

Before we dive into the project's code, have a look at what we're trying to build.

On the left side of the screen, you see a graphical representation of a typical thermometer. It has a scale ranging from 5.5 to 40 degrees Celsius. The thermometer isn't a static image. The bar in the middle will grow or shrink depending on the current temperature.

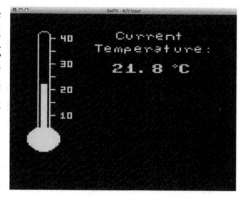

On the right side of the screen, we display the current temperature as text. All in all, we have to output some text, and we have to draw some graphics. It's a perfect opportunity to meet TVout's most important functions, so let's see how it works.

Video/TvThermometer/TvThermometer.ino

```
#include <TVout.h>
#include <fontALL.h>
#include "thermometer.h"

const float SUPPLY_VOLTAGE = 5.0;
const float MIN_TEMP = 5.5;
const float MAX_TEMP = 40.0;
const unsigned int SCREEN_WIDTH = 120;
const unsigned int SCREEN_HEIGHT = 96;
const unsigned int TEMP_SENSOR_PIN = A0;
const unsigned int SCALE_X_MIN = 8;
const unsigned int SCALE_Y_MIN = 6;
const unsigned int SCALE_Y_MAX = 75;
const unsigned int SCALE_WIDTH = 3;
const unsigned int SCALE_HEIGHT = SCALE_Y_MAX - SCALE_Y_MIN;

float current_temperature = 0.0;
unsigned long last_measurement = millis();
TVout TV;
```

At the beginning of our program, we include a few header files. TVout.h declares TVout's main class and all of its methods. fontALL.h contains the definition of all fonts that TVout offers. If you don't want to output any text, you don't have to include it. The thermometer.h file makes the graphical representation of our thermometer available to our program. I'll explain its content later.

After we've included all necessary header files, we define a few constants and variables:

- SUPPLY_VOLTAGE defines the Arduino's supply voltage, and TEMP_SENSOR_PIN contains the number of the pin to which you've connected the TMP36 sensor.

- MIN_TEMP and MAX_TEMP define the minimum and maximum temperatures (in degrees Celsius) that the TV thermometer can display.

- SCREEN_WIDTH and SCREEN_HEIGHT define the screen's width and height. Note that the Arduino isn't capable of displaying really big screen resolutions. A width of 120 to 132 pixels and a height of 96 pixels is a reasonable compromise.

- SCALE_X_MIN defines the minimum X position of the thermometer's scale. SCALE_Y_MIN and SCALE_Y_MAX define the minimum and maximum Y positions of the thermometer's scale. We'll need these constants to draw a rectangle representing the current temperature later.

- SCALE_WIDTH and SCALE_HEIGHT define the width and height of the thermometer's scale.

- The variable current_temperature holds the last temperature we measured. last_measurement contains the time stamp in milliseconds when we last measured the current temperature. We need this because we don't want to measure the temperature permanently, but only every few seconds.

- TV is an instance of the TVout class, and we'll use it for accessing the TV screen using the Arduino.

Next we define the setup function:

Video/TvThermometer/TvThermometer.ino
```
void setup() {
  TV.begin(PAL, SCREEN_WIDTH, SCREEN_HEIGHT);
  TV.bitmap(0, 1, thermometer);
  TV.select_font(font4x6);
  TV.set_cursor(20, 4);
  TV.print("40");
  TV.set_cursor(20, 24);
  TV.print("30");
  TV.set_cursor(20, 44);
  TV.print("20");
  TV.set_cursor(20, 64);
  TV.print("10");
}
```

We call the begin method of the TV object. We set the analog TV standard to PAL, and we set the screen's width and height. If your TV set prefers NTSC, you have to replace the first argument with NTSC. After that, we invoke the bitmap method to draw the thermometer image to the screen. Its X position is 0, and its Y position is 1.

The thermometer's image doesn't contain numbers next to its scale, so we add the numbers in our program. Therefore, we have to select the font we're going to use by using the select_font method. TVout's font capabilities are quite impressive. It comes with three fixed-width fonts (4x6, 6x8, and 8x8 pixels) that are sufficient for most purposes. It also supports variable-width fonts, and it even allows you to define your own. Here we use a font that's 4 pixels wide and 6 pixels high. The set_cursor method moves the cursor to a certain screen position, and print prints text to the current cursor position.

The loop function implements the rest of our thermometer's business logic.

Video/TvThermometer/TvThermometer.ino

```
Line 1  void loop() {
   -      unsigned long current_millis = millis();
   -      if (abs(current_millis - last_measurement) >= 1000) {
   -        current_temperature = get_temperature();
   5        last_measurement = current_millis;
   -        int y_pos = mapfloat(
   -          current_temperature, MIN_TEMP, MAX_TEMP, SCALE_Y_MAX, SCALE_Y_MIN);
   -        TV.draw_rect(
   -          SCALE_X_MIN, SCALE_Y_MIN, SCALE_WIDTH, SCALE_HEIGHT, BLACK, BLACK);
   10       TV.draw_rect(
   -          SCALE_X_MIN, y_pos, SCALE_WIDTH, SCALE_Y_MAX - y_pos, WHITE, WHITE);
   -        TV.select_font(font6x8);
   -        TV.set_cursor(53, 1);
   -        TV.print("Current");
   15       TV.set_cursor(40, 11);
   -        TV.print("Temperature:");
   -        TV.select_font(font8x8);
   -        TV.set_cursor(50, 25);
   -        TV.print(current_temperature, 1);
   20       TV.print(" C");
   -        TV.draw_circle(88, 27, 1, WHITE);
   -      }
   -  }

   25  const float mapfloat(
   -      float x, float in_min, float in_max, float out_min, float out_max)
   -  {
   -      return (x - in_min) * (out_max - out_min) / (in_max - in_min) + out_min;
   -  }
   30
   -  const float get_temperature() {
   -      const int sensor_voltage = analogRead(TEMP_SENSOR_PIN);
   -      const float voltage = sensor_voltage * SUPPLY_VOLTAGE / 1024;
   -      return (voltage * 1000 - 500) / 10;
   35  }
```

We make sure that we measure the current temperature only once per second. Whenever we determine the current temperature, we calculate the new upper Y position of the thermometer's scale in line 6. The map_float function maps the current temperature to a value on our thermometer's scale.

Then we use the draw_rect method (which draws a rectangle on the screen) twice. The first call erases the thermometer's scale completely. This is necessary because the temperature can rise or fall. We could clear and redraw the whole screen every time, but that would be overkill. The second call draws a white rectangle on our scale that represents the current temperature.

Next, we output the current temperature as text. We use TVout's select_font, set_cursor, and print methods to output the text "Current Temperature" in a font that is 6 pixels wide and 8 pixels high. After that, we output the current temperature in degrees Celsius using the 8x8 font. The TVout library doesn't define a symbol for degrees Celsius, so we use the draw_circle method in line 21 to draw a small circle to simulate a degrees symbol.

We're done! That's all the code we need to make the TV thermometer work. The only thing I haven't explained in detail is how outputting the thermometer image works. You'll learn more about that in the next section.

Working with Graphics in TVout

In TvThermometer.ino we've included the thermometer.h file without explaining what it contains. Here's how it looks:

Video/TvThermometer/thermometer.h
```
#ifndef THERMOMETER_H
#define THERMOMETER_H
extern const unsigned char thermometer[];
#endif
```

Quite disappointing, isn't it? The file declares only a single variable named thermometer. This variable is an array of unsigned character values, and the extern keyword tells the compiler that we only want to declare the variable. That is, we can refer to it in our program, but we still have to define it to allocate some memory.

We actually define the thermometer variable in thermometer.cpp (we've skipped a few lines for brevity):

Video/TvThermometer/thermometer.cpp
```
Line 1  #include <Arduino.h>
     -  #include <avr/pgmspace.h>
     -  #include "thermometer.h"
     -  PROGMEM const unsigned char thermometer[] = {
     5    20, 94,
     -      B00000000, B11110000, B00000000,
     -      B00000001, B00001000, B00000000,
     -      B00000010, B00000100, B00000000,
     -      B00000010, B00000100, B00000000,
    10      B00000010, B00000100, B00000000,
     -      B00000010, B00000111, B10000000, // 40.0
     -      B00000010, B00000100, B00000000,
     -      B00000010, B00000100, B00000000,
     -      B00000010, B00000100, B00000000,
    15      B00000010, B00000100, B00000000,
     -      B00000010, B00000100, B00000000,
```

```
-      B00000010, B00000100, B00000000,
-      B00000010, B00000100, B00000000,
-      B00000010, B00000100, B00000000,
20     B00000010, B00000100, B00000000,
-      // ...
-      B00000010, B00000100, B00000000, // 5.5
-      B00000111, B11111110, B00000000,
-      B00001111, B11111111, B00000000,
25     B00011111, B11111111, B10000000,
-      B00111111, B11111111, B11000000,
-      B01111111, B11111111, B11100000,
-      B01111111, B11111111, B11100000,
-      B11111111, B11111111, B11110000,
30     B11111111, B11111111, B11110000,
-      B11111111, B11111111, B11110000,
-      B11111111, B11111111, B11110000,
-      B11111111, B11111111, B11110000,
-      B11111111, B11111111, B11110000,
35     B01111111, B11111111, B11100000,
-      B01111111, B11111111, B11100000,
-      B00111111, B11111111, B11000000,
-      B00011111, B11111111, B10000000,
-      B00001111, B11111111, B00000000,
40     B00000111, B11111110, B00000000,
-      B00000001, B11111000, B00000000,
-      B00000001, B11111000, B00000000,
-    };
```

This file looks weird at first, but it's really simple. First, we include Arduino.h because we'll need to declare binary constants later. After that, we include avr/pgmspace.h because we want to store our image data in the Arduino's flash RAM. Eventually, we include thermometer.h because we need the declaration of our thermometer image data.

In line 4, we eventually define the thermometer variable we declared in thermometer.h. The definition differs slightly from the declaration because it contains the PROGMEM directive.[5] This directive tells the compiler to copy the data stored in the thermometer variable to the Arduino's flash memory. Usually, when you define a variable in an Arduino program, it occupies memory in the SRAM. Most Arduinos don't have a lot of SRAM (the Arduino Uno only has 2 KB), so it's a valuable resource and you shouldn't waste it. As a rule of thumb, you should store all constant data in the Arduino's flash RAM. Use SRAM only for information that might change during program execution.

---

5.   http://arduino.cc/en/Reference/PROGMEM

Image data like our thermometer usually doesn't change, so you should always store it in flash RAM using the PROGMEM directive. TVout expects image data in raw format. The first two bytes contain the width and height of an image. The data that follows contains the image data line by line. In thermometer.cpp, each line of image data contains three bytes, because the image is 20 pixels wide, and 20 pixels occupy three bytes. Consequently, the file contains 94 lines each representing a single line of the thermometer image. Because we've used binary literals to encode the image data, you can actually see how the image looks when reading the source code. A 1 represents a white pixel, and a 0 represents a black pixel.

Drawing Images for Your Arduino Programs

You can draw simple images directly in the source code by editing binary numbers. As soon as your images get more complex, you need some tool support. For graphics that are still fairly simple but that are too complex to edit the binary numbers in the source code, you can use any drawing program, of course, but most modern tools are way too complicated for this job.

I've created the thermometer image with a fairly simple online tool named Piskel.[6] It's open source, it's easy to use, and it feels just right for creating Arduino graphics. You can see it in action in Figure 25, *You can find good online editors for pixel graphics*, on page 142.

Applications like Piskel really help to create images for your Arduino programs, but they usually store these images in .gif or .png files. In the next section, you'll learn how to convert these files into source code.

Turning Pixels into C++ Code

After you've finished your pixel art, you still have to convert it into a C/C++ file. You could do it manually, but that wouldn't be very pragmatic, would it? It'd be much better to write a small program that does the conversion automatically.

You could write such a program in any modern programming language; we'll use Ruby here. Processing graphics in Ruby is easy thanks to the rmagick library. This library is a binding to ImageMagick,[7] a powerful tool for transforming images. Before you can install rmagick, you have to install ImageMagick.

---

6. http://www.piskelapp.com/
7. http://www.imagemagick.org/

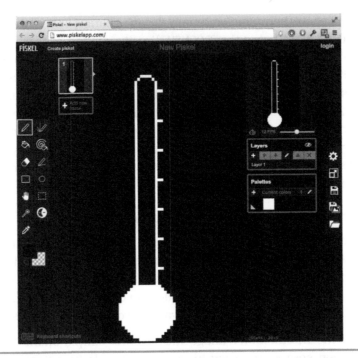

Figure 25—You can find good online editors for pixel graphics.

When ImageMagick is available on your system, you can install the rmagick library using the following command:

```
maik> gem install rmagick
```

Now you can use rmagick in your Ruby programs. We'll use it to convert a graphics file into a C++ file:

Video/img2cpp.rb
```
Line 1  require 'RMagick'
     -  include Magick
     -
     -  image = Image::read(ARGV[0]).first
     5
     -  puts '#include "thermometer.h"'
     -  puts 'PROGMEM const unsigned char thermometer[] = {'
     -  puts "  #{image.columns}, #{image.rows},"
     -
    10  (0..image.rows).each do |y|
     -    print '  B'
     -    (0..image.columns).each do |x|
     -      pixel = image.pixel_color(x, y)
     -      print pixel.red == 0 ? '0' : '1'
    15      print ', B' if (x + 1) % 8 == 0
```

```
-      end
-      print '0' * (8 - (image.columns % 8))
-      puts ','
-    end
20
-    puts '};'
```

First, the program loads the rmagick library and imports the RMagick namespace. We do this to save some typing, because now we don't have to fully qualify all classes that live in the RMagick namespace. In line 4, we read an image whose name we have to pass as a command-line argument. The image file's format doesn't matter, because ImageMagick understands nearly all image file formats. The image variable contains a representation of the image that doesn't depend on the original file format any longer.

Next, we output the first three lines of the C++ file we'd like to generate. These lines are mostly static. Only the third line contains some variable parts—that is, the image's width and the height.

Then we process the image's pixels using two nested loops. The outer loop iterates through each row of the image, and the inner loop through each column. In line 13 we read the current pixel, and in the next line we use a cheap trick to determine whether the pixel is black or white. We know that our images consist only of black and white pixels, so it's sufficient to check only one color component. If the red component is 0, the pixel has to be black. If it's 1, the pixel has to be white. We transform every pixel into a bit value, and if the number of pixels in an image row isn't divisible by 8 without a remainder, we fill the remaining bits with zeros.

You can run the program like this:

```
maik> ruby img2cpp.rb thermometer.png > thermometer.cpp
```

This call turns the thermometer.png file into a C++ file you can add to your Arduino project without any further modifications. That's how software developers approach boring and error-prone tasks.

In the next chapter, you'll learn how to connect a Wii Nunchuk to your Arduino, and we'll use the TVout library to turn the Arduino into a video game console.

What If It Doesn't Work?

Even if this chapter's hardware is simple, a few things can still go wrong. If you don't see a video signal at all on your TV set, make sure you've selected the right input source. Usually its name is AV or Composite. When in doubt, try all of them.

Then check whether you've swapped the resistors. Connect the 470Ω resistor to pin D7 and the 1kΩ resistor to D9. Also, make sure the resistors have the right values.

If you see a distorted video signal, make sure you haven't accidentally used NTSC instead of PAL or vice versa. Also, check all solder joints on the modified RCA cable. When in doubt, add more solder.

Exercises

- Use the TVout library to visualize some other sensor's data. You can try to build the parking-distance control from Chapter 5, *Sensing the World Around Us*, on page 77, using the TVout library.

- Modify the TV thermometer so that it switches between degrees Celsius and degrees Fahrenheit every few seconds. Don't just change the text; change the graphics, too.

CHAPTER 9

Tinkering with the Wii Nunchuk

One of the most entertaining electronic activities is simply tinkering: taking an existing product and turning it into something different or using it for an unintended purpose. Sometimes you have to open the product and void its warranty; other times you can safely make it part of your own project.

In this chapter, you'll learn how to hijack a Nintendo Nunchuk controller. It's a perfect candidate for tinkering: it comes with a three-axis accelerometer, an analog joystick, and two buttons, and it is very cheap (less than $20 at the time of this writing). Even better: because of its good design and its easy-to-access connectors, you can easily integrate it into your own projects.

You'll use an ordinary Nunchuk controller and transfer the data it emits to our computer using an Arduino. You'll learn how to wire it to the Arduino, how to write software that reads the controller's current state, and how to build your own video game console. You don't even need a Nintendo Wii to do all of this—you need only a Nunchuk controller (shown in Figure 26, *A Nintendo Nunchuk controller*, on page 146).

What You Need

- An Arduino board, such as the Uno, Duemilanove, or Diecimila
- A USB cable to connect the Arduino to your computer
- A Nintendo Nunchuk controller
- Four wires
- The modified RCA cable you built in Chapter 8, *Generating Video Signals with an Arduino*, on page 127

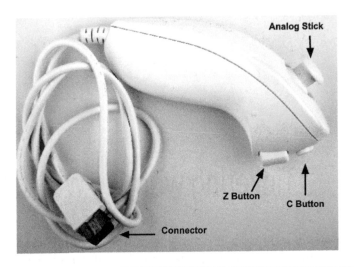

Figure 26—A Nintendo Nunchuk controller

Wiring a Wii Nunchuk

Wiring a Nunchuk to an Arduino really is a piece of cake. You don't have to open the Nunchuk or modify it in any way. You only have to put four wires into its connector and then connect the wires to the Arduino:

It has six connectors, but only four of them are active: GND, 3.3V, Data, and Clock. Here's the pinout of a Nunchuk plug:

Put a wire into each connector and then connect the wires to the Arduino. Connect the data wire to analog pin 4 and the clock wire to analog pin 5. The GND wire has to be connected to the Arduino's ground pin, and the 3.3V wire belongs to the Arduino's 3.3V pin.

That's really all you have to do to connect a Nunchuk controller to an Arduino. In the next section, you'll see that the two wires connected to analog pins 4 and 5 are all we need to interface with the controller.

Talking to a Nunchuk

No official documentation shows how a Nunchuk works internally or how you can use it in a non-Wii environment. But some smart hackers and makers on the Internet invested a lot of time into reverse-engineering what's happening inside the controller.

All in all, it's really simple, because the Nunchuk uses the Two-Wire Interface (TWI), also known as I^2C (Inter-Integrated Circuit) protocol.[1] It enables devices to communicate via a master/slave data bus using only two wires. You transmit data on one wire (Data), while the other synchronizes the communication (Clock).

The Arduino IDE comes with a library named Wire that implements the I^2C protocol. It expects the data line to be connected to analog pin 4 and the clock line to analog pin 5. We'll use it shortly to communicate with the Nunchuk, but before that, we'll have a look at the commands the controller understands.[2]

To be honest, the Nunchuk understands only a single command: "Give me all your data." Whenever it receives this command, it returns 6 bytes that have the following meanings:

Bit	7	6	5	4	3	2	1	0
Byte 1	Joystick x position							
Byte 2	Joystick y position							
Byte 3	X acceleration bits 9..2							
Byte 4	Y acceleration bits 9..2							
Byte 5	Z acceleration bits 9..2							
Byte 6	Z accel. bits 1..0		Y accel. bits 1..0		X accel. bits 1..0		C status	Z status

---

1. http://en.wikipedia.org/wiki/I2c
2. At http://todbot.com/blog/2010/09/25/softi2cmaster-add-i2c-to-any-arduino-pins/, you can find a library that allows you to use any pair of pins for I^2C communication.

- Byte 1 contains the analog stick's x-axis value, and in byte 2 you'll find the stick's y-axis value. Both are 8-bit numbers and range from about 29 to 225.

- Acceleration values for the x-, y-, and z-axes are three 10-bit numbers. Bytes 3, 4, and 5 contain their eight most significant bits. You can find the missing two bits for each of them in byte 6.

- Byte 6 has to be interpreted bit-wise. Bit 0 (the least significant bit) contains the status of the Z-button. It's 0 if the button was pressed; otherwise, it is 1. Bit 1 contains the C-button's status.

The remaining six bits contain the missing least significant bits of the acceleration values. Bits 2 and 3 belong to the x-axis, bits 4 and 5 belong to Y, and bits 6 and 7 belong to Z.

Now that you know how to interpret the data you get from the Nunchuk, you can start to build a Nunchuk class to control it.

Improve People's Lives with Tinkering

Because of its popularity, peripheral equipment for modern game consoles often is unbelievably cheap. Also, it's no longer limited to classic controllers; you can buy things such as snowboard simulators or cameras. So, it comes as no surprise that creative people have built many interesting projects using hardware that was originally built for playing games.

An impressive and useful tinkering project is the EyeWriter.[a] It uses the PlayStation Eye (a camera for Sony's PlayStation 3) to track the movement of human eyes.

A team of hackers built it to enable their paralyzed friend to draw graffiti using his eyes. Because of a disease, this friend, an artist, is almost completely physically paralyzed and can move only his eyes. With the EyeWriter, he can create amazing artwork again.

It's not an Arduino project, but it's definitely worth a look.

---

a.   http://www.eyewriter.org/

Building a Nunchuk Class

The interface of our Nunchuk class (and the main part of its implementation) looks as follows:

Tinkering/NunchukDemo/nunchuk.h
```
Line 1  #ifndef __NUNCHUK_H__
     -  #define __NUNCHUK_H__
     -  #define NUNCHUK_BUFFER_SIZE 6
```

```
 5  class Nunchuk {
 -  public:
 -    void initialize();
 -    bool update();
 -
10    int joystick_x() const { return _buffer[0]; }
 -    int joystick_y() const { return _buffer[1]; }
 -
 -    int x_acceleration() const {
 -      return ((int)(_buffer[2]) << 2) | ((_buffer[5] >> 2) & 0x03);
15    }
 -
 -    int y_acceleration() const {
 -      return ((int)(_buffer[3]) << 2) | ((_buffer[5] >> 4) & 0x03);
 -    }
20
 -    int z_acceleration() const {
 -      return ((int)(_buffer[4]) << 2) | ((_buffer[5] >> 6) & 0x03);
 -    }
 -    bool z_button() const { return !(_buffer[5] & 0x01); }
25    bool c_button() const { return !(_buffer[5] & 0x02); }
 -
 -  private:
 -    void request_data();
 -    char decode_byte(const char);
30
 -    unsigned char _buffer[NUNCHUK_BUFFER_SIZE];
 -  };
 -
 -  #endif
```

This small C++ class is all you need to use a Nunchuk controller with your Arduino. It starts with a double-include prevention mechanism: it checks whether a preprocessor macro named _NUNCHUK_H_ has been defined already using #ifndef. If it hasn't been defined, we define it and continue with the declaration of the Nunchuk class. Otherwise, the preprocessor skips the declaration, so you can safely include this header file more than once in your application.

In line 3, we create a constant for the size of the array we need to store the data the Nunchuk returns. We define this array in line 31, and in this case, we define the constant using the preprocessor instead of the const keyword, because array constants must be known at compile time in C++.

Then the actual declaration of the Nunchuk class begins. To initiate the communication channel between the Arduino and the Nunchuk, you have to invoke the initialize method once. Then you call update whenever you want the Nunchuk to send new data. You'll see the implementation of these two methods shortly.

We have public methods for getting all of the attributes the Nunchuk returns: the x and y positions of the analog stick, the button states, and the acceleration values of the x-, y-, and z-axes. All of these methods operate on the raw data you can find in the buffer in line 31. Their implementation is mostly trivial, and it requires only a single line of code. Only the assembly of the 10-bit acceleration values needs some tricky bit operations (see *Bit Operations*, on page 251).

At the end of the class declaration, you'll find two private helper methods named request_data and decode_byte. We need them to implement the initialize and update methods:

Tinkering/NunchukDemo/nunchuk.cpp

```
Line 1  #include <Arduino.h>
   -    #include <Wire.h>
   -    #include "nunchuk.h"
   -    #define NUNCHUK_DEVICE_ID 0x52
   5
   -    void Nunchuk::initialize() {
   -      Wire.begin();
   -      Wire.beginTransmission(NUNCHUK_DEVICE_ID);
   -      Wire.write((byte)0x40);
  10      Wire.write((byte)0x00);
   -      Wire.endTransmission();
   -      update();
   -    }
   -
  15  bool Nunchuk::update() {
   -      delay(1);
   -      Wire.requestFrom(NUNCHUK_DEVICE_ID, NUNCHUK_BUFFER_SIZE);
   -      int byte_counter = 0;
   -      while (Wire.available() && byte_counter < NUNCHUK_BUFFER_SIZE)
  20        _buffer[byte_counter++] = decode_byte(Wire.read());
   -      request_data();
   -      return byte_counter == NUNCHUK_BUFFER_SIZE;
   -    }
   -
  25  void Nunchuk::request_data() {
   -      Wire.beginTransmission(NUNCHUK_DEVICE_ID);
   -      Wire.write((byte)0x00);
   -      Wire.endTransmission();
   -    }
  30
   -    char Nunchuk::decode_byte(const char b) {
   -      return (b ^ 0x17) + 0x17;
   -    }
```

After including all of the libraries we need, we define the NUNCHUK_DEVICE_ID constant. I^2C is a master/slave protocol; in our case, the Arduino will be the master, and the Nunchuk will be the slave. The Nunchuk registers itself at the data bus using a certain ID (0x52), so we can address it when we need something.

In initialize, we establish the connection between the Arduino and the Nunchuk by sending a handshake. In line 7, we call Wire's begin method, so the Arduino joins the I^2C bus as a master. (If you pass begin an ID, it joins the bus as a slave having this ID.) Then we'll begin a new transmission to the device identified by NUNCHUCK_DEVICE_ID: our Nunchuk.

We send two bytes (0x40 and 0x00) to the Nunchuk, and then we end the transmission. This is the whole handshake procedure, and now we can ask the Nunchuk for its current status by calling update. In the following figure, we see the message flow between an Arduino and a Nunchuk.

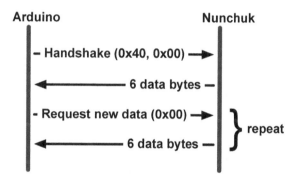

update first pauses for a millisecond to let things settle. Then we request six bytes from the Nunchuk, calling Wire.requestFrom. This doesn't actually return the bytes, but we have to read them in a loop and fill our buffer. Wire.available returns the number of bytes available on the data bus, and Wire.read returns the current byte. We cannot use the bytes we get from the Nunchuk directly, because the controller obfuscates them. "Decrypting" them is easy, as you can see in decode_byte.

Finally, we call request_data to tell the Nunchuk to prepare new data. It transmits a single zero byte to the Nunchuk, which means "prepare the next six bytes."

Before we actually use our Nunchuk class in the next section, take a look at the documentation of the Wire library. In the Arduino IDE's menu, choose Help > Reference and click the Libraries link.

> ## Scientific Applications Using Wii Equipment
>
> Because of the Wii's accuracy and low price, many scientists use the Wii for things other than gaming. Some hydrologists use it for measuring evaporation from a body of water.[a] Usually, you'd need equipment costing more than $500 to do that.
>
> Some doctors at the University of Melbourne had a closer look at the Wii Balance Board, because they were looking for a cheap device to help stroke victims recover.[b] They published a scientific paper verifying that the board's data is clinically comparable to that of a lab-grade "force platform" for a fraction of the cost.
>
> ---
>
> a. http://www.wired.com/wiredscience/2009/12/wiimote-science/
> b. http://www.newscientist.com/article/mg20527435.300-wii-board-helps-physios-strike-a-balance-after-strokes.html

Using Our Nunchuk Class

Let's use the Nunchuk class to see what data the controller actually returns:

Tinkering/NunchukDemo/NunchukDemo.ino

```
#include <Wire.h>
#include "nunchuk.h"

const unsigned int BAUD_RATE = 19200;
Nunchuk nunchuk;

void setup() {
  Serial.begin(BAUD_RATE);
  nunchuk.initialize();
}

void loop() {
  if (nunchuk.update()) {
    Serial.print(nunchuk.joystick_x());
    Serial.print(" ");
    Serial.print(nunchuk.joystick_y());
    Serial.print(" ");
    Serial.print(nunchuk.x_acceleration());
    Serial.print(" ");
    Serial.print(nunchuk.y_acceleration());
    Serial.print(" ");
    Serial.print(nunchuk.z_acceleration());
    Serial.print(" ");
    Serial.print(nunchuk.z_button());
    Serial.print(" ");
    Serial.println(nunchuk.c_button());
  }
}
```

No big surprises here: we define a global Nunchuk object and initialize it in the setup function. In loop, we call update to request the controller's current status and output all attributes to the serial port.

Compile and upload the program, and then open the serial monitor and play around with the Nunchuk. Move the stick, move the controller, and press the buttons, and you should see something like this:

```
46 109 428 394 651 1 1
49 132 414 380 656 1 0
46 161 415 390 651 1 0
46 184 429 377 648 1 0
53 199 404 337 654 1 0
53 201 406 359 643 1 0
```

You have successfully connected a Nunchuk controller to your Arduino. It really isn't rocket science, and in the next section you'll learn how to use it to control your own video games.

The next time you buy a new piece of hardware, try to imagine how to use it in a different context. Often it's easier than you think. Oh, and whenever you create a class such as our Nunchuk class, consider turning your code into a library and making it available on the Internet. (See Chapter 4, *Building a Morse Code Generator Library*, on page 61, to learn how to create your own libraries.)

Creating Your Own Video Game Console

Now that you know how to generate video output and how to control the Wii Nunchuk, it seems natural to build your own little video game console. You only have to combine the Nunchuk circuit and the circuit for generating the video signal. See Figure 27, *Circuit of our video game console*, on page 154.

Note that you still don't need a breadboard. Simply connect the Nunchuk to the Arduino as shown on page 146 and connect the RCA cable as shown on page 133. That's all you have to do to create your own video game console. Now let's write some games for it.

Creating Your Own Video Game

TVout and our Nunchuk library are all we need to write entertaining games for our video game console. In this section we'll build Pragduino, a simple game that demonstrates most of the skills you need to write more complex games.

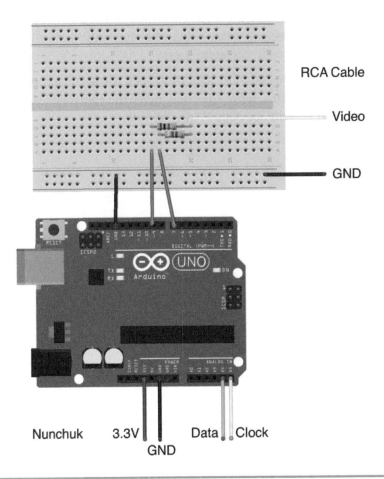

RCA Cable

Video

GND

Nunchuk   3.3V   Data Clock

GND

Figure 27—Circuit of our video game console

The player controls crosshairs using the Nunchuk's analog stick and has to shoot circles using the Nunchuk's Z button. The circles appear at random positions and stay there for 1.5 seconds. A status bar at the top of the screen shows how much time is left until the current circle disappears. The game ends after ten rounds, and the game's goal is to hit as many circles as possible.

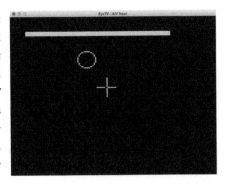

Before we dive into the game's code, make sure you've installed the TVout library as described in *Using the TVout Library*, on page 133. You also have to make the code of your Nunchuk library available. We haven't turned it into a complete library in this chapter, but the book's code archive contains an enhanced version. Download the book's code from the book's website and unzip it. Copy the code/Tinkering/Nunchuk directory to the libraries folder of your Arduino IDE. Alternatively, you can create a folder named Nunchuk in your IDE's libraries folder and copy the nunchuk.h and nunchuk.cpp files to it. In both cases you have to restart the IDE.

That's all the preparation you need to implement the Pragduino game, so let's get started.

Setting the Stage for the Game

Most games need to handle a lot of global state, and Pragduino is no exception, so its code starts with a list of constant and variable definitions:

Tinkering/Pragduino/Pragduino.ino
```
#include <Wire.h>
#include <TVout.h>
#include <fontALL.h>
#include "nunchuk.h"

const int WIDTH = 128;
const int HEIGHT = 96;
const int CH_LEN = 8;
const int MAX_TARGET = 10;
const int TARGET_LIFESPAN = 1500;
```

As usual, we include all header files we need and define a few constants. WIDTH and HEIGHT contain the screen dimensions, and CH_LEN contains the length of a single crosshair element. (The crosshairs consist of four elements.) MAX_TARGET contains the number of circles you have to shoot, and TARGET_LIFESPAN contains a circle's lifespan measured in milliseconds.

Next we define several global variables:

Tinkering/Pragduino/Pragduino.ino
```
Line 1  TVout tv;
     -  Nunchuk nunchuk;
     -
     -  boolean up, down, left, right, c_button, z_button;
     5  int chx, chy;
     -  int chvx, chvy;
     -  int target_x, target_y, target_r;
     -  unsigned int target_count;
     -  unsigned int hits;
```

```
10  unsigned long target_creation;
-
-   enum GameState {
-     INTRO, STARTING, RUNNING, DONE
-   };
15
-   GameState state;
```

In game programming you often have to manage a lot of global variables—even in a small game like ours. First, we define a TVout instance named tv and a Nunchuk instance named nunchuk. After that, we define Boolean variables for all Nunchuk properties we're interested in. They all work the same—we set up to true, for example, if the user pushes the Nunchuk's analog stick upward.

chx and chy contain the current position of the crosshairs. chvx and chvy contain its X and Y velocity. Similarly, target_x and target_y contain the position of the current target. Because the target is a circle, we also need a radius, which we store in target_r.

target_count contains the number of targets we've created already, and in hits you can find the number of targets the player has hit so far. Targets disappear automatically after a short period of time, so we need a place to store the creation time of the current target. This place is target_creation.

In line 12, we define an enumeration that lists our game's potential states. If the game is in the INTRO state, it displays a title screen and waits for the player to press the Z button. If the player presses the Z button, the game changes to the STARTING state. It outputs a "READY?" message and waits for another button press to give the player some time to prepare.

The RUNNING state is where all the action is. In this state the game loop creates new targets, checks the player's moves, and so on. After all targets have appeared, the game state changes to DONE. The player will see a game-over screen and the number of targets that he or she has hit.

We need to initialize all of these global variables whenever a new game starts. The following functions will do that:

Tinkering/Pragduino/Pragduino.ino

```
void init_game() {
  up = down = left = right = c_button = z_button = false;
  chx = WIDTH / 2;
  chy = HEIGHT / 2;
  chvx = 1;
  chvy = 1;
  state = INTRO;
  target_count = 0;
```

```
    hits = 0;
    create_target();
  }

  void create_target() {
    target_r = random(7, 11);
    target_x = random(target_r, WIDTH - target_r);
    target_y = random(target_r, HEIGHT - target_r);
    target_count++;
    target_creation = millis();
  }
```

The init_game function sets most of the global variables to constant values. create_target is a bit more interesting. It creates a new target at a random position and having a random size. We'll use it later on in the game loop whenever we need to create a new target. Note that the function ensures that the target always stays within the screen's bounds. Also, it uses the millis function to determine the target's creation time.

Adding the Setup and Loop Functions

Like all Arduino programs our little game needs setup and loop functions:

```
Tinkering/Pragduino/Pragduino.ino
Line 1  void setup() {
   -      randomSeed(analogRead(A0));
   -      tv.begin(PAL, WIDTH, HEIGHT);
   -      nunchuk.initialize();
   5      init_game();
   -    }
   -
   -    void loop() {
   -      check_controls();
  10      switch (state) {
   -        case INTRO:    intro();       break;
   -        case STARTING: start_game();  break;
   -        case RUNNING:  update_game(); break;
   -        case DONE:     game_over();   break;
  15      }
   -      tv.delay_frame(1);
   -    }
   -
   -    void check_controls() {
  20      up = down = left = right = c_button = z_button = false;
   -      if (nunchuk.update())
   -      {
   -        if (nunchuk.joystick_x() < 70)
   -          left = true;
  25        if (nunchuk.joystick_x() > 150)
   -          right = true;
```

```
        if (nunchuk.joystick_y() > 150)
-          up = true;
-        if (nunchuk.joystick_y() < 70)
30         down = true;
-        c_button = nunchuk.c_button();
-        z_button = nunchuk.z_button();
-      }
- }
```

setup initializes the random number generator using some noise from analog pin A0. Then it initializes the screen and the Nunchuk, and finally it calls init_game to set all global variables to reasonable values.

The loop function calls check_controls to read the current state of the Nunchuk. Then it checks the game's current state in a switch statement and delegates its work to the function responsible for handling the current state.

In line 16, loop calls a function of the TVout library you haven't seen before. delay_frame waits for the beginning of the next vertical blanking interval—that is, for the moment when the TV set's electron beam wanders from the bottom of the screen back to the top. We only want to wait for the beginning of the next frame, so we pass 1 to delay_frame. This is necessary to prevent flickering, because it ensures that the creation of the game's graphics in memory stays in sync with the actual output on the screen.

Handling the Different Game States

Handling the game's different states is vital, so we define separate functions for dealing with each game state:

Tinkering/Pragduino/Pragduino.ino
```
Line 1  void intro() {
-          tv.select_font(font8x8);
-          tv.printPGM(28, 20, PSTR("Pragduino"));
-          tv.select_font(font6x8);
5          tv.printPGM(16, 40, PSTR("A Pragmatic Game"));
-          tv.select_font(font4x6);
-          tv.printPGM(18, 74, PSTR("Press Z-Button to Start"));
-          if (z_button) {
-            state = STARTING;
10           z_button = false;
-            delay(200);
-          }
- }
-
15  void start_game() {
-          tv.clear_screen();
-          tv.select_font(font8x8);
-          tv.printPGM(40, 44, PSTR("READY?"));
```

```
   -       if (z_button) {
20           init_game();
   -         state = RUNNING;
   -       }
   -     }
   -
25   void game_over() {
   -     tv.clear_screen();
   -     tv.select_font(font8x8);
   -     tv.printPGM(28, 38, PSTR("Game Over"));
   -     int x = (WIDTH - 7 * 8) / 2;
30     if (hits > 9)
   -       x = (WIDTH - 8 * 8) / 2;
   -     tv.printPGM(x, 50, PSTR("Hits: "));
   -     tv.print(x + 6 * 8, 50, hits);
   -     if (z_button) {
35       state = STARTING;
   -       z_button = false;
   -       delay(200);
   -     }
   -   }
40
   -   void update_game() {
   -     tv.clear_screen();
   -     tv.draw_circle(target_x, target_y, target_r, WHITE);
   -     move_crosshairs();
45     draw_crosshairs();
   -     check_target();
   -     if (target_count == MAX_TARGET + 1) {
   -       state = DONE;
   -       z_button = false;
50       delay(200);
   -     }
   -   }
```

The intro, start_game, and game_over functions are very similar. They print a message to the screen, then they wait for a Z button press. If the Z button was pressed, they move to the next state. Before they move to the next state, they set z_button to false and wait for 200 milliseconds. This is necessary to debounce the Z button.

All three functions use yet another TVout method. Look at line 3, for example. Here we use TVout's printPGM method. It works like the regular print method, but it reads the string to be output from the Arduino's flash memory and not from its precious SRAM. For applications that display a lot of constant messages, this can save a lot of memory.

To transfer the string into flash memory, we use the PSTR macro. It ensures that the strings we output using printPGM will be copied to flash memory when the program gets compiled.

Writing the Game Loop

The most central function of our game is update_game. It implements the actual game loop and first clears the screen by calling clear_screen. Then it uses draw_circle to draw the current target. move_crosshairs calculates the new position of the crosshairs depending on the player's movement. draw_crosshairs outputs the crosshairs to the screen.

check_target determines the state of the current target—in other words, it checks whether the user has hit the target, whether the target has been on the screen for too long, or whether nothing special has happened. If all targets have been shown already, the game is over.

To control the crosshairs, we use the following helper functions:

Tinkering/Pragduino/Pragduino.ino

```
void move_crosshairs() {
  if (left) chx -= chvx;
  if (right) chx += chvx;
  if (up) chy -= chvy;
  if (down) chy += chvy;

  if (chx <= CH_LEN)
    chx = CH_LEN + 1;
  if (chx >= WIDTH - CH_LEN)
    chx = WIDTH - CH_LEN - 1;
  if (chy <= CH_LEN)
    chy = CH_LEN + 1;
  if (chy >= HEIGHT - CH_LEN)
    chy = HEIGHT - CH_LEN - 1;
}

void draw_crosshairs() {
  tv.draw_row(chy, chx - CH_LEN, chx - 1, WHITE);
  tv.draw_row(chy, chx + 1, chx + CH_LEN, WHITE);
  tv.draw_column(chx, chy - CH_LEN, chy - 1, WHITE);
  tv.draw_column(chx, chy + 1, chy + CH_LEN, WHITE);
}
```

move_crosshairs checks all global variables related to the current Nunchuk state. It updates the position of the crosshairs depending on the variable values. Then it ensures that the crosshairs stay within the screen's bounds.

The draw_crosshairs function actually draws the crosshairs on the screen. Instead of using a bitmap to draw the crosshairs, we use two new TVout methods. draw_row outputs a horizontal line, and we use it to output the two horizontal lines of the crosshairs. Similarly, we use draw_column to draw the two vertical lines. We leave the pixel at the crossing point empty to make the crosshairs look a bit nicer.

You might wonder why we didn't use a bitmap. The problem with bitmaps is that they don't look nice when they overlap. Even if the bitmap looks like crosshairs, it still is a square. If you move a crosshairs bitmap over a circle, the bitmap will hide a big part of the circle's pixels.

To complete the game's source code, we need two functions for managing the targets:

Tinkering/Pragduino/Pragduino.ino

```
bool target_hit() {
  if (z_button)
    return (target_x - chx) * (target_x - chx) +
           (target_y - chy) * (target_y - chy) < target_r * target_r;
  return false;
}

void check_target() {
  if (target_hit()) {
    hits++;
    create_target();
  }
  int remaining_time = millis() - target_creation;
  if (remaining_time >= TARGET_LIFESPAN) {
    create_target();
  }
  int w = map(TARGET_LIFESPAN - remaining_time, 0, TARGET_LIFESPAN, 0, WIDTH);
  tv.draw_rect(0, 0, w, 3, WHITE, WHITE);
}
```

target_hit checks whether the player has hit the current target. This can only happen if the player presses the Z button. If this is the case, we use a simple distance calculation to see whether the crosshairs are in the circle.

To manage the current target's lifecycle, we use check_target. If the target was hit, we increment the hits counter and create the next target. After that, we calculate the time the current target will stay on the screen unless it gets hit. If this time is greater than the target's lifespan, we create a new target. At the end of the function, we turn the remaining time into a status bar at the top of the screen.

With less than 200 lines of code, you've written a complete game for your new video game console. It's definitely not a blockbuster, but it's actually fun and a great opportunity to learn about the very basics of game programming.

Also, it should give you enough confidence to implement more advanced games. You can find a lot of classic games on the web that use nearly the same hardware we used in this chapter.[3]

What If It Doesn't Work?

From a maker's perspective, this chapter is an easy one. Still, things can go wrong, especially with the wiring. Make sure you've connected the right pins on the Arduino and on the Nunchuk. Also check that the wires tightly fit into the Nunchuk's and the Arduino's sockets. When in doubt, use wire with a larger diameter.

Also, check *What If It Doesn't Work?*, on page 143, for all things that can go wrong when generating video signals with the Arduino.

Exercises

- Rewrite the game we implemented in Chapter 7, *Writing a Game for the Motion-Sensing Game Controller*, on page 111, so it supports the Nunchuk controller. It should support both the analog stick and the accelerometer. Perhaps you can switch between them using the Nunchuk buttons.

- Tinkering with Nintendo's Wii Motion is more complicated.[4] But it's a nice and cheap way to sharpen your tinkering skills.

- The TVout library has basic audio support. Connect a piezo buzzer to digital pin 11 and use the tone and noTone functions to add sound capabilities to the video game console. Also, add some sound effects to Pragduino.

---

3.   See http://nootropicdesign.com/hackvision/games.html.
4.   http://randomhacksofboredom.blogspot.com/2009/07/motion-plus-and-nunchuck-together-on.html

CHAPTER 10

Networking with Arduino

With a stand-alone Arduino, you can create countless fun and useful projects. But as soon as you turn the Arduino into a networking device, you open up a whole new world of possibilities.

You now have access to all of the information on the Internet, so you could turn your Arduino into a nice, geeky weather station simply by reading data from a weather service. You can also turn the Arduino into a web server that provides sensor data for other devices or computers on your network.

We'll start with a "naked" Arduino that doesn't have any network capabilities. As you'll see, you can still attach it to the Internet and Tweet[1] messages as long as you connect it to a PC.

For our second project, we'll improve the situation dramatically with an Ethernet shield. Your Arduino will become a full-blown network device that can directly access IP services, such as a Daytime service. This will turn your Arduino into a very accurate clock.

The skills you learn in this chapter are the basis for more advanced techniques and the projects you'll create in the next chapter.

---

1.   http://twitter.com

What You Need

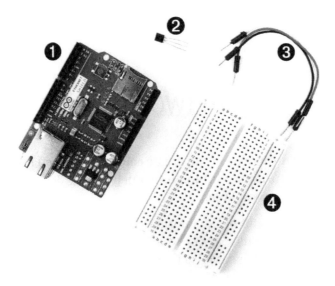

1. An Ethernet shield for the Arduino
2. A TMP36 temperature sensor
3. Some wires
4. A breadboard
5. An Arduino board, such as the Uno, Duemilanove, or Diecimila
6. A USB cable to connect the Arduino to your computer

Using Your PC to Transfer Sensor Data to the Internet

Remember when you connected your PC to the Internet, oh, around twenty years ago? It all started with a 38,400 baud modem, Netscape Navigator 3, and one of those AOL floppy disks or CD-ROMs you got in the mail. Today you probably have broadband access via cable, satellite, or DSL, and it's probably available everywhere in your house via Wi-Fi. So, we'll start by using your existing connection to connect your Arduino to the Internet.

In the following figure, you can see a typical setup for connecting an Arduino to the Internet. A program runs on your PC and communicates with the Arduino using the serial port. Whenever the application needs Internet access, the program on the PC deals with it. Using this architecture, you can Tweet interesting sensor data.

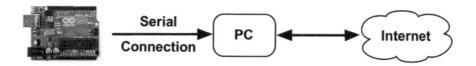

We'll build a system that Tweets a message when the temperature in your working room or office exceeds a certain threshold—32 degrees Celsius (90 degrees Fahrenheit). Build the temperature sensor example from *Increasing Precision Using a Temperature Sensor*, on page 86, again (try to do it without looking at the circuit) and upload the following sketch to your Arduino:

Ethernet/TwitterTemperature/TwitterTemperature.ino
```
Line 1  #define CELSIUS
    -   const unsigned int TEMP_SENSOR_PIN = 0;
    -   const unsigned int BAUD_RATE = 9600;
    -   const float SUPPLY_VOLTAGE = 5.0;
    5   void setup() {
    -     Serial.begin(BAUD_RATE);
    -   }

    -   void loop() {
   10     const int sensor_voltage = analogRead(TEMP_SENSOR_PIN);
    -       const float voltage = sensor_voltage * SUPPLY_VOLTAGE / 1024;
    -       const float celsius = (voltage * 1000 - 500) / 10;
    -   #ifdef CELSIUS
    -     Serial.print(celsius);
   15     Serial.println(" C");
    -   #else
    -     Serial.print(9.0 / 5.0 * celsius + 32.0);
    -     Serial.println(" F");
    -   #endif
   20     delay(5000);
    -   }
```

This is nearly the same sketch we've used before. Keep in mind that you have to set SUPPLY_VOLTAGE to 3.3 in line 4 if you're using an Arduino that runs with 3.3V instead of 5V.

We support both Celsius and Fahrenheit values now, and you can use a preprocessor constant to control which unit should be used. If you set the constant CELSIUS in the first line, the application outputs the temperature in degree Celsius. If you remove the first line or turn it into a comment line, the application will use Fahrenheit.

To change the application's behavior, we use the #ifdef preprocessor directive. It checks whether a certain preprocessor constant has been set, and then it compiles code conditionally. In our case, it will compile the Celsius-to-Fahrenheit formula in line 17 only if the constant CELSIUS has not been set.

Upload the sketch, and it will output the current temperature to the serial port every five seconds. Its output looks as follows:

```
27.15 C
26.66 C
27.15 C
```

What we need now is a program running on your PC that reads this output and Tweets a message as soon as the temperature is greater than 32 degrees Celsius (90 degrees Fahrenheit). We could use any programming language that is capable of reading from a serial port and that supports Twitter, but because Processing[2] has excellent support for Twitter and the serial port, we'll use it for this project.

The Arduino and the Internet of Things (IoT)

Today for most people the Internet is a network of computers that can be used for looking up entertaining, useful, or interesting information. In recent years the nature of the Internet has changed tremendously. More and more autonomous and automated devices have joined the Internet. For many people it's normal already to use a smartphone to surf the web, and in a not-too-distant future, devices such as toasters and refrigerators will be part of the Internet, too. This is the Internet of Things, where everyday objects are able to send and receive data over a network connection.

With the advent of cheap open-source hardware and sensors, web services for publishing sensor data have become popular over the past few years. Such services allow you to publish, read, and analyze sensor data. People from all over the world publish data from their weather stations, environmental sensors, and so on, and they make it available for free on the Internet.

These web services offer even more functions today and make it easy to turn an Arduino into a full-blown member of the Internet of Things—that is, you can integrate your Arduino with Google Mail, Facebook, eBay, and so on.

Popular services are Xively[a] and Temboo.[b] In principle, they all work the same: you register an account, and you get back an API key. Then you can use this key to authenticate against the service and upload sensor data or use other functions of their API. Usually, these services also offer special Arduino libraries that help you to build your applications.

a.   http://xively.com
b.   https://www.temboo.com/

Registering an Application with Twitter

Before we start coding, we have to register our application at the Twitter website to get API keys and an OAuth access token.[3] OAuth is an authentication scheme that allows applications to use other applications' resources. In our case, we'll grant our very own application the right to update our Twitter feed without using our Twitter username and password.

To get all of the information needed, create a new application in the applications section of the Twitter website.[4] After you've logged in, click the Create New App button and fill out the form:

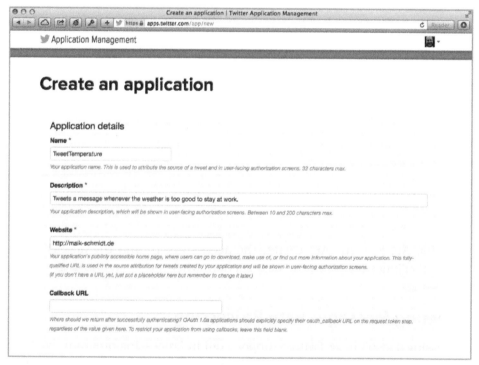

After you've created your new application, go to the Permissions tab and set the application's access level to Read and Write. Then navigate to the API Keys tab and press the Create My Access Token button. It can take a few moments-refresh the page a few times until the access token is available.

The API Keys tab should contain all information that you need to allow your application to modify your Twitter status. It should look similar to this:

---

3.   http://en.wikipedia.org/wiki/Oauth
4.   https://apps.twitter.com

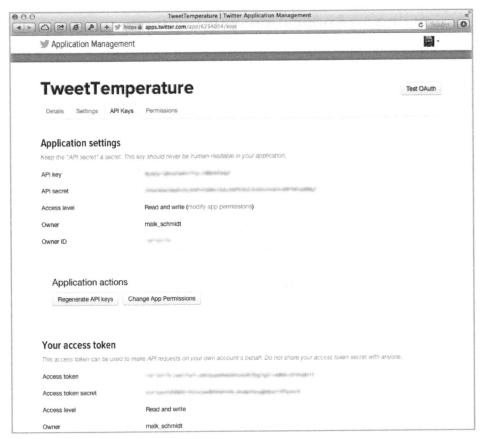

Copy the API key, the API secret, the access token, and the access token secret. You'll need them in the next section, when we Tweet messages using Processing.

Tweeting Messages with Processing

Processing doesn't have Twitter support, but in Processing programs we have direct access to Java libraries, and you can find several good Twitter libraries for Java. One of them is Twitter4J.[5] We'll use it because it's very mature and has excellent OAuth support.

Download Twitter4J from its website[6] and unpack it to a temporary folder. Depending on the version you've downloaded, you'll find a file named twitter4j-core-x.y.z.jar or twitter4j-core-x.y.z-SNAPSHOT.jar in the folder. Open the Processing IDE, create a new sketch, and then drag and drop the jar file to the IDE. (The

---

5. http://twitter4j.org/
6. http://twitter4j.org/en/index.html#download

jar file will automatically be copied to a local folder named code.) That's all you have to do to give your application access to the Twitter4J library.

We proceed with some boilerplate code:

Ethernet/TweetTemperature/TweetTemperature.pde
```
import processing.serial.*;

final float  MAX_WORKING_TEMP = 32.0;
final int    LINE_FEED = 10;
final int    BAUD_RATE = 9600;
final int    FONT_SIZE = 32;
final int    WIDTH = 320;
final int    HEIGHT = 240;
final String API_KEY = "<YOUR API KEY>";
final String API_SECRET = "<YOUR API SECRET>";
final String ACCESS_TOKEN = "<YOUR ACCESS TOKEN>";
final String ACCESS_TOKEN_SECRET = "<YOUR ACCESS TOKEN SECRET>";

Serial _arduinoPort;
float _temperature;
boolean _isCelsius;
PFont _font;

void setup() {
  size(WIDTH, HEIGHT);
  _font = createFont("Arial", FONT_SIZE, true);
  println(Serial.list());
  _arduinoPort = new Serial(this, Serial.list()[0], BAUD_RATE);
  _arduinoPort.clear();
  _arduinoPort.bufferUntil(LINE_FEED);
  _arduinoPort.readStringUntil(LINE_FEED);
}

void draw() {
  background(255);
  fill(0);
  textFont(_font, FONT_SIZE);
  textAlign(CENTER, CENTER);
  if (_isCelsius)
    text(_temperature + " \u2103", WIDTH / 2, HEIGHT / 2);
  else
    text(_temperature + " \u2109", WIDTH / 2, HEIGHT / 2);
}
```

As usual, we import the serial libraries for communicating with the Arduino, and then we define some constants we'll need later. Most of them contain the credentials we need to access the Twitter service. With MAX_WORKING_TEMP, you can define at which temperature the application starts to Tweet. This can be a degrees Celsius or Fahrenheit value. The rest defines a few values we need for the user interface, such as the screen width, the screen height, and the font size.

After that, we define a few member variables. _arduinoPort contains a reference to the Serial object we use to communicate with the Arduino. _temperature contains the last temperature value we received from the Arduino, and _isCelsius is true if the value we read was in degrees Celsius. We need the _font variable to define the font we use to output the temperature on the screen.

In the setup method, we set the window size and create the font we're going to use. Then we print out a list of all serial devices available. We initialize our _arduinoPort variable with the first one we find, hoping that it's the Arduino. You could also loop through the list automatically and search for something that looks like an Arduino port name, but that'd be fragile, too.

We call the clear method to empty the serial port's buffer. With bufferUntil, we make sure that we get notified about serial events only when we've received a linefeed character. The call to readStringUntil ensures that we start with a fresh serial buffer that doesn't contain an incomplete line of data.

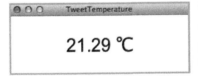

The draw method prints the last temperature we received on the screen. It sets the background color to white using background and the text color to black using fill. Then it sets the font and ensures the text we are printing is centered horizontally and vertically. Eventually, we print the temperature using the text method. To make the result look nicer, we use the official Unicode characters for degrees Celsius (\u2103) and Fahrenheit (\u2109).

Now let's implement the business logic of our "Take me to the beach" alarm:

Ethernet/TweetTemperature/TweetTemperature.pde
```
void serialEvent(Serial port) {
  final String arduinoData = port.readStringUntil(LINE_FEED);
  if (arduinoData != null) {
    final String[] data = split(trim(arduinoData), ' ');
    if (data.length == 2 &&
        (data[1].equals("C") || data[1].equals("F")))
    {
      _isCelsius = data[1].equals("C");
      _temperature = float(data[0]);
      if (Float.isNaN(_temperature))
        return;
      println(_temperature);
      int sleepTime = 5 * 60 * 1000;
      if (_temperature > MAX_WORKING_TEMP) {
        tweetAlarm();
```

```
      sleepTime = 120 * 60 * 1000;
    }
    try {
      Thread.sleep(sleepTime);
    }
    catch(InterruptedException ignoreMe) {}
  }
 }
}

void tweetAlarm() {
  ConfigurationBuilder cb = new ConfigurationBuilder();
  cb.setDebugEnabled(true)
    .setOAuthConsumerKey(API_KEY)
    .setOAuthConsumerSecret(API_SECRET)
    .setOAuthAccessToken(ACCESS_TOKEN)
    .setOAuthAccessTokenSecret(ACCESS_TOKEN_SECRET);
  TwitterFactory tf = new TwitterFactory(cb.build());
  Twitter twitter = tf.getInstance();
  try {
    Status status = twitter.updateStatus(
      "Someone, please, take me to the beach!"
    );
    println(
      "Successfully updated status to '" + status.getText() + "'."
    );
  }
  catch (TwitterException e) {
    e.printStackTrace();
  }
}
```

Whenever new data arrives on the serial port, the Processing runtime environment calls the serialEvent method. There we try to read a line of text, and then we check whether it contains a decimal number followed by a blank and a *C* or an *F* character. This ensures we've read an actual temperature data set and not some digital garbage.

If we got a syntactically correct temperature data set, we convert it into a float object and check to see whether it's greater than MAX_WORKING_TEMP. (No one should be forced to work at temperatures that high!) If yes, we call tweetAlarm and Tweet a message to encourage some followers to rescue us. Then we wait for two hours until our next check. Otherwise, we wait five minutes and check the temperature again.

tweetAlarm updates our Twitter status and is simple. In good old Java tradition, we create a new Twitter instance using a TwitterFactory. The factory expects a ConfigurationBuilder object that we have initialized with our Twitter application

Tweeting Arduinos

A useful and interesting hardware kit is Botanicalls.[a] It checks whether your plants need water, and if they do, it sends a reminder message via http://twitter.com/. As soon as you water the plant, Botanicalls dutifully sends a "Thank You" message. Although the official version of Botanicalls is a specialized piece of hardware, you can build it using an Arduino.[b]

Botanicalls certainly make your life easier. Whether the Tweeting Vending Machine[c] improves your life is a matter of taste. Users of this modified vending machine have to identify themselves using an RFID card. Whenever they buy some sweets, the vending machine Tweets their name and what they've bought.

_____

a. http://www.botanicalls.com/

b. http://www.botanicalls.com/archived_kits/twitter/

c. http://www.popsugar.com/tech/Tweeting-Vending-Machine-34558986

credentials. Finally, we invoke updateStatus. If everything went fine, we print a success message to the console. If anything goes wrong, updateStatus will raise an exception, and we'll print its stack trace for debugging purposes.

That's all the code we need, so connect your Arduino to your PC and run it! The following figure shows what happens on Twitter when the temperature in my working room is higher than 32 degrees Celsius. (For your first tests, you might have to change 32.0 to a smaller value. If you don't have to change it, why aren't you at the beach?)

Using a full-blown PC as an Internet relay for your Arduino is convenient, but it's also overkill for most applications. In the next section, you'll learn how to turn an Arduino into a real networking device.

Communicating Over Networks Using an Ethernet Shield

In the previous section, you learned how to build network applications with an Arduino by using your PC's network connection. This approach works nicely, but it also has a few disadvantages. The biggest problem is that you need a complete PC, while for many applications the Arduino's hardware capabilities would be sufficient. In this section, you'll learn how to solve this problem with an Ethernet shield.

Usually, you can't connect a naked Arduino to a network. Not only are its hardware capabilities too limited, but also most Arduino boards don't have an Ethernet port. That means you can't plug an Ethernet cable into them, and to overcome this limitation, you have to use an Ethernet shield. Such shields come with an Ethernet chip and Ethernet connectors and turn your Arduino into a networking device immediately. You only have to plug it in.

You can choose from several products (the following figure shows some of them); they all are good and serve their purpose well. For prototyping, I prefer the "official" shield,[7] because it comes with sockets for all pins and has a microSD card slot. Alternatively, you can use the Arduino Ethernet,[8] an Arduino board that comes with an Ethernet port and doesn't need a separate shield.

Hardware is only one aspect of turning an Arduino into a network device. We also need some software for network communication. The Arduino IDE comes with a convenient Ethernet library that contains a few classes related to networking. We'll use it now to access a Daytime service on the Internet.

A Daytime service[9] returns the current date and time as an ASCII string. Daytime servers listen on either TCP or UDP port 13. You can find many Daytime services on the Internet; one of them runs at *time.nist.gov*. Before

7.   http://www.arduino.cc/en/Main/ArduinoEthernetShield
8.   http://www.arduino.cc/en/Main/ArduinoBoardEthernet
9.   http://en.wikipedia.org/wiki/DAYTIME

we use the service programmatically with an Arduino, see how it works using the telnet command:

```
maik> telnet time.nist.gov 13
Trying 192.43.244.18...
Connected to time.nist.gov.
Escape character is '^]'.
56965 14-11-04 20:33:03 00 0 0 867.4 UTC(NIST) *
Connection closed by foreign host.
```

As soon as the telnet command connects to the Daytime server, it sends back the current time and date.[10] Then the service shuts down the connection immediately.

Here's an implementation of exactly the same behavior for an Arduino with an Ethernet shield:

Ethernet/TimeServer/TimeServer.ino
```
Line 1  #include <SPI.h>
     -  #include <Ethernet.h>
     -  const unsigned int BAUD_RATE = 9600;
     -  const unsigned int DAYTIME_PORT = 13;
     5
     -  byte mac[] = { 0xDE, 0xAD, 0xBE, 0xEF, 0xFE, 0xED };
     -  IPAddress my_ip(192, 168, 2, 120);
     -  IPAddress time_server(192, 43, 244, 18); // time.nist.gov
     -  EthernetClient client;
     10
     -  void setup() {
     -    Serial.begin(BAUD_RATE);
     -    Ethernet.begin(mac, my_ip);
     -  }
     15
     -  void loop() {
     -    delay(1000);
     -    Serial.print("Connecting...");
     -
     20   if (client.connect(time_server, DAYTIME_PORT) <= 0) {
     -      Serial.println("connection failed.");
     -    } else {
     -      Serial.println("connected.");
     -      delay(300);
     25     while (client.available()) {
     -        char c = client.read();
     -        Serial.print(c);
     -      }
     -
```

---

10. See http://www.nist.gov/physlab/div847/grp40/its.cfm for a detailed description of the date string's format.

```
30    Serial.println("Disconnecting.");
-     client.stop();
-   }
- }
```

First, we include the Ethernet library and define a constant for the Daytime service port. (We also have to include the SPI library, because the Ethernet library depends on it.) Then we define a few global variables:

- mac contains the MAC address we're going to use for the Ethernet shield. A MAC address is a 48-bit number that uniquely identifies a network device.[11] Usually the manufacturer sets this identifier, but for the Ethernet shield, we have to set it ourselves; we use an arbitrary number.

  Important note: the MAC address has to be unique on your network. If you connect more than one Arduino, make sure they all have different MAC addresses! Also note that the Arduino Ethernet and the latest versions of the Ethernet shields have a MAC address that can be found on a sticker on their back side.

- Whenever you connect your PC to the Internet, it probably gets a new IP address via the Dynamic Host Configuration Protocol (DHCP).[12] For most Arduino applications, a DHCP implementation is comparatively costly, so you usually assign an IP address manually. (See how to use DHCP in *Using DHCP and DNS*, on page 177.) In most cases, this will be a local address in the *192.168.x.y* range; we store this address in the my_ip variable using the Arduino's IPAddress class. In older versions of the Arduino IDE, you had to use a byte array to store IP addresses. You can still do so, because byte arrays will be converted to IPAddress objects automatically if needed.

- To turn domain names such as *time.nist.gov* into an IP address, you need access to the Domain Name System (DNS). The Arduino's standard library supports DNS, but we'll find out the IP address ourselves. (See how to use DNS in *Using DHCP and DNS*, on page 177.) We assign it to time_server. The telnet command already turned the Daytime service domain name into an IP address for us. Alternatively, you can use one of the following commands to determine a domain name's IP address:

```
maik> host time.nist.gov
time.nist.gov has address 192.43.244.18
maik> dig +short time.nist.gov
```

---

11. http://en.wikipedia.org/wiki/Mac_address
12. http://en.wikipedia.org/wiki/Dynamic_Host_Configuration_Protocol

```
192.43.244.18
maik> resolveip time.nist.gov
IP address of time.nist.gov is 192.43.244.18
maik> ping -c 1 time.nist.gov
PING time.nist.gov (192.43.244.18): 56 data bytes
64 bytes from 192.43.244.18: icmp_seq=0 ttl=48 time=173.598 ms

--- time.nist.gov ping statistics ---
1 packets transmitted, 1 packets received, 0.0% packet loss
round-trip min/avg/max/stddev = 173.598/173.598/173.598/0.000 ms
```

Back to the source code! In line 9, we create a new EthernetClient object. This class is part of the Ethernet library and allows us to create network clients that connect to a certain IP address and port. In former versions of the Arduino IDE, this class was named Client.

Now we have to initialize the Ethernet shield itself; we do this in line 13 in the setup function. We have to invoke Ethernet.begin, passing it our MAC and IP address. Then we initialize the serial port so that we can output some debug messages. At this point, we've initialized all the components we need, so we can finally connect to the Daytime server and read its output.

Please note that you can also pass the IP address of your network gateway and your subnet mask to Ethernet.begin. This is necessary if you don't connect the Arduino directly to the Internet but use a router or a cable modem instead. In this case, you can pass the gateway address as follows:

```
// ...
byte mac[] = { 0xDE, 0xAD, 0xBE, 0xEF, 0xFE, 0xED };
IPAddress my_ip(192, 168, 2, 120);
IPAddress time_server(192, 43, 244, 18); // time.nist.gov
// Insert IP address of your domain name system below:
IPAddress dns(8, 8, 8, 8);
// Insert IP address of your cable or DSL router below:
IPAddress gateway(192, 168, 13, 254);

EthernetClient client(time_server, DAYTIME_PORT);
void setup() {
  Ethernet.begin(mac, my_ip, dns, gateway);
  Serial.begin(BAUD_RATE);
}
// ...
```

The loop function of our sketch starts with a short delay, allowing all components to initialize properly. This is necessary because the Ethernet shield is an autonomous device that is capable of working in parallel to the Arduino. In line 20, we try to connect to the Daytime service. If the connection cannot be established, we print an error message. Otherwise, we wait for 300 milliseconds to give the service some preparation time, and then we read and print its output character by character.

The client's interface is similar to that of the Serial class. The available function checks whether some bytes are still available, and read returns the next byte. At the end, we call stop to disconnect from the service, and then we start again.

Note that our program isn't completely robust. If the server needs longer than 300 milliseconds to deliver its data, our program will not read it. In our case it's not a big deal, but for more critical applications, you'd better wait until data is available and add a timeout mechanism.

Compile and upload the program to the Arduino. Then open the serial monitor, and you should see something like this:

```
Connecting...connected.
56807 14-11-04 16:34:18 50 0 0 259.2 UTC(NIST) *
Disconnecting.
Connecting...connected.
56807 14-11-04 16:34:20 50 0 0 515.5 UTC(NIST) *
Disconnecting.
```

We're finished! Our Arduino is directly connected to the Internet, and it even does something useful: we've turned it into a very accurate clock.

All in all, networking with an Arduino doesn't differ much from networking with a PC, if you use the Ethernet shield. In the next section, you'll learn how to use services such as DHCP and DNS with an Arduino.

Using DHCP and DNS

In the preceding section, you learned how to access IP services the "hard" way. That is, you had to know your own IP address and the services's IP address, too. For your home projects, this is convenient and efficient.

As soon as you create projects that have to run in unknown environments, you have to use a more flexible approach. If you're going to build an actual product based on a networking Arduino, you certainly don't want your customers to enter an unused IP address and upload a new sketch before they can use it.

In such cases you need a more flexible solution. In this section you'll determine service addresses using the Domain Name System (DNS), and you'll obtain the Arduino's IP address using the Dynamic Host Configuration Protocol (DHCP).

Here's a version of our time server example that uses DHCP and DNS:

More Fun with Networking Arduinos

Wearables and e-textiles are getting more and more popular, and they're still a good way to impress your colleagues and friends. Different types of interactive T-shirts are available in every well-stocked geek shop. Some of them show the current Wi-Fi strength, while others come with a full-blown built-in electronic rock guitar.

With an Arduino LilyPad,[a] a Bluetooth dongle, and an Android phone, you can build a T-shirt that displays the current number of unread emails in your inbox.[b]

Not only can you show the number of unread email messages, you can also use the LilyPad and an XBee module to teach children important information about bees and their behavior.[c]

---

a. http://arduino.cc/en/Main/ArduinoBoardLilyPad
b. http://blog.makezine.com/2010/03/30/email-counting-t-shirt/
c. http://www.instructables.com/id/Interactive-Bee-Game/

Ethernet/TimeServerDnsDhcp/TimeServerDnsDhcp.ino

```
Line 1  #include <SPI.h>
     -  #include <Ethernet.h>
     -
     -  const unsigned int BAUD_RATE = 9600;
     5  const unsigned int DAYTIME_PORT = 13;
     -
     -  byte mac[] = { 0xDE, 0xAD, 0xBE, 0xEF, 0xFE, 0xED };
     -  char* time_server = "time.nist.gov";
     -  EthernetClient client;
    10
     -  void setup() {
     -    Serial.begin(BAUD_RATE);
     -    if (Ethernet.begin(mac) == 0) {
     -      for (;;) {
    15        Serial.println("Could not obtain an IP address using DHCP.");
     -        delay(1000);
     -      }
     -    } else {
     -      print_ip_address(Ethernet.localIP());
    20    }
     -  }
     -
     -
     -  void loop() {
    25    delay(1000);
     -    Serial.print("Connecting...");
     -    if (client.connect(time_server, DAYTIME_PORT) <= 0) {
     -      Serial.println("connection failed.");
     -    } else {
    30      Serial.println("connected.");
```

```
  -       delay(300);
  -
  -       while (client.available()) {
  -         char c = client.read();
 35         Serial.print(c);
  -       }
  -
  -       Serial.println("Disconnecting.");
  -       client.stop();
 40     }
  -   }
  -
  -   void print_ip_address(IPAddress ip) {
  -       const unsigned int OCTETS = 4;
 45       Serial.print("We've got the following IP address: ");
  -       for (unsigned int i = 0; i < OCTETS; i++) {
  -         Serial.print(ip[i]);
  -         if (i != OCTETS - 1)
  -           Serial.print(".");
 50       }
  -       Serial.println();
  -   }
```

This program does the same as the program in the previous section, but it doesn't contain any explicit IP addresses. Apart from that, it doesn't differ much from the original version. The first difference is in line 8. Here we no longer declare the variable time_server as an IPAddress object but as a string. The string contains the name of the server we're going to connect to.

In line 13, we no longer pass our own IP address to Ethernet's begin method. In this case, begin tries to obtain an unique IP address using a DHCP server in the local network. If it cannot obtain an IP address, we start an endless loop that prints an error message every second. Otherwise, we print the IP address we've got, using a small helper function named print_ip_address.

Eventually, in line 27, we pass our time_server string to the connect method. Note that we didn't change the line; we've only changed the type of the time_server variable. If connect gets a string and not an IPAddress object, it tries to look up the IP address belonging to the server name stored in the string using DNS.

Run the program, and you'll see output similar to the following:

```
We've got the following IP address: 192.168.2.113
Connecting...connected.

56807 14-11-04 16:34:18 50 0 0 259.2 UTC(NIST) *
Disconnecting.
```

You might ask yourself why you shouldn't enjoy the convenience of DHCP and DNS all the time. First of all, DHCP and DNS are two more things that can go wrong. Debugging embedded systems is hard enough already, so you shouldn't make it harder by using services that you don't absolutely need. For most applications, hardwired IP addresses will do the job.

Another reason is code size. DHCP and DNS support will increase significantly the size of the resulting binary file. Adding DHCP support to our time service program increased its size by nearly 3,500 bytes. Still, DHCP and DNS are useful tools for certain applications, and it's great that they're now part of the Arduino's standard library.

In the next chapter, you'll learn how to implement another important network protocol: you will send emails using an Arduino.

Alternative Networking Technologies

Ethernet is one of the most popular and most powerful networking technologies. Using an Ethernet shield, you can easily connect your Arduino to the Internet both as a client and as a server.

Depending on your project's needs, it's sometimes better to use a wireless connection. With a Wi-Fi shield,[a] you can easily turn your Arduino into a wireless networking device.

But often you don't need the full power of Ethernet, especially if you need only short-range communication in a personal area network. You can choose from a variety of options, but Bluetooth and ZigBee[b] are probably the most popular. Excellent solutions for both of them are available for the Arduino.

Finally, you can even participate in cellular networks with your Arduino. Plug in a GSM shield[c] and your SIM card, and you are ready to go.

---

a.   http://arduino.cc/en/Main/ArduinoWiFiShield
b.   http://en.wikipedia.org/wiki/Zigbee
c.   http://arduino.cc/en/Main/ArduinoGSMShield

What If It Doesn't Work?

Networks are complex and complicated beasts, and many things can go wrong when trying the examples in this chapter. The most common problems are the following:

- You have chosen the wrong serial port in the Processing application. By default, the application uses the first serial port it can find. It might be that you have connected your Arduino to another port. In this case, you have to change the index 0 in the statement arduinoPort = new Serial(this, Serial.list()[0], BAUD_RATE); accordingly.

- You forgot to plug the Ethernet cable into the Ethernet shield.

- Your network router has a MAC whitelist that allows only certain MAC addresses to access the network. Make sure that the MAC address you use in your sketches is whitelisted. Check your router's documentation.

- You have used the same MAC address twice on your network.

- You've used an IP address that isn't allowed in your network or that is used already by another device. Double-check your IP address.

- You've used the wrong credentials for accessing a service such as Twitter. Make sure you use the right OAuth tokens.

- Twitter doesn't allow duplicate Tweets. So, whenever your application fails to Tweet a message, make sure you haven't Tweeted it recently.

- Networks have become very reliable over the last couple of decades, but sometimes they are still fragile. So, it might well be that connections fail or that you run into timeouts. Try increasing the delays in your sketches.

Exercises

- Search the Web for other Ethernet shield projects and build at least one of them. A very ambitious project tries to implement a complete web browser on the Arduino, for example.[13]

- Register an account at Xively, Temboo, or any other IoT service. Work through their tutorials and create at least one Arduino application.

- Try at least one additional networking technology, such as Bluetooth, Wi-Fi, or XBee, with your Arduino.

---

13. http://hackaday.io/project/3116-pip-arduino-web-browser

CHAPTER 11

Creating a Burglar Alarm with Email Notification

In the preceding chapter, you learned how to access networking services with the Arduino in various ways. Adding networking capabilities to an Arduino enables you to create countless useful projects. In this chapter, you'll use your newly gained knowledge to build a real-world project: a burglar alarm that uses email notification.

The burglar alarm will send you an email whenever it detects movement in your living room during your absence. To achieve this, you first have to learn how to send emails. You already know a lot about networking with an Arduino, so this won't be too difficult.

You also need to know how to detect motion. So you'll also learn how passive infrared (PIR) sensors work and how you can control them with an Arduino.

At the end of the chapter, not only will you have learned some useful skills, but you'll also feel much safer when the burglar alarm is running.

What You Need

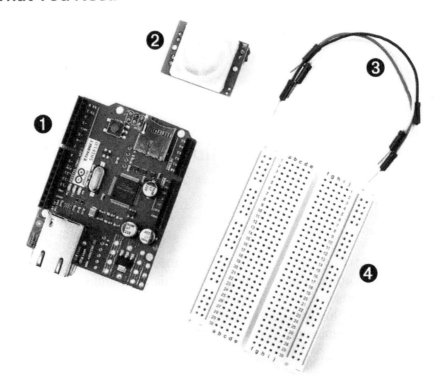

1. An Ethernet shield for the Arduino
2. A PIR motion sensor
3. Some wires
4. A breadboard
5. An Arduino board, such as the Uno, Duemilanove, or Diecimila
6. A USB cable to connect the Arduino to your computer

Emailing from the Command Line

Although email is an important service, only a few people know how it actually works behind the scenes. To send emails from an Arduino, we could choose the easy path and use a PC as an email relay, as we did in *Tweeting Messages with Processing*, on page 168, to Tweet messages. As real hackers, we'll follow a more sophisticated path and implement a subset of the Simple Mail Transfer Protocol (SMTP).[1]

---

1. http://en.wikipedia.org/wiki/Smtp

SMTP is a typical Internet protocol. It uses only text, and it is mainly line-based; that is, you exchange information line by line. A typical email consists of only a few attributes: a sender, a receiver, a subject, and a message body. To transmit an email, you have to send a request to an SMTP server. The request has to adhere to the SMTP specification.

Before we send an email using an Arduino and an Ethernet shield, you should learn how to send an email from a command line using the telnet command. To do so, you have to find an SMTP server that actually allows you to send emails. This isn't as easy as it sounds.

The biggest problem is that over the years, SMTP servers got very good at detecting spam messages. Often you can't send an email manually using a telnet session because the SMTP server thinks it's spam. Usually, the SMTP server will accept your commands, but eventually it will tell you that it won't send your email.

Also, many SMTP servers today insist on encrypted connections, which is a good thing. Implementing the cryptographic algorithms on an Arduino is quite difficult and uses a lot of resources.

So, even with your email provider's SMTP server, you might run into big problems when you try to use it for sending emails from your Arduino.

To overcome such issues, you can use a special SMTP service, such as SMTP2GO.[2] Most of these services support unencrypted connections and do not restrict access in any way. Of course, you have to pay for the service if the number of emails you send exceeds a certain limit. Most services offer a free account that allows you to send a few emails per day or per month. As of this writing, SMTP2GO allows you to send twenty emails per day for free. If your burglar alarm sends more than twenty emails per day, you should consider moving to a new neighborhood anyway.

To follow this chapter's email examples, I strongly suggest you register an account at a free SMTP service, such as SMTP2GO. If you have access to an unrestricted SMTP server already, you can use that one, of course.

The following telnet session shows you how to send an email using SMTP2GO:

```
maik> telnet smtpcorp.com 2525
Trying 207.58.147.66...
Connected to smtpcorp.com.
Escape character is '^]'.
220 smtpcorp.com ESMTP Exim 4.80 Sun, 01 Jun 2014 18:22:28 +0000
```

---

2.   http://www.smtp2go.com/

```
EHLO
250-smtpcorp.com Hello dslb-088-077-003-169.pools.example.net [88.77.3.169]
250-SIZE 52428800
250-8BITMIME
250-PIPELINING
250-AUTH CRAM-MD5 PLAIN LOGIN
250-STARTTLS
250 HELP
AUTH LOGIN
334 VXNlcm5hbWU6
bm90bXl1c2VybmFtZQ==
334 UGFzc3dvcmQ6
bm90bXlwYXNzd29yZA==
235 Authentication succeeded
MAIL FROM:<arduino@example.com>
250 OK
RCPT TO:<info@example.com>
250 Accepted <info@example.com>
DATA
354 Enter message, ending with "." on a line by itself
from:arduino@example.com
to:info@example.com
subject:This is a test

Really, it is a test!
.
250 OK id=1WrAQ9-4gfLuZ-5U
QUIT
221 smtpcorp.com closing connection
Connection closed by foreign host.
```

Although it's more complex, this session is similar to our Daytime example. We only send more complex commands. (By the way, you don't have to write the commands in uppercase.) Please note that we're connecting to port 2525, which is not the standard SMTP port (25). Check your SMTP service provider's website to see what port you have to use.

We start the session using EHLO. We use the EHLO command to tell the SMTP server that we'd like to use a slightly extended version of SMTP that supports authentication.

After that, we send the AUTH LOGIN command to tell the SMTP server that we'd like to send our username and password. The SMTP server sends back the string VXNlcm5hbWU6. It looks a bit weird at first, but it's only the string "Username:" encoded using Base64.[3]

---

3. http://en.wikipedia.org/wiki/Base64 At http://www.freeformatter.com/base64-encoder.html, you can convert text into Base64 strings.

We send our username and encode it using Base64, too. The SMTP server's reply is UGFzc3dvcmQ6 ("Password:"), so we send our password (encoded using Base64).

Note that although Base64 data looks cryptic, it's not encrypted at all. It's as insecure as plain text, and there are software developers who can read Base64 data as quickly as regular text. You can find countless Base64 converters on the Web, and there's a Base64 library for nearly every programming language.

After the authentication succeeds, we tell the server that we'd like to send an email using MAIL FROM:. The email address we provide with this command will be used by the server in case our email bounces back. Note that the server sends back a response line for every request. These responses always start with a three-digit status code.

The RCPT TO: command sets the recipient's email address. If you'd like to send an email to more than one recipient, you have to repeat the command for each of them.

With the DATA command, we tell the server that we now start to transmit the email's attributes. Email attributes are mainly a list of key/value pairs where key and value are delimited by a colon. So in the first three lines, we set the attributes "from," "to," and "subject," and they all have the meaning you'd expect when sending an email.

You separate the email's body from the attributes using a blank line. To mark the end of the email body, send a line containing a single period. Send the QUIT command to end the session with the SMTP server.

You should find a new email in your inbox or in your spam folder. If not, try another SMTP server first. Things can still go wrong, and although simple in theory, SMTP can be a complex beast in practice. SMTP servers often return helpful error messages that might help you quickly solve your problem.

If you want to give your current SMTP server a try, you have to find out its address first. Open a terminal and enter the following:

```
maik> nslookup
> set type=mx
> gmail.com
Server:    192.168.2.1
Address:   192.168.2.1#53
Non-authoritative answer:
gmail.com mail exchanger = 5 gmail-smtp-in.l.google.com.
gmail.com mail exchanger = 10 alt1.gmail-smtp-in.l.google.com.
gmail.com mail exchanger = 20 alt2.gmail-smtp-in.
> exit
```

This command returns a list of all mail exchange servers (MX) that belong to the domain gmail.com (replace it with the domain of your email provider) and that are available on your network. In this case they all belong to Google Mail, and you cannot use them to send emails from your Arduino, because Google Mail insists on an encrypted connection.

Provided your email provider is less restrictive, you can try to send an email using no authentication and no encryption at all. Open a connection to the SMTP standard port 25 and replace the server name smtp.example.com and all email addresses accordingly in the following telnet session:

```
maik> telnet smtp.example.com 25
Trying 93.184.216.119...
Connected to smtp.example.com.
Escape character is '^]'.
220 mx.example.com ESMTP q43si10820020eeh.100
HELO
250 mx.example.com at your service
MAIL FROM: <arduino@example.com>
250 2.1.0 OK q43si10820020eeh.100
RCPT TO: <info@example.com>
250 2.1.5 OK q43si10820020eeh.100
DATA
354  Go ahead q43si10820020eeh.100
from: arduino@example.com
to: info@example.com
subject: This is a test

Really, this is a test!
.
250 2.0.0 OK 1286819789 q43si10820020eeh.100
QUIT
221 2.0.0 closing connection q43si10820020eeh.100
Connection closed by foreign host.
```

Here we send the HELO command (the spelling is correct) to establish a session with the SMTP server that doesn't need authentication information. The rest of the conversation looks exactly like our previous example.

Sometimes you have to try a few things before you're able to send an email from your command line. Don't proceed until you succeed, because sending email from your command line is the basis for the next section, in which you'll learn how to send emails with an Arduino.

Emailing Directly from an Arduino

To send an email from the Arduino, we'll basically implement the telnet session from the previous chapter. Instead of hardwiring the email's attributes into the networking code, we'll create create something more advanced.

We start with an Email class:

Ethernet/Email/email.h
```
#ifndef __EMAIL__H_
#define __EMAIL__H_

class Email {
  String _from, _to, _subject, _body;

  public:

  Email(
    const String& from,
    const String& to,
    const String& subject,
    const String& body
  ) : _from(from), _to(to), _subject(subject), _body(body) {}

  const String& getFrom()    const { return _from; }
  const String& getTo()      const { return _to; }
  const String& getSubject() const { return _subject; }
  const String& getBody()    const { return _body; }
};

#endif
```

This class encapsulates an email's four most important attributes—the email addresses of the sender and the recipient, a subject, and a message body. We store all attributes as String objects.

Wait a minute...a String class? Yes! The Arduino IDE comes with a full-blown string class.[4] It doesn't have as many features as the C++ or Java string classes, but it's still way better than messing around with char pointers. You'll see how to use it in a few paragraphs.

The rest of our Email class is pretty straightforward. In the constructor, we initialize all instance variables, and we have methods for getting every single attribute. We now need an SmtpService class for sending Email objects:

---

4.   http://arduino.cc/en/Reference/StringObject

Ethernet/Email/smtp_service.h

```
Line 1  #ifndef __SMTP_SERVICE__H_
    -   #define __SMTP_SERVICE__H_
    -
    -   #include "email.h"
    5
    -   class SmtpService {
    -     boolean      _use_auth;
    -     IPAddress    _smtp_server;
    -     unsigned int _port;
   10     String       _username;
    -     String       _password;
    -
    -     void read_response(EthernetClient& client) {
    -       delay(4000);
   15       while (client.available()) {
    -         const char c = client.read();
    -         Serial.print(c);
    -       }
    -     }
   20
    -     void send_line(EthernetClient& client, String line) {
    -       const unsigned int MAX_LINE = 256;
    -       char buffer[MAX_LINE];
    -       line.toCharArray(buffer, MAX_LINE);
   25       Serial.println(buffer);
    -       client.println(buffer);
    -       read_response(client);
    -     }
    -
   30   public:
    -
    -     SmtpService(
    -       const IPAddress&   smtp_server,
    -       const unsigned int port) : _use_auth(false),
   35                                  _smtp_server(smtp_server),
    -                                  _port(port) { }
    -
    -     SmtpService(
    -       const IPAddress&   smtp_server,
   40       const unsigned int port,
    -       const String&      username,
    -       const String&      password) : _use_auth(true),
    -                                      _smtp_server(smtp_server),
    -                                      _port(port),
   45                                      _username(username),
    -                                      _password(password) { }
    -
    -     void send_email(const Email& email) {
    -       EthernetClient client;
```

```
50      Serial.print("Connecting...");

        if (client.connect(_smtp_server, _port) <= 0) {
          Serial.println("connection failed.");
        } else {
55        Serial.println("connected.");
          read_response(client);
          if (!_use_auth) {
            Serial.println("Using no authentication.");
            send_line(client, "helo");
60        }
          else {
            Serial.println("Using authentication.");
            send_line(client, "ehlo");
            send_line(client, "auth login");
65          send_line(client, _username);
            send_line(client, _password);
          }
          send_line(
            client,
70          "mail from: <" + email.getFrom() + ">"
          );
          send_line(
            client,
            "rcpt to: <" + email.getTo() + ">"
75        );
          send_line(client, "data");
          send_line(client, "from: " + email.getFrom());
          send_line(client, "to: " + email.getTo());
          send_line(client, "subject: " + email.getSubject());
80        send_line(client, "");
          send_line(client, email.getBody());
          send_line(client, ".");
          send_line(client, "quit");
          client.println("Disconnecting.");
85        client.stop();
        }
      }
    };

90  #endif
```

Admittedly, this is a lot of code, but we'll walk through it step by step. First, the SmtpService class encapsulates the SMTP server's IP address and its port. These attributes are required in any case. In addition, we store a username and a password in case someone's going to use an authenticated connection.

To communicate with an SMTP server, we have to read its responses, and we do that using the private read_response method starting on line 13. It waits for four seconds (SMTP servers usually are very busy, because they have to send a lot of spam), and then it reads all the data sent back by the server and outputs it to the serial port for debugging purposes.

Before we can process responses, we have to send requests. send_line, beginning in line 21, sends a single command to an SMTP server. You have to pass the connection to the server as an EthernetClient instance, and the line you'd like to send has to be a String object.

To send the data stored in a String object, we need to access the character data it refers to. We can use toCharArray or getBytes to retrieve this information. These two methods do not return a pointer to the string's internal buffer. Instead, they expect you to provide a sufficiently large char array and its size. That's why we copy line's content to buffer before we output it to the serial and Ethernet ports. After we've sent the data, we read the server's response and print it to the serial port.

There aren't any surprised in the public interface. There are two constructors. The first, on line 32, expects the SMTP server's IP address and its port. If you use it, the SmtpService class assumes you're not using authentication.

To authenticate against the SMTP service using a username and a password, you have to use the second constructor, starting in line 38. In addition to the SMTP server's IP address and port, it expects the username and password encoded in Base64.

The send_email method is the largest piece of code in our class, but it's also one of the simplest. It mimics exactly our telnet session. The only thing worth mentioning is line 57. Here we check whether authentication information has been provided in the constructor. If not, we send the HELO command. If authentication information has been provided, we send the EHLO command and the corresponding authentication information.

Let's use our classes now to actually send an email:

Ethernet/Email/Email.ino
```
Line 1  #include <SPI.h>
     -  #include <Ethernet.h>
     -  #include "smtp_service.h"
     -
     5  const unsigned int SMTP_PORT = 2525;
     -  const unsigned int BAUD_RATE = 9600;
     -  const String       USERNAME = "bm90bXllc2VybmFtZQ=="; // Encoded in Base64.
     -  const String       PASSWORD = "bm90bXlwYXNzd29yZA=="; // Encoded in Base64.
     -
    10  byte mac[] = { 0xDE, 0xAD, 0xBE, 0xEF, 0xFE, 0xED };
     -  IPAddress my_ip(192, 168, 2, 120);
```

```
     // Insert IP address of your SMTP server below!
     IPAddress smtp_server(0, 0, 0, 0);
15
     SmtpService smtp_service(smtp_server, SMTP_PORT, USERNAME, PASSWORD);

     void setup() {
       Ethernet.begin(mac, my_ip);
20     Serial.begin(BAUD_RATE);
       delay(1000);
       Email email(
         "arduino@example.com",
         "info@example.net",
25       "Yet another subject",
         "Yet another body"
       );
       smtp_service.send_email(email);
     }
30
     void loop() {}
```

No surprises here. We define constants for the SMTP port, the MAC address, the username, the password, and so on; then we create an SmtpService instance. In the setup function, we initialize the Ethernet shield and the serial port, then wait for a second to let things settle down. In line 22, we create a new Email object and pass it to the send_email method.

Figure 28, *A typical SMTP session on the Arduino*, on page 194 shows this in action (including authentication).

Now we know how to send emails with an Arduino, but to build our burglar alarm, we still have to learn how to detect motion.

Detecting Motion Using a Passive Infrared Sensor

Detecting motion is a useful technique, and you probably already know devices that turn on the light in your garden or at your door whenever someone is near enough. Most use *passive infrared sensors* (PIR)[5] for motion detection.

Nearly every object emits infrared light and a PIR sensor measures exactly this kind of light. Detecting motion is comparatively easy if you're already able to receive the infrared radiation emitted by objects in the sensor's field of view. If the sensor receives the infrared light emitted by a wall and suddenly a human being or an animal moves in front of the wall, the infrared light signal will change.

---

5. http://en.wikipedia.org/wiki/Passive_infrared_sensor

```
⊙ ⊙ ⊙                    /dev/tty.usbmodem24321
|                                                              ( Send )
Connecting...connected.
220 smtpcorp.com ESMTP Exim 4.84 Wed, 24 Sep 2014 19:04:37 +0000
Using authentication.
ehlo
250-smtpcorp.com Hello
250-SIZE 52428800
250-8BITMIME
250-PIPELINING
250-AUTH CRAM-MD5 PLAIN LOGIN
250-STARTTLS
250 HELP
auth login
334 VXNlcm5hbWU6

334 UGFzc3dvcmQ6

235 Authentication succeeded
mail from: <arduino@example.com>
250 OK
rcpt to: <contact@maik-schmidt.de>
250 Accepted <contact@maik-schmidt.de>
data
354 Enter message, ending with "." on a line by itself
from: arduino@example.com
to: contact@maik-schmidt.de
subject: Yet another subject

Yet another body
.
250 OK id=
quit
221 smtpcorp.com closing connection

☑ Autoscroll              ( No line ending ⬍ ) ( 9600 baud   ⬍ )
```

Figure 28—A typical SMTP session on the Arduino

Off-the-shelf sensors hide these details, so you can use a single digital pin to check whether someone is moving in the sensor's field of view. The Parallax PIR sensor[6] is a good example of such a device, and we can use it as the basis of our burglar alarm.

Figure 29—Top and bottom of a passive infrared sensor

---

6. http://www.parallax.com/product/555-28027

The PIR sensor has three pins: power, ground, and signal. Connect power to the Arduino's 5V supply, ground to one of the Arduino's GND pins, and signal to digital pin 2. In the following figure, you see a circuit diagram that connects a PIR sensor from Adafruit[7] to an Arduino. Note that PIR sensors from different vendors often differ in the order of their connectors. The PIR sensor in Figure 29, *Top and bottom of a passive infrared sensor,* is different, so you should always make sure you connect the correct pins.

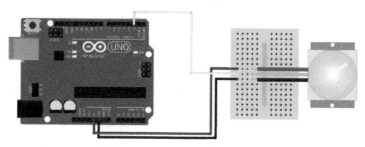

The PIR sensor usually also has a jumper that you can use for changing its behavior. For our project, it has to be in position H; the jumper has to cover the pin next to the H. (Lady Ada has an excellent tutorial on PIR sensors.)[8]

Then enter the following code in the Arduino IDE:

Ethernet/MotionDetector/MotionDetector.ino

```
const unsigned int PIR_INPUT_PIN = 2;
const unsigned int BAUD_RATE = 9600;

class PassiveInfraredSensor {
  int _input_pin;

  public:
  PassiveInfraredSensor(const int input_pin) {
    _input_pin = input_pin;
    pinMode(_input_pin, INPUT);
  }
  const bool motion_detected() const {
    return digitalRead(_input_pin) == HIGH;
  }
};

PassiveInfraredSensor pir(PIR_INPUT_PIN);

void setup() {
  Serial.begin(BAUD_RATE);
}
```

---

7. http://www.adafruit.com/products/189
8. https://learn.adafruit.com/pir-passive-infrared-proximity-motion-sensor

```
     void loop() {
       if (pir.motion_detected()) {
25       Serial.println("Motion detected");
       } else {
         Serial.println("No motion detected");
       }
       delay(200);
30   }
```

With the constant PIR_INPUT_PIN, you can define the digital pin you've connected your PIR sensor to. In line 4, we begin the definition of a class named Passive-InfraredSensor that encapsulates all things related to PIR sensors.

We define a member variable named _input_pin that stores the number of the digital pin we've connected our sensor to. Then we define a constructor that expects the pin number as an argument and assigns it to our member variable.

The only method we need to define is motion_detected. It returns true if it has currently detected a motion and false otherwise. So, it has to check only whether the current state of the sensor's digital pin is HIGH or LOW.

Compile the sketch and upload it to your Arduino. You should see an output similar to the following screenshot when you start to wave your hand in front of the sensor.

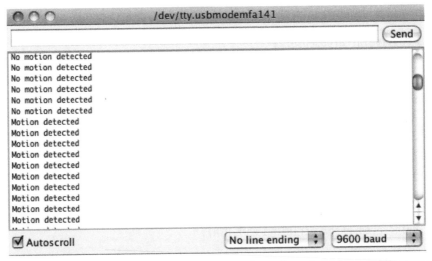

Now we've built the two main components of our burglar alarm, and the only thing left to do is to bring them both together. We'll do that in the next section.

Bringing It All Together

With our PassiveInfraredSensor and SmtpService classes, it's a piece of cake to build a burglar alarm with email notifications. Connect the PIR sensor to the Ethernet shield, as shown in the following figure.

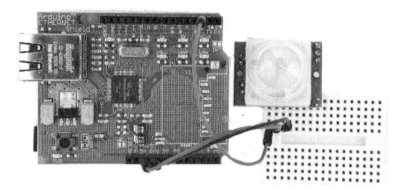

Then enter the following code in your Arduino IDE:

Ethernet/BurglarAlarm/burglar_alarm.h

```
Line 1  #ifndef __BURGLAR_ALARM_H__
   -    #define __BURGLAR_ALARM_H__
   -    #include "pir_sensor.h"
   -    #include "smtp_service.h"
   5
   -    class BurglarAlarm {
   -      PassiveInfraredSensor _pir_sensor;
   -      SmtpService           _smtp_service;
   -      void send_alarm() {
  10        Email email(
   -          "arduino@example.com",
   -          "info@example.net",
   -          "Intruder Alert!",
   -          "Someone's moving in your living room!"
  15        );
   -        _smtp_service.send_email(email);
   -      }
   -
   -    public:
  20      BurglarAlarm(
   -        const PassiveInfraredSensor& pir_sensor,
   -        const SmtpService&           smtp_service) :
   -          _pir_sensor(pir_sensor),
   -          _smtp_service(smtp_service)
  25      {
   -      }
   -
   -
   -
```

```
-      void check() {
30       Serial.println("Checking");
-        if (_pir_sensor.motion_detected()) {
-          Serial.println("Intruder detected!");
-          send_alarm();
-        }
35   }
-   };
-   #endif
```

This defines a class named BurglarAlarm that aggregates all the code we've written so far. It encapsulates a SmtpService instance and a PassiveInfraredSensor object. Its most complex method is send_alarm, which sends a predefined email.

The rest of the BurglarAlarm class is pretty straightforward. Beginning on line 20, we define the constructor that initializes all private members. If the PIR sensor detects movement, the check method sends an email.

Let's use the BurglarAlarm class:

Ethernet/BurglarAlarm/BurglarAlarm.ino
```
#include <SPI.h>
#include <Ethernet.h>
#include "burglar_alarm.h"

const unsigned int PIR_INPUT_PIN = 2;
const unsigned int SMTP_PORT = 25;
const unsigned int BAUD_RATE = 9600;
const String       USERNAME = "bm90bXllc2VybmFtZQ=="; // Encoded in Base64.
const String       PASSWORD = "bm90bXlwYXNzd29yZA=="; // Encoded in Base64.

byte mac[] = { 0xDE, 0xAD, 0xBE, 0xEF, 0xFE, 0xED };
IPAddress my_ip(192, 168, 2, 120);

// Insert IP address of your SMTP server below!
IPAddress smtp_server(0, 0, 0, 0);
PassiveInfraredSensor pir_sensor(PIR_INPUT_PIN);
SmtpService           smtp_service(smtp_server, SMTP_PORT, USERNAME, PASSWORD);
BurglarAlarm          burglar_alarm(pir_sensor, smtp_service);

void setup() {
  Ethernet.begin(mac, my_ip);
  Serial.begin(BAUD_RATE);
  delay(20 * 1000);
}

void loop() {
  burglar_alarm.check();
  delay(3000);
}
```

First we include all of the libraries we need, and we define constants for the PIR sensor pin and our MAC address. Then we define SmtpService and PassiveInfraredSensor objects and use them to define a BurglarAlarm instance. Note that we pass a username and a password, implying that we're using an authenticated SMTP connection to send our emails. If you use an unauthenticated connection, you can safely remove the USERNAME and PASSWORD parameters and all of their occurrences.

In the setup method, we define the serial port and the Ethernet shield. I've also added a delay of twenty seconds, which gives you enough time to leave the room before the alarm begins to work.

The loop function is simple, too. It delegates all the work to BurglarAlarm's check method. In the following figure, you can see what happens when the burglar alarm detects an intruder.

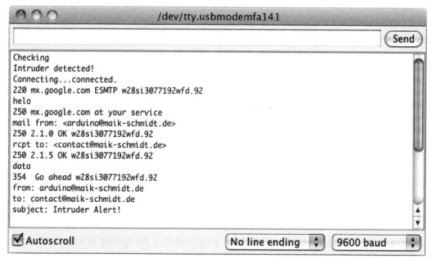

Did you notice how easy object-oriented programming on an embedded device can be? We've cleanly hidden in two small classes the complexity of both email and the PIR sensor. To build the burglar alarm, we then only had to write some glue code.

One word regarding privacy: do not abuse the project in this chapter to observe other people without their knowledge. Not only is it unethical, but in many countries it's even illegal!

In this and the preceding chapter, you learned different ways to connect the Arduino to the Internet. Some of them require an additional PC, while others need an Ethernet shield, but they all open the door to a whole new range of embedded computing applications.

Networking is one of those techniques that may have a direct impact on the outside world. In the next chapter, you'll learn about another technique that has similar effects: you'll learn how to control devices remotely.

What If It Doesn't Work?

The burglar alarm is a networking project, so you should check all the things mentioned in *What If It Doesn't Work?*, on page 180. In addition, you should double-check the connection parameters and authentication information for your email provider. Did you use the correct IP address for your email provider? Did you use the right SMTP port? Did you use the right username and password? Did you use the right Base64 version of the username and password?

PIR sensors are fairly simple devices. Still, you can wire them the wrong way, so if the motion detection doesn't work, double-check the wiring.

Exercises

- Build a project similar to the burglar alarm, but use another type of sensor. There's tons of inspiration out there on the Web.[9]

- Add the current timestamp to the burglar alarm email. Get the timestamp from a Daytime service.

- Add support for DHCP and DNS to the burglar alarm.

- Add support for Base64 to the burglar alarm, so you no longer have to manually encode your username and password. A Base64 library is available.[10]

- Add a piezo buzzer to the project and emit a beeping sound whenever a burglar is detected.

- Get a TTL Serial Camera[11] and attach photos of the burglar to your emails. This is a fairly advanced exercise. You have to learn how to control the camera, and you also have to learn how to send email attachments.

---

9. http://www.tigoe.net/pcomp/code/arduinowiring/873
10. https://github.com/adamvr/arduino-base64
11. https://learn.adafruit.com/ttl-serial-camera/overview

CHAPTER 12

Creating Your Own Universal Remote
Control

Remote controls add a lot of convenience to our lives, but they aren't without annoyances. Sometimes remotes don't have a certain function that you'd like, such as a sleep timer. Plus, remote controls seem to reproduce at the same rate as rabbits. They quickly occupy your whole coffee table, and you have to feed them with expensive batteries that you don't have at home when you need them during a football game. Universal remote controls reduce the pain, but even the most expensive products aren't perfect.

Although we use remote controls every day, few of us understand how they work. In this chapter, you'll find out how remote controls work from the inside out, and then you'll build your own universal remote control that's better than a store-bought one because you can fully customize it to your needs. You can easily add all of your favorite functions, and you can add functions that other remotes don't offer. If a commercial product doesn't support a certain vendor, you're usually stuck. With your own remote, you can easily add new protocols. You can even support not only infrared, but also more transmission technologies, such as Bluetooth or Wi-Fi.

We get started by learning the basics of infrared signaling. You'll build an infrared circuit to grab control codes from any remote you have on hand. Once you grab the control codes, you can emit them using an infrared LED, and you'll start to build your own universal remote control.

Then we'll even take the idea of a remote control a step further. Once we have a universal remote, we'll control the Arduino itself using the serial port or an Ethernet connection. This way, you can control the Arduino using a web browser, so you can control your TV set or DVD player using a web browser.

What You Need

1. One or more infrared remote controls. They can be from your TV set or your DVD player, for example.
2. An Ethernet shield for the Arduino.
3. An infrared receiver, such as the PNA4602 or the TSOP38238.
4. A 100Ω resistor.
5. An infrared LED.
6. Some wires.
7. A breadboard.
8. An Arduino board, such as the Uno, Duemilanove, or Diecimila.
9. A USB cable to connect the Arduino to your computer.

Understanding Infrared Remote Controls

To wirelessly control a device such as a TV set, you need a sender and a receiver. The receiver usually is built into the device to be controlled, and the sender is part of a separate remote control. Although you can choose from a variety of technologies, such as Bluetooth or Wi-Fi, most modern remote controls still use infrared light for communication.

Using infrared to transmit signals has several advantages. It is invisible to human beings, so it won't bother you. Also, you can generate it cheaply with infrared LEDs that can be integrated easily into electronic circuits. So, for many purposes, such as controlling devices in a typical household, it's an excellent choice.

But infrared also has some drawbacks. It doesn't work through walls or doors, and the distance between the remote control and the operated device is fairly limited. Even more importantly, the infrared signal is subject to interference from other light sources.

To keep possible distortions caused by other light sources to a minimum, the infrared signal has to be modulated. That means you turn the LED on and off at a certain frequency, usually somewhere between 36 kHz and 40 kHz.

That's one of the problems that complicates building a robust infrared remote control. The biggest problem is that vendors have invented countless incompatible protocols. They all use different frequencies, and they all interpret data differently. Some interpret "light on" as a 1 bit, while others treat it as 0, and they all define their own commands that have different lengths. So, to work successfully with different remote control protocols, you need to know how to obtain all of these properties for a specific remote control.

To get this information, we'll take a pragmatic approach. In the next two sections, you'll learn how to read infrared signals from a commercial-grade remote control, and you'll also learn how to reproduce them.

Grabbing Remote Control Codes

Because remote controls from different vendors rarely use the same protocol or even the same commands, before we start sending remote control codes ourselves, we should know what we have to send to achieve a certain result. We have to get as much information as possible about the remote control we'd like to emulate.

We have two options for obtaining remote control codes for a specific device: we could use a remote control database on the Internet, such as the Linux Infrared Remote Control project,[1] or we could use an infrared receiver to read them directly from our device's remote. We'll choose the latter approach because you can learn a lot from it.

Infrared receivers are fairly complex on the inside, but they're easy to use. They automatically observe the infrared light spectrum at a certain frequency (usually between 36 kHz and 40 kHz), and they report their observations using a single pin. So, when

---

1.   http://www.lirc.org/

you're using such a receiver, you don't have to deal with all the complicated transmission details. You can focus on reading and interpreting the incoming signals.

The image that follows shows how to connect a TSOP38238 receiver to an Arduino. It's cheap, it's easy to use, and it works at a frequency of 38 kHz, so it detects signals from a broad range of devices. Connect its ground connector to one of the Arduino's GND pins, the power supply to the Arduino's 5V pin, and the signal pin to digital pin 11.

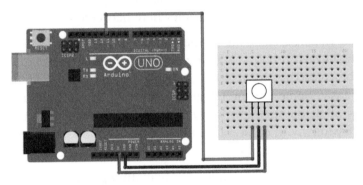

You might be tempted to write a sketch that reads and outputs all incoming data on pin 11, and I won't stop you. Call digitalRead in the loop method and output the results to the serial port. Point your TV set's remote to the receiver and see what happens.

You'll probably have a hard time understanding the data you see. The problem is that decoding the incoming data isn't easy. Even if the receiver has already processed the data, it still has to be transformed and interpreted according to some complicated rules. Also, Arduino's digitalRead method is too slow to deal with all types of incoming signals. You have to directly access the microcontroller to get the best results.

Fortunately, we don't have to do this ourselves, because the IRremote library[2] hides the nasty details. It supports the most popular infrared protocols, and it can both receive and send data.

After you've downloaded and extracted the zip file,[3] rename the resulting directory to IRremote. Copy the directory IRremote to either ~/Documents/Arduino/libraries (on a Mac) or My Documents\Arduino\libraries (on a Windows box). Then restart your IDE.

2. https://github.com/shirriff/Arduino-IRremote
3. https://github.com/shirriff/Arduino-IRremote/archive/master.zip

If you're using Arduino 1.6.0, IRremote collides with one of the Arduino IDE's new standard libraries named RobotIRremote. In this case you have to delete RobotIRremote to make this chapter's examples run. On a Mac you need to delete /Applications/Arduino.app/Contents/Resources/Java/libraries/RobotIRremote/. On a Windows machine, it's something like C:\Program Files (x86)\Arduino\libraries\RobotIRremote'.

With the following sketch, you can then decode incoming infrared signals, if the IRremote library supports their encoding:

RemoteControl/InfraredDumper/InfraredDumper.ino

```
Line 1   #include <IRremote.h>

      -  const unsigned int IR_RECEIVER_PIN = 11;
      -  const unsigned int BAUD_RATE = 9600;
      5
      -  IRrecv ir_receiver(IR_RECEIVER_PIN);
      -  decode_results results;
      -
      -  void setup() {
     10    Serial.begin(BAUD_RATE);
      -    ir_receiver.enableIRIn();
      -  }
      -
      -  void dump(const decode_results* results) {
     15    const int protocol = results->decode_type;
      -    Serial.print("Protocol: ");
      -    if (protocol == UNKNOWN) {
      -      Serial.println("not recognized.");
      -    } else  if (protocol == NEC) {
     20      Serial.println("NEC");
      -    } else if (protocol == SONY) {
      -      Serial.println("SONY");
      -    } else if (protocol == RC5) {
      -      Serial.println("RC5");
     25    } else if (protocol == RC6) {
      -      Serial.println("RC6");
      -    } else if (protocol == DISH) {
      -      Serial.println("DISH");
      -    } else if (protocol == SHARP) {
     30      Serial.println("SHARP");
      -    } else if (protocol == PANASONIC) {
      -      Serial.print("PANASONIC (");
      -      Serial.print("Address: ");
      -      Serial.print(results->panasonicAddress, HEX);
     35      Serial.println(")");
      -    } else if (protocol == JVC) {
      -      Serial.println("JVC");
      -    } else if (protocol == SANYO) {
      -      Serial.println("SANYO");
     40    } else if (protocol == MITSUBISHI) {
```

```
   -      Serial.println("MITSUBISHI");
   -    } else if (protocol == SAMSUNG) {
   -      Serial.println("SAMSUNG");
   -    } else if (protocol == LG) {
45        Serial.println("LG");
   -    }
   -    Serial.print("Value: ");
   -    Serial.print(results->value, HEX);
   -    Serial.print(" (");
50      Serial.print(results->bits, DEC);
   -    Serial.println(" bits)");
   -  }
   -
   -  void loop() {
55    if (ir_receiver.decode(&results)) {
   -      dump(&results);
   -      ir_receiver.resume();
   -    }
   -  }
```

First, we define an IRrecv object named ir_receiver that reads from pin 11. We also define a decode_result object that we'll use to store the attributes of incoming infrared signals. In setup, we initialize the serial port, and we initialize the infrared receiver by calling enableIRIn.

Then we define the dump method that formats and outputs the content of a decode_result object to the serial port. decode_result is one of the core data types of the IRremote library. It encapsulates data such as the protocol type, the length of a command code, and the command code itself. In line 15, we read the protocol type that has been used to encode the incoming signal. When we receive a new signal, we output all of these attributes to the serial port.

The loop method is simple. We call decode to check whether we've received a new signal. If yes, we call dump to output it to the serial port, and then we call resume to wait for the next signal.

Compile and upload the sketch to your Arduino. Start the serial monitor and point a remote control at the receiver. Push some of the remote's buttons and see what happens. Figure 30, *Capture the IR codes of a Samsung remote*, on page 207 shows happens when you point a recent Samsung remote at the receiver and press menu, up, down, left, right, and play.

If you're using a remote from a different vendor, your results will differ. Nearly all modern remotes send a unique 32-bit value for each command, but there are exceptions, too. For example, Panasonic devices send not only a command value, but also an address. Also, remote control behavior differs regarding command repetition. If you press and hold a key on a Samsung remote, it will send the same code over and over again as long as you press the key. An Apple remote will send the key's command code only once, and after that it sends the code 0xffffffff as long as you press the key.

Figure 30—Capture the IR codes of a Samsung remote

After you've grabbed a remote's control codes, you can use them to build your own remote. You'll learn how to do that in the next section.

Cloning a Remote

As soon as you know the protocol and the command codes a remote uses, you can clone it. You need only an infrared LED that doesn't differ much from the LEDs we've used before. The only difference is that it emits "invisible" light. The figure shows how to connect it to pin 3 of an Arduino. (The library we're using in this section expects the infrared LED to be connected to pin 3.) Note that you can't use an LED without a resistor. (See *Current, Voltage, and Resistance*, on page 239, to learn more about it.)

We could try to generate the infrared signals ourselves, but that'd be tedious and error-prone. It's better to use the existing implementation in the IRremote library. We'll use it to create our own TvRemote class that encapsulates all of the gory protocol details. Here's the class:

```
Line 1  #include <IRremote.h>

        class TvRemote {

  5       enum {
            CMD_LEN    = 32,         GUIDE    = 0xE0E0F20D,
            POWER      = 0xE0E040BF, TOOLS    = 0xE0E0D22D,
            SOURCE     = 0xE0E0807F, INFO     = 0xE0E0F807,
            HDMI       = 0xE0E0D12E, OPTIONS  = 0xE0E016E9,
 10         ONE        = 0xE0E020DF, UP_K     = 0xE0E006F9,
            TWO        = 0xE0E0A05F, LEFT_K   = 0xE0E0A659,
            THREE      = 0xE0E0609F, RIGHT_K  = 0xE0E046B9,
            FOUR       = 0xE0E010EF, DOWN_K   = 0xE0E08679,
            FIVE       = 0xE0E0906F, RETURN   = 0xE0E01AE5,
 15         SIX        = 0xE0E050AF, EXIT     = 0xE0E0B44B,
            SEVEN      = 0xE0E030CF, A        = 0xE0E036C9,
            EIGHT      = 0xE0E0B04F, B        = 0xE0E028D7,
            NINE       = 0xE0E0708F, C        = 0xE0E0A857,
            TXT        = 0xE0E034CB, D        = 0xE0E06897,
 20         ZERO       = 0xE0E08877, PIP      = 0xE0E004FB,
            PRE_CH     = 0xE0E0C837, SEARCH   = 0xE0E0CE31,
            VOL_UP     = 0xE0E0E01F, DUAL     = 0xE0E000FF,
            VOL_DOWN   = 0xE0E0D02F, USB_HUB  = 0xE0E025DA,
            MUTE       = 0xE0E0F00F, P_SIZE   = 0xE0E07C83,
 25         CH_LIST    = 0xE0E0D629, SUBTITLE = 0xE0E0A45B,
            PROG_UP    = 0xE0E048B7, REWIND   = 0xE0E0A25D,
            PROG_DOWN  = 0xE0E008F7, PAUSE    = 0xE0E052AD,
            MENU       = 0xE0E058A7, FORWARD  = 0xE0E012ED,
            SMART_TV   = 0xE0E09E61, RECORD   = 0xE0E0926D,
 30         PLAY       = 0xE0E0E21D, STOP     = 0xE0E0629D
          };

          IRsend tv;

 35       void send_command(const long command) {
            tv.sendSAMSUNG(command, CMD_LEN);
          }

          public:

 40       void guide()   { send_command(GUIDE); }
          void power()   { send_command(POWER); }
          void tools()   { send_command(TOOLS); }
          void source()  { send_command(SOURCE); }
 45       void info()    { send_command(INFO); }
          void hdmi()    { send_command(HDMI); }
          void zero()    { send_command(ZERO); }
          void one()     { send_command(ONE); }
          void two()     { send_command(TWO); }
```

```
50   void three()      { send_command(THREE); }
-    void four()       { send_command(FOUR); }
-    void five()       { send_command(FIVE); }
-    void six()        { send_command(SIX); }
-    void seven()      { send_command(SEVEN); }
55   void eight()      { send_command(EIGHT); }
-    void nine()       { send_command(NINE); }
-    void up()         { send_command(UP_K); }
-    void left()       { send_command(LEFT_K); }
-    void right()      { send_command(RIGHT_K); }
60   void down()       { send_command(DOWN_K); }
-    void ret()        { send_command(RETURN); }
-    void exit()       { send_command(EXIT); }
-    void a()          { send_command(A); }
-    void b()          { send_command(B); }
65   void c()          { send_command(C); }
-    void d()          { send_command(D); }
-    void txt()        { send_command(TXT); }
-    void pip()        { send_command(PIP); }
-    void pre_ch()     { send_command(PRE_CH); }
70   void search()     { send_command(SEARCH); }
-    void vol_up()     { send_command(VOL_UP); }
-    void vol_down()   { send_command(VOL_DOWN); }
-    void dual()       { send_command(DUAL); }
-    void usb_hub()    { send_command(USB_HUB); }
75   void mute()       { send_command(MUTE); }
-    void p_size()     { send_command(P_SIZE); }
-    void ch_list()    { send_command(CH_LIST); }
-    void subtitle()   { send_command(SUBTITLE); }
-    void prog_up()    { send_command(PROG_UP); }
80   void prog_down()  { send_command(PROG_DOWN); }
-    void pause()      { send_command(PAUSE); }
-    void rewind()     { send_command(REWIND); }
-    void forward()    { send_command(FORWARD); }
-    void menu()       { send_command(MENU); }
85   void smart_tv()   { send_command(SMART_TV); }
-    void record()     { send_command(RECORD); }
-    void play()       { send_command(PLAY); }
-    void stop()       { send_command(STOP); }
-  };
```

The code starts with an enumeration that contains all the constants we need: the length of each control code (CMD_LEN) and the control codes themselves. There's one entry in the enumeration for each key on our remote control.

In line 33, we define an IRsend object named tv that we'll use to send commands using the send_command method. send_command uses IRsend's sendSAMSUNG method because in this example we're using a Samsung remote control. If you're using a device from Sony or Sharp, you have to adjust the code accordingly. Note that at the time of this writing, the IRremote library is able to decode remote controls from Sanyo, Mitsubishi, and LG, but it doesn't support sending commands to devices from these manufacturers.

After we've established the basis, we can implement all commands with a single function call, so implementing power, menu, play, and so on is a piece of cake.

Using the TvRemote class is easy, too. In the following sketch, we use it to control a Samsung TV from the Arduino's serial monitor:

RemoteControl/TvRemote/TvRemote.ino

```
const unsigned int BAUD_RATE = 9600;

TvRemote tv;
String command = "";
boolean input_available = false;

void setup() {
  Serial.begin(BAUD_RATE);
}

void serialEvent() {
  while (Serial.available()) {
    const char c = Serial.read();
    if (c == '\n')
      input_available = true;
    else
      command += c;
  }
}

void loop() {
  if (input_available) {
    Serial.print("Received command: ");
    Serial.println(command);
    if (command == "guide")            tv.guide();
    else if (command == "power")       tv.power();
    else if (command == "tools")       tv.tools();
    else if (command == "source")      tv.source();
    else if (command == "info")        tv.info();
    else if (command == "hdmi")        tv.hdmi();
    else if (command == "zero")        tv.zero();
    else if (command == "one")         tv.one();
    else if (command == "two")         tv.two();
    else if (command == "three")       tv.three();
    else if (command == "four")        tv.four();
    else if (command == "five")        tv.five();
    else if (command == "six")         tv.six();
    else if (command == "seven")       tv.seven();
```

```
  -         else if (command == "eight")        tv.eight();
 40         else if (command == "nine")         tv.nine();
  -         else if (command == "up")           tv.up();
  -         else if (command == "left")         tv.left();
  -         else if (command == "right")        tv.right();
  -         else if (command == "down")         tv.down();
 45         else if (command == "ret")          tv.ret();
  -         else if (command == "exit")         tv.exit();
  -         else if (command == "a")            tv.a();
  -         else if (command == "b")            tv.b();
  -         else if (command == "c")            tv.c();
 50         else if (command == "d")            tv.d();
  -         else if (command == "txt")          tv.txt();
  -         else if (command == "pip")          tv.pip();
  -         else if (command == "pre_ch")       tv.pre_ch();
  -         else if (command == "search")       tv.search();
 55         else if (command == "vol_up")       tv.vol_up();
  -         else if (command == "vol_down")     tv.vol_down();
  -         else if (command == "dual")         tv.dual();
  -         else if (command == "usb_hub")      tv.usb_hub();
  -         else if (command == "mute")         tv.mute();
 60         else if (command == "p_size")       tv.p_size();
  -         else if (command == "ch_list")      tv.ch_list();
  -         else if (command == "subtitle")     tv.subtitle();
  -         else if (command == "prog_up")      tv.prog_up();
  -         else if (command == "prog_down")    tv.prog_down();
 65         else if (command == "pause")        tv.pause();
  -         else if (command == "rewind")       tv.rewind();
  -         else if (command == "forward")      tv.forward();
  -         else if (command == "menu")         tv.menu();
  -         else if (command == "smart_tv")     tv.smart_tv();
 70         else if (command == "record")       tv.record();
  -         else if (command == "play")         tv.play();
  -         else if (command == "stop")         tv.stop();
  -         else Serial.println("Command is unknown.");
  -
 75         command = "";
  -         input_available = false;
  -     }
  - }
```

In lines 3 to 5, we define a global TvRemote object named tv, a string named command that holds the current command, and a Boolean flag named input_available that is true when the sketch has received a new command. As usual, we initialize the serial port in the setup function.

The Arduino calls the serialEvent function defined in line 11 when new data arrives at the serial port. (Learn more about serialEvent in *Serial Communication Using Various Languages*, on page 255.) We append that data to the command variable, and when we encounter a newline character, we also set the input_available flag to true. This way, the loop function can determine whether a new command has been received and which command it was.

In loop, we wait for commands. When a new command arrives, we check whether it's supported. If it is supported, we send the corresponding control code. Otherwise, we print an error message.

Compile and upload the sketch, and you can control the TV of your choice—a Samsung TV, in this example—using any serial monitor, which is quite cool already. The interface is still awkward for less geeky people, so in the next section, you'll learn how to create a more user-friendly interface.

Controlling Infrared Devices Remotely with Your Browser

We've already created several projects that you can control using a serial monitor. For programmers, that's a nice and convenient interface, but as soon as you want to present your projects to your nontechnical friends, you'd better have something more user-friendly and colorful.

Now we'll implement a Google Chrome app to create a nice user interface for our cloned remote control. Before you proceed, you should read Appendix 4, *Controlling the Arduino with a Browser*, on page 267, if you haven't already.

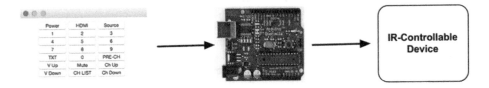

The Chrome app's manifest.json file contains no surprises. It defines the application name and grants the application access to the serial port.

RemoteControl/TvRemoteUI/manifest.json
```json
{
  "manifest_version": 2,
  "name": "TV Remote Emulator",
  "version": "1",
  "permissions": [ "serial" ],
  "app": {
    "background": {
      "scripts": ["background.js"]
    }
  },
  "minimum_chrome_version": "33"
}
```

The same is true for the application's background.js file. It renders the following HTML file when the application is launched.

RemoteControl/TvRemoteUI/main.html

```html
<!DOCTYPE html>
<html lang="en">
  <head>
    <meta charset="utf-8"/>
    <link rel="stylesheet" type="text/css" href="css/style.css"/>
    <title>TV Remote Emulator</title>
  </head>
  <body>
    <div id="main">
      <div>
        <button id="power" type="button">Power</button>
        <button id="hdmi" type="button">HDMI</button>
        <button id="source" type="button">Source</button>
      </div>
      <div>
        <button id="one" type="button">1</button>
        <button id="two" type="button">2</button>
        <button id="three" type="button">3</button>
      </div>
      <div>
        <button id="four" type="button">4</button>
        <button id="five" type="button">5</button>
        <button id="six" type="button">6</button>
      </div>
      <div>
        <button id="seven" type="button">7</button>
        <button id="eight" type="button">8</button>
        <button id="nine" type="button">9</button>
      </div>
      <div>
        <button id="txt" type="button">TXT</button>
        <button id="zero" type="button">0</button>
        <button id="pre_ch" type="button">PRE-CH</button>
      </div>
      <div>
        <button id="vol_up" type="button">V Up</button>
        <button id="mute" type="button">Mute</button>
        <button id="prog_up" type="button">Ch Up</button>
      </div>
      <div>
        <button id="vol_down" type="button">V Down</button>
        <button id="ch_list" type="button">CH LIST</button>
        <button id="prog_down" type="button">Ch Down</button>
      </div>
    </div>
    <script src="js/jquery-1.11.1.min.js"></script>
```

```
    <script src="js/serial_device.js"></script>
    <script src="js/remote.js"></script>
  </body>
</html>
```

This HTML document defines seven rows that contain three buttons each. Also, it loads several JavaScript files. It loads the jQuery library and the SerialDevice class we defined in *Writing a SerialDevice Class*, on page 274. In addition, it loads a file named remote.js that defines what happens when a user clicks a button on our virtual remote.

RemoteControl/TvRemoteUI/js/remote.js
```
Line 1  $(function() {
   -      var BAUD_RATE = 9600;
   -      var remote = new SerialDevice("/dev/tty.usbmodem24311", BAUD_RATE);
   -
   5      remote.onConnect.addListener(function() {
   -        console.log("Connected to: " + remote.path);
   -      });
   -
   -      remote.connect();
  10
   -      $("[type=button]").on("click", function(event){
   -        var buttonType = $(event.currentTarget).attr("id");
   -        console.log("Button pressed: " + buttonType);
   -        remote.send(buttonType + "\n");
  15      });
   -    });
```

In remote.js, we use jQuery's $ function in the first line to make sure all Java-Script code gets executed after the whole HTML page has been loaded. Then we define a new SerialDevice instance named remote and connect to it. Make sure you're using the right serial port name here.

The rest of the code attaches callback functions to all of the buttons we've defined. We use jQuery's $ function to select all elements having the type button. Then we call the on function for each button element and pass it the parameter click to add a callback function that gets called when the button gets clicked.

In the callback function for click events, we use the event's currentTarget property in line 12 to determine which button has actually been clicked. We read the button's ID attribute and use it as the command we send to the Arduino. If the user clicks the button with the ID one, the program will send the command one to the Arduino. The Arduino will then send the corresponding code via infrared. Using a consistent naming scheme for the button elements in the HTML page has really paid off. To add another button, you only have to modify the HTML page. Add a new button element and set its ID attribute to the name of the Arduino command that emits the corresponding remote control code.

To align the buttons of our virtual remote control and to make the Chrome app look nice, we use the following stylesheet:

RemoteControl/TvRemoteUI/css/style.css
```
#main {
  width: 18em;
  margin-left: auto;
  margin-right: auto;
}

button {
  width: 6em;
}
```

The stylesheet mainly ensures that all buttons have the same width. Run the Chrome app, and you'll see something like the following figure:

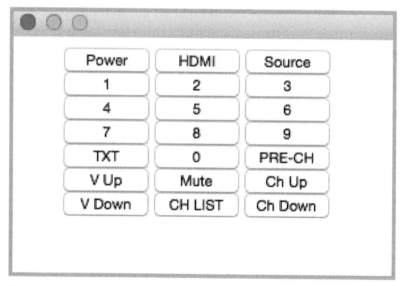

Upload the sketch from *Cloning a Remote*, on page 207, to your Arduino and start the Chrome app. Click any button to perform the corresponding action. That's an interface even your grandma could use, isn't it?

You still need to connect the Arduino to your computer's serial port to control it with a web browser. In the next section, you'll learn how to overcome this and control an Arduino without a serial connection.

Building an Infrared Proxy

All of our previous remote control approaches have one major drawback: they all depend on a serial connection to a PC. In this section, you'll learn how to replace this connection with an Ethernet connection, so you no longer need a PC but only Internet access. You will directly plug your Ethernet cable into an Ethernet shield connected to the Arduino, so it is available on your network. Then you'll connect an infrared LED to the Ethernet shield using the same circuit as shown in *Cloning a Remote*, on page 207.

You don't necessarily have to use your PC's web browser to access the Arduino. You could also use the browser on your PlayStation Portable or on your iPhone. Yes, you can now control your TV set using your game consoles or your smartphone. Oh, and you could replace the Ethernet shield with a Wi-Fi shield so you don't have to connect your Arduino physically to your network router.

Before we dive into the code, we should do a little planning ahead and make clear what we'd like to achieve. We'll build an infrared proxy—a device that receives commands via Ethernet and turns them into infrared signals. (See the image on page 212.) To make it easy to integrate the device into a network, we'll make it accessible via HTTP. This way, we can control it using a regular web browser.

We'll implement only a very small portion of the HTTP standard on the Arduino—we'll support only a certain URL scheme. The URLs we'll support look as follows:

```
http://«arduino-ip»/«protocol-name»/«command-length»/«command-code»
```

We'll replace *«arduino-ip»* with the IP address of the Arduino's Ethernet shield. The element *«protocol-name»* can be one of the supported protocols ("NEC," "SONY," "RC5," "RC6," "DISH," "JVC," or "SAMSUNG"). *«command-length»* specifies the length of the command code in bits, and *«command-code»* contains the command code itself as a hexadecimal number.

Note that the sketch currently doesn't support Panasonic devices because they don't fit our URL scheme.

Let's assume we'd like to send the code for the power key on a Samsung remote, and our Arduino has the IP address 192.168.2.42. Then we'd have to point our web browser to the following URL:

```
http://192.168.2.42/SAMSUNG/32/E0E040BF
```

In this case, the protocol name is SAMSUNG, the length of the command code is 32 bits, and the command code is E0E040BF (the hexadecimal number we grabbed in *Grabbing Remote Control Codes*, on page 203).

We already used the Arduino as a web client in Chapter 10, *Networking with Arduino*, on page 163, but now we need to turn it into a web server. The server waits for new HTTP requests like the one shown previously, parses the URL, and emits the corresponding infrared signal.

We'll hide all of these details in a class named InfraredProxy, and to keep things as easy and as concise as possible, we'll make use of both the Ethernet and the IRremote library. The InfraredProxy class is still one of the book's most sophisticated examples of Arduino code. Here's its interface:

RemoteControl/InfraredProxy/infrared_proxy.h

```
#include <SPI.h>
#include <Ethernet.h>
#include <IRremote.h>

class InfraredProxy {
  private:
  IRsend _infrared_sender;

    void read_line(EthernetClient& client, char* buffer, const int buffer_length);
    bool send_ir_data(const char* protocol, const int bits, const long value);
    bool handle_command(char* line);

    public:
    void receive_from_server(EthernetServer server);
};
```

After including all libraries needed, we declare the InfraredProxy class. We define a member variable named _infrared_sender that stores an IRsend object we need to emit infrared control codes. Then we declare three private helper methods and the receive_from_server method, which is the only public method of the InfraredProxy class.

Let's have a look at the implementation of all methods. We'll start with read_line:

RemoteControl/InfraredProxy/infrared_proxy.cpp
```cpp
void InfraredProxy::read_line(
  EthernetClient& client, char* buffer, const int buffer_length)
{
  int buffer_pos = 0;
  while (client.available() && (buffer_pos < buffer_length - 1)) {
    const char c = client.read();
    if (c == '\n')
      break;
    if (c != '\r')
      buffer[buffer_pos++] = c;
  }
  buffer[buffer_pos] = '\0';
}
```

read_line reads one line of data sent by a client. A line ends either with a newline character (\n) or with a carriage return character followed by a newline character (\r\n). read_line expects the EthernetClient object to read data from, a character buffer to store the data in (buffer), and the maximum length of the character buffer (buffer_length). The method ignores all newline and carriage return characters, and it sets the line's last character to \0 so the buffer to be filled will always be a null-terminated string.

send_ir_data is responsible for sending infrared commands:

RemoteControl/InfraredProxy/infrared_proxy.cpp
```cpp
bool InfraredProxy::send_ir_data(
  const char* protocol, const int bits, const long value)
{
  bool result = true;
  if (!strcasecmp(protocol, "NEC"))
    _infrared_sender.sendNEC(value, bits);
  else if (!strcasecmp(protocol, "SONY"))
    _infrared_sender.sendSony(value, bits);
  else if (!strcasecmp(protocol, "RC5"))
    _infrared_sender.sendRC5(value, bits);
  else if (!strcasecmp(protocol, "RC6"))
    _infrared_sender.sendRC6(value, bits);
  else if (!strcasecmp(protocol, "DISH"))
    _infrared_sender.sendDISH(value, bits);
  else if (!strcasecmp(protocol, "SHARP"))
    _infrared_sender.sendSharp(value, bits);
  else if (!strcasecmp(protocol, "JVC"))
    _infrared_sender.sendJVC(value, bits, 0);
  else if (!strcasecmp(protocol, "SAMSUNG"))
    _infrared_sender.sendSAMSUNG(value, bits);
  else
    result = false;
  return result;
}
```

It emits an infrared command specified by a protocol type (protocol), the length of the code measured in bits (bits), and the code value to be sent (value). Depending on the name of the protocol, the method delegates all the real work to our IRsend instance.

handle_command implements one of the most difficult aspects of our InfraredProxy—it parses the URL addressed by the HTTP request:

```
RemoteControl/InfraredProxy/infrared_proxy.cpp
```
```
bool InfraredProxy::handle_command(char* line) {
  strsep(&line, " ");
  char* path = strsep(&line, " ");

  char* args[3];
  for (char** ap = args; (*ap = strsep(&path, "/")) != NULL;)
    if (**ap != '\0')
      if (++ap >= &args[3])
        break;
  const int  bits = atoi(args[1]);
  const long value = strtoul(args[2], NULL, 16);
  return send_ir_data(args[0], bits, value);
}
```

To understand what this method does, you have to understand how HTTP requests work. If you wander up to your web browser's address bar and enter a URL like http://192.168.2.42/SAMSUNG/32/E0E040BF, your browser will send an HTTP request that looks like this:

```
GET /SAMSUNG/32/E0E040BF HTTP/1.1
host: 192.168.2.42
```

The first line is a GET request, and handle_command expects a string containing such a request. It extracts all the information encoded in the given path (/SAMSUNG/32/E0E040BF) and uses it to emit an infrared signal. Parsing the information is tricky, but using C's strsep function, it's not too difficult. strsep separates strings delimited by certain characters. It expects a string containing several separated strings and a string containing all delimiters. To get the separated strings, you have to call strsep repeatedly until it returns NULL. That is, whenever you invoke strsep, it returns the next string or NULL.

We use strsep in two different contexts. In the first case, we extract the path from the GET command: we strip off the string "GET" and the string "HTTP/1.1." Both are separated from the path by a blank character. In line 2, we call strsep to remove the "GET" at the beginning of the string. We don't even store the function's return value, because we know it's "GET" anyway.

In line 3, we read the next separated string, which contains the actual path. If you were to pass the request GET http://192.168.2.42/SAMSUNG/32/E0E040BF HTTP/1.1 to handle_command, path would contain /SAMSUNG/32/E0E040BF now.

At this stage, we have a string consisting of three strings separated by a slash character (/). It's time to use strsep again, and if you understand what happens in lines 6 to 9, then you can call yourself familiar with both C and the strsep function. In the end, the array args contains all three path elements. We can pass the protocol name directly to send_ir_data, but we have to turn the bit length and the value of the code into int and long values before. For the conversion, we use the atoi and strtoul functions. We use the latter one to convert a hexadecimal value to a decimal value.

Now we have defined all helper methods we need, and we only have to implement the only public method of the InfraredProxy class:

RemoteControl/InfraredProxy/infrared_proxy.cpp

```
Line 1  void InfraredProxy::receive_from_server(EthernetServer server) {
   -      const int MAX_LINE = 256;
   -      char line[MAX_LINE];
   -      EthernetClient client = server.available();
   5      if (client) {
   -        while (client.connected()) {
   -          if (client.available()) {
   -            read_line(client, line, MAX_LINE);
   -            Serial.println(line);
   10           if (line[0] == 'G' && line[1] == 'E' && line[2] == 'T')
   -              handle_command(line);
   -            if (!strcmp(line, "")) {
   -              client.println("HTTP/1.1 200 OK\n");
   -              break;
   15           }
   -          }
   -        }
   -        delay(1);
   -        client.stop();
   20     }
   -    }
```

The receive_from_server method finally implements the core logic of our InfraredProxy class. It expects an instance of the EthernetServer class that is defined in the Ethernet library. It waits for a client to connect using EthernetServer's available method in line 4. Whenever the server is connected to a client, it checks whether the client has new data using EthernetClient's available method in line 7.

receive_from_server reads the data sent by the client line by line, calling read_line. It prints each line to the serial port for debugging purposes, and for every line it checks whether the line begins with GET. If yes, it calls handle_command; otherwise, it checks whether the line is empty, because all HTTP messages are terminated by an empty line. In this case, receive_from_server sends back an "OK" response, waits for a millisecond to give the client some time to process the response, and then disconnects from the client by calling stop.

Admittedly, that was a lot of code, but the effort was well worth it. Using the InfraredProxy is really simple now:

RemoteControl/InfraredProxy/InfraredProxy.ino
```
#include <SPI.h>
#include <Ethernet.h>
#include <IRremote.h>
#include "infrared_proxy.h"

const unsigned int PROXY_PORT = 80;
const unsigned int BAUD_RATE = 9600;

byte mac[] = { 0xDE, 0xAD, 0xBE, 0xEF, 0xFE, 0xED };
IPAddress ip(192, 168, 2, 42);

EthernetServer server(PROXY_PORT);
InfraredProxy ir_proxy;

void setup() {
  Serial.begin(BAUD_RATE);
  Ethernet.begin(mac, ip);
  server.begin();
}

void loop() {
  ir_proxy.receive_from_server(server);
}
```

As usual, we define the MAC and IP addresses we'd like to use. Then we define an EthernetServer object, passing it the port it should listen to, 80 (the standard HTTP port). Also, we initialize a new InfraredProxy object.

In the setup method, we initialize the serial port for debugging purposes. We also initialize the Ethernet shield, and we call EthernetServer's begin method to start our server's listener. In loop, we call only the InfraredProxy's receive_from_server method, passing it our EthernetServer instance.

Let's finally test the code! Attach the Ethernet shield to your Arduino, and attach the infrared LED circuit to the shield. Configure the MAC and IP addresses, compile the InfraredProxy sketch, and upload it to your Arduino. Point your web browser to http://192.168.2.42/SAMSUNG/32/E0E040BF (adjust the URL to your local settings!) and see what happens to your TV set or whatever device you want to control. In the following figure, you can see a typical output of the infrared proxy on the serial monitor. Note that the web browser sends not only one but two requests. The second one is for downloading the website's Favicon,[4] and we can safely ignore it.

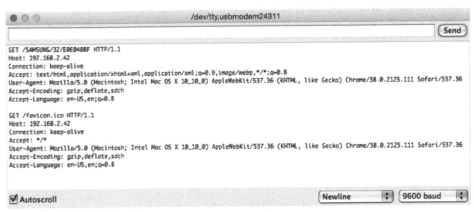

Although we've used only a minimal amount of hardware (a cheap and simple infrared LED), this chapter's projects are very useful and fairly sophisticated, at least from a software development point of view. Now not only can we control any device that understands infrared signals, but we also can do it using a computer's serial port or even a web browser.

Also, you no longer need to connect the Arduino to your computer's USB port. The infrared proxy needs only the USB port to get some power. Plug an AC adapter into your Arduino, and you can get rid of your USB cable.

For the first time, we've controlled real-world devices using an Arduino. We'll continue to do so in the next chapter, where you'll learn how to control motors.

Control Everything

All of the projects in this chapter are based on devices you can control already using an infrared remote control. But you can also add an infrared receiver to existing devices or build completely new gadgets that come with an infrared receiver.

In principle, you could control your refrigerator or your microwave oven with a remote control. But have you ever thought about a remote-controlled lawnmower?[a] I bet not.

a. http://www.instructables.com/id/Arduino-RC-Lawnmower/

---

4. http://en.wikipedia.org/wiki/Favicon

What If It Doesn't Work?

If you cannot make this chapter's code run, you should download the code from the book's website and try to run it. Make sure you're using the correct serial port in the code/RemoteControl/TvRemoteUI/js/remote.js file.

In this chapter, we mainly used LEDs and an Ethernet shield, so all of the advice from Chapter 3, *Building Binary Dice*, on page 39, and Chapter 10, *Networking with Arduino*, on page 163, also applies to this chapter.

In addition, you have to be careful of more things. The distance between an infrared LED and its receiver is important. To be on the safe side, you should position the LED near the receiver. It should also be placed right in front of the receiver, and you should make sure there's not too much ambient light that might disturb the infrared signal.

For debugging purposes, it's useful to replace an invisible infrared LED with a regular LED from time to time. This way, you can see whether your circuit works in principle.

If you're trying to control a Mac, you should unpair any other remote controls in the Security area of the Mac's System Preferences window.

Finally, you might be using a device that uses a protocol that isn't supported by the IRremote library. In this case, you have to add it. This can be tricky, but IRremote is open source, so at least it's possible.

Exercises

- Build an emulator for a remote control you find in your household. Make its commands available via serial port and via Ethernet.

- Instead of controlling the Arduino via a serial monitor or web browser, control it using a Nintendo Nunchuk. You could move the analog stick up and down to control your TV set's volume, and you could move it left or right to change the channel.

- Design a real universal remote control based on an Arduino. Look for a touchscreen, a button pad, an SD card shield, and a Bluetooth module. I bet you didn't think you could build a device like this—but you know everything you need to do it now.

CHAPTER 13

Controlling Motors with Arduino

So far, we've created projects that have had an impact on the real world. We've made LEDs shine, and we've controlled devices using infrared light. In this chapter, we'll create an even more intense experience: we'll control motors that will actually move things. We won't go so far as to build a full-blown autonomous robot, but we'll create a small device that does something useful and funny.

First, though, you'll learn about the basics of different motor types and their pros and cons. Today you can choose from a variety of motor types for your projects, and this chapter starts with a brief description of their differences.

We'll concentrate on servo motors, because you can use them for a wide range of projects and they're cheap and easy to use. You'll learn to use the Arduino servo library and to control a servo using the serial port.

Based on these first steps, we'll then build a more sophisticated project. It's a blaming device that uses nearly the same hardware as the first project in the chapter but more elaborate software. You'll probably find many applications for it in your office!

What You Need

1. A servo motor, such as the Hitec HS-322HD
2. Some wires
3. A TMP36 temperature sensor (it's optional, and you need it only for the exercises)
4. An Arduino board, such as the Uno, Duemilanove, or Diecimila
5. A USB cable to connect the Arduino to your computer

Introducing Motors

Depending on your project's needs, you can choose from a variety of motors. For hobby electronics, you'll usually use DC motors, servo motors, or stepper motors. (In the following figure, you see a few different types of motors.) They differ mainly in speed, precision of control, power consumption, reliability, and price.

Figure 31—Motor types from left to right:
standard servo, continuous rotation servo, stepper, DC motor

DC motors are fast and efficient, so you can use them in drill machines, electric bicycles, or remote-control cars. You can control DC motors easily, because they have only two connectors. Connect one to a power supply and the other to ground, and the motor will start to spin. Swap the connections, and the motor will spin the other direction. Add more voltage, and the motor will spin faster; decrease voltage, and it will spin slower.

DC motors aren't a good choice if you need precise control. In such cases, it's better to use a stepper motor, which allows for precise control in a range of 360 degrees. Although you might not have noticed it, you're surrounded by stepper motors. You hear them when your printer, scanner, or disk drive is at work. Controlling stepper motors isn't rocket science, but it is more complicated than controlling DC motors and servos.

Servo motors are the most popular among hobbyists, because these motors are a good compromise between DC motors and steppers. They're affordable, reliable, and easy to control. You can move standard servos only in a range of 180 degrees, but that's sufficient for many applications. With continuous rotation servos, you can increase the range to 360 degrees, but you lose the ease of control.

In the next section, you'll learn how easy it is to control standard servo motors with an Arduino.

First Steps with a Servo Motor

The Arduino IDE comes with a library for controlling servo motors that we'll use for our first experiments. The following figure shows a basic circuit for connecting an Arduino to a servo motor. Connect the ground wire to one of the Arduino's GND pins, connect power to the Arduino's 5V pin, and connect the control line to pin 9.

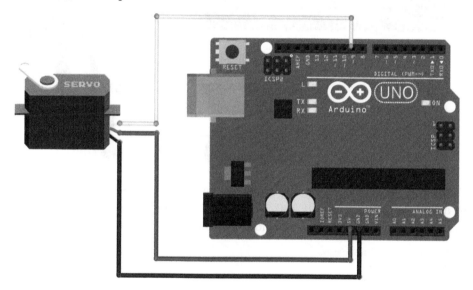

Please note that this works only for a 5V servo! Many cheap servos use 9V, and in that case you need an external power supply, and you can no longer connect the servo to the Arduino's 5V pin. If you have a 9V servo, attach an external power supply, such as an AC-to-DC adapter or a DC power supply, to your Arduino's power jack. Then connect the servo to the Vin pin.[1] You should also check the specifications of your Arduino board. For example, you should not use an Arduino BT[2] to control motors, because it can only handle a maximum of 5.5V.

---

1. http://www.arduino.cc/playground/Learning/WhatAdapter
2. http://arduino.cc/en/Main/ArduinoBoardBluetooth

Here's a picture of a servo motor connected to an Arduino using wires. You can also use pin headers, but wires give you more flexibility.

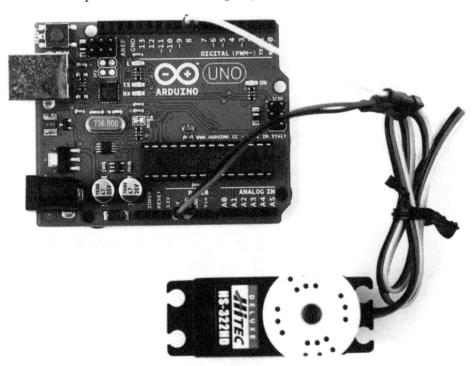

Controlling servo motors is convenient, because you can set the motor's shaft to an angle between 0 and 180. With the following sketch, you can send a degree value via the serial port and move the servo motor accordingly:

Motors/SerialServo/SerialServo.ino

```
Line 1  #include <Servo.h>
     -
     -  const unsigned int MOTOR_PIN = 9;
     -  const unsigned int MOTOR_DELAY = 15;
     5  const unsigned int SERIAL_DELAY = 5;
     -  const unsigned int BAUD_RATE = 9600;
     -
     -  Servo servo;
     -
    10  void setup() {
     -    Serial.begin(BAUD_RATE);
     -    servo.attach(MOTOR_PIN);
     -    delay(MOTOR_DELAY);
     -    servo.write(1);
    15    delay(MOTOR_DELAY);
     -  }
     -
```

```
   -    void loop() {
   -      const unsigned int MAX_ANGLE = 3;
  20      char degrees[MAX_ANGLE + 1];
   -
   -      if (Serial.available()) {
   -        int i = 0;
   -        while (Serial.available() && i < MAX_ANGLE + 1) {
  25          const char c = Serial.read();
   -          if (c != -1 && c != '\n')
   -            degrees[i++] = c;
   -          delay(SERIAL_DELAY);
   -        }
  30        degrees[i] = 0;
   -        int value = atoi(degrees);
   -        if (value == 0)
   -          value = 1;
   -        Serial.print(value);
  35        Serial.println(" degrees.");
   -        servo.write(value);
   -        delay(MOTOR_DELAY);
   -      }
   -    }
```

We include the Servo library, and in line 8, we define a new Servo object. In the setup function, we initialize the serial port, and we attach the Servo object to the pin we have defined in MOTOR_PIN. After that, we wait for 15 milliseconds so the servo motor has enough time to process our command. Then we call write to move the servo back to 1 degree. We could also move it back to 0 degrees, but some of the servos I've worked with make some annoying noise in this position.

The main purpose of the loop function is to read new degree values from the serial port. These values are in a range from 0 to 180, and we read them as ASCII values. So, we need a string that can contain up to four characters. (Remember, strings are null-terminated in C.) That's why we declare the degrees string with a length of four in line 20.

Then we wait for new data to arrive at the serial port and read it character by character until no more data is available or until we have read enough. We terminate the string with a zero byte and print the value we've read to the serial port. Finally, we convert the string into an integer value using atoi and pass it to the write method of the Servo object in line 36. Then we wait again for the servo to do its job.

Compile and upload the sketch, then open the serial monitor. After the servo has initialized, send some degree values, such as 45, 180, or 10. See how the

> ## Arduino Arts
>
> You can use the Arduino not just for gadgets or fun projects, but also in artistic ways. Especially in the new-media art area, you will find many amazing projects built with the Arduino. One of them is Anthros,[a] a responsive environment that observes a small area using a webcam. The area contains some "tentacles," and whenever a person crosses the area, the tentacles move in the person's direction. Servos move the tentacles, and an Arduino controls the servos.
>
> For all people interested in new-media art, Alicia Gibb's thesis, "New Media Art, Design, and the Arduino Microcontroller: A Malleable Tool,"[b] is a must-read.
>
> ───────────
>
> a.   http://makezine.com/2010/04/19/arduino-powered-kinetic-sculpture/
> b.   http://aliciagibb.com/thesis/

motor moves to the angle you've specified. To see the effect a bit better, form a wire or some paper into an arrow and attach it to the motor's gear.

It's easy to control a servo via the serial port, and the circuit we've built can be the basis for many useful and fun projects. In the next section, we'll use it to build an automatic blaming device.

Building a Blaminatr

Finger-pointing isn't nice, but it can be oddly satisfying. In this section, we'll build a device that I call *Blaminatr*. Instead of blaming someone directly, you can tell the Blaminatr to do so. In the following figure, you can see the device in action. Tell it to blame me, and it moves an arrow so it points to "Maik."

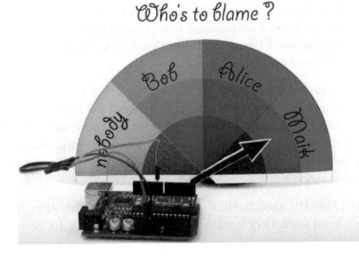

Blaminatrs are perfect office toys that you can use in many situations. For software developers, it can be a good idea to attach one to your continuous integration (CI) system. Continuous integration systems, such as Jenkins,[3] help you continuously check whether your software is in good shape.

Whenever a developer checks in changes, the CI automatically compiles the software and runs all tests. Then it publishes the results via email or as an RSS feed. You can easily write a small piece of software that subscribes to such a feed. Whenever someone breaks the build, you'll find a notification in the feed, and you can use the Blaminatr to point to the name of the developer who has committed the latest changes.[4]

In the previous section, you learned all about the servo motor you need to build the Blaminatr. Now we need only some creativity to build the device's display, and we need more elaborate software. We start with a class named Team that represents the members of our team; that is, the potential "blamees":

Motors/Blaminatr/Blaminatr.ino

```
Line 1   const unsigned int MAX_MEMBERS = 10;

         class Team {
           const char** _members;
     5     unsigned int _num_members;
           unsigned int _positions[MAX_MEMBERS];
         public:
         Team(const char** members) {
           _members = members;
    10       _num_members = 0;
           const char** member = _members;
           while (*member++)
             _num_members++;

    15       const unsigned int share = 180 / _num_members;
           unsigned int pos = share / 2;
           for (unsigned int i = 0; i < _num_members; i++) {
             _positions[i] = pos;
             pos += share;
    20     }
         }

         int get_position(const char* name) const {
           int position = 0;
    25     for (unsigned int i = 0; i < _num_members; i++) {
             if (!strcmp(_members[i], name)) {
```

3. http://jenkins-ci.org//
4. At http://urbanhonking.com/ideasfordozens/2010/05/19/the_github_stoplight/, you can see an alternative project. It uses a traffic light to indicate your project's current status.

```
         position = _positions[i];
         break;
       }
30   }
     return position;
   }
};
```

The code defines several member variables: _members contains a list of up to ten team member names, _num_members contains the actual number of people on the team, and we store the position (angle) of the team member's name on the Blaminatr display in _positions.

The constructor expects an array of strings that contains the team members' names and that is terminated by a NULL pointer. We store a reference to the list, and then we calculate the number of team members. We iterate over the array until we find a NULL pointer. All this happens in lines 10 to 13.

Then we calculate the position of each team member's name on the Blaminatr's display. Every team member gets his or her fair share on the 180-degree display, and the Blaminatr will point to the share's center, so we divide the share by 2. We store the positions in the _positions array that corresponds to the _members array. That means the first entry of _positions contains the position of the first team member, and so on.

With the get_position method, we get back the position belonging to a certain name. We walk through the _members array and check whether we have found the right member using the strcmp function. As soon as we've found it, we return the corresponding entry of the _positions array. If we can't find a team member with the name we are looking for, we return 0.

Implementing a Blaminatr class is easy now:

Motors/Blaminatr/Blaminatr.ino
```
#include <Servo.h>
const unsigned int MOTOR_PIN = 9;
const unsigned int MOTOR_DELAY = 15;

class Blaminatr {
  Team  _team;
  Servo _servo;

  public:

  Blaminatr(const Team& team) : _team(team) {}

  void attach(const int sensor_pin) {
    _servo.attach(sensor_pin);
```

```
      delay(MOTOR_DELAY);
    }

    void blame(const char* name) {
      _servo.write(_team.get_position(name));
      delay(MOTOR_DELAY);
    }
};
```

A Blaminatr object aggregates a Team object and a Servo object. The constructor initializes the Team instance while we can initialize the Servo instance by calling the attach method.

The most interesting method is blame. It expects the name of the team member to blame, calculates his position, and moves the servo accordingly. Let's put it all together now:

Motors/Blaminatr/Blaminatr.ino

```
Line 1  const unsigned int MAX_NAME = 30;
     -  const unsigned int BAUD_RATE = 9600;
     -  const unsigned int SERIAL_DELAY = 5;
     -
     5  const char* members[] = { "nobody", "Bob", "Alice", "Maik", NULL };
     -  Team team(members);
     -  Blaminatr blaminatr(team);
     -
     -  void setup() {
    10    Serial.begin(BAUD_RATE);
     -    blaminatr.attach(MOTOR_PIN);
     -    blaminatr.blame("nobody");
     -  }
     -
    15  void loop() {
     -    char name[MAX_NAME + 1];
     -    if (Serial.available()) {
     -      unsigned int i = 0;
     -      while (Serial.available() && i < MAX_NAME + 1) {
    20        const char c = Serial.read();
     -        if (c != -1 && c != '\n')
     -          name[i++] = c;
     -        delay(SERIAL_DELAY);
     -      }
    25      name[i] = 0;
     -      Serial.print(name);
     -      Serial.println(" is to blame.");
     -      blaminatr.blame(name);
     -    }
    30  }
```

We define a list of member names that is terminated by a NULL pointer. The list's first entry is "nobody," so we don't have to deal with the rare edge case when nobody is to blame. Then we use members to initialize a new Team object and pass this object to the Blaminatr's constructor.

More Motors Projects

Motors are fascinating. Search the Net, and you'll find numerous projects combining the Arduino with motors. Most of them probably deal with robots[a] or remote-controlled cars.

You'll also find useful and exciting project like the USB hourglass.[b] It uses an Arduino and a servo motor to turn a sand timer, and it observes the falling sand using an optical sensor. Whenever all the sand has fallen through, the device turns the timer automatically.

That's all nice, but the device's main purpose is to generate true random numbers. Falling sand is a perfect basis for generating true randomness (see *Generating Random Numbers*, on page 48), and the USB hourglass uses the signals from its optical sensor to generate random numbers, sending them to the serial port.

---

a. http://makezine.com/projects/building-a-simple-arduino-robot/
b. http://makezine.com/2009/12/23/usb-hourglass-random-number-generat/

In the setup function, we initialize the serial port and attach the Blaminatr's servo motor to the pin we defined in MOTOR_PIN. Also, we initialize the Blaminatr by blaming "nobody."

The loop function is nearly the same as in *First Steps with a Servo Motor*, on page 227. The only difference is that we do not control a servo directly, but instead call blame in line 28.

That's it! You can now start to draw your own display and create your own arrow. Attach them directly to the motor or—even better—put everything into a nice box. Compile and upload the software and start to blame.

Of course, you can use motors for more serious projects. You can use them to build robots running on wheels or similar devices. But you cannot attach too many motors to a "naked" Arduino, because it isn't meant for driving bigger loads. So if you have a project in mind that needs a significant number of motors, you should consider buying a motor shield[5] or using a special shield, such as the Robotics Shield Kit.[6]

---

5. You can find them at http://adafruit.com or http://makershed.com.
6. http://www.parallax.com/product/130-35000

What If It Doesn't Work?

Working with motors is surprisingly easy, but a lot of things still can go wrong. The biggest problem is that motors consume a lot of power, so you cannot simply attach every motor to an Arduino. Also, you cannot easily drive more than one motor, especially not with the small amount of power you get from a USB port. If your motor doesn't run as expected, check its specification and attach an AC or DC adapter to your Arduino if necessary.

You also shouldn't attach too much weight to your motor. Moving an arrow made of paper is no problem, but you might run into problems if you attach bigger and heavier things. Also, be careful not to put any obstacles in the motor's way. The motor's shaft always needs to move freely.

Some motors have to be adjusted from time to time, and usually you have to do that with a very small screwdriver. Refer to the motor's specifications for detailed instructions.

Exercises

- Add an Ethernet shield to the Blaminatr so you can blame people via the Internet and not only via the serial port. Pointing your web browser to an address such as http://192.168.1.42/blame/Maik should blame me.

- Create a thermometer based on a TMP36 temperature sensor and a servo motor. Its display could look like the image below; that is, you have to move an arrow that points to the current temperature.

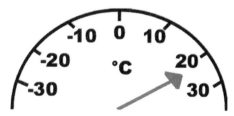

- Use an IR receiver to control the Blaminatr. You could use the channel key of your TV set's remote control to move the Blaminatr from one name to the other.

Part III

Appendixes

Part III

Appendices

Electronics and Soldering Basics

You didn't need a lot of theory or background to create your first Arduino projects. But it's a good idea to learn about electricity and about soldering if you want to build bigger and more sophisticated projects.

In this appendix, you'll learn the basics of electricity, and you'll learn about Ohm's law, which is probably the most important law in electronics. Also, you'll learn more about resistors, and you'll see that soldering isn't as difficult as it might seem.

Current, Voltage, and Resistance

To build your first projects with the Arduino, you didn't need to know much about electricity. But at some point, you'll need to understand what current, voltage, and resistance are all about. For example, you already know that you always have to put a resistor in front of an LED, but you might not know exactly why, and you might not know how to calculate the resistor's size for a given LED. Let's remedy that.

Electrical Circuits

An electrical circuit resembles a water circuit in many respects. In the following figure,[1] you can see a water circuit on the left and an electrical circuit on the right. Isn't it fascinating how similar they are and that you can even find a connection between them when you use a water-driven dynamo that acts as a power supply? Let's take a closer look at their most important attributes.

---

1. Lightbulb image is from Benji Park at https://openclipart.org/detail/26218/Lightbulb_Bright-by-bpcomp.

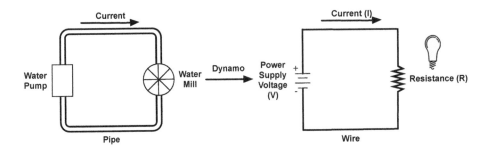

While water flows in a water circuit, electrons flow in an electrical circuit. Voltage is electricity's equivalent of water pressure and is measured in volts (V). Voltage is the initial cause for a current, and the higher the voltage, the faster the current flows.

In electronics, current is the amount of electricity flowing through an electric line. It is the equivalent of the actual flow of water in a water circuit. While we measure the water flow in liters per minute, we measure current in amperes. One ampere means that approximately 6.24×10^{18} electrons are flowing per second.

Every component in a circuit—be it water or electricity—resists some amount of current. In a water circuit, it's the pipes the water is flowing through or perhaps a water mill. In an electrical circuit, it is the wire or a light bulb. Resistance is an important physical phenomenon that is closely related to current and voltage. We measure it in ohms, and its official symbol is Ω.

The German physicist Georg Ohm found that current depends on voltage and resistance. He postulated the following form that we call *Ohm's law* today (we use I as the current's letter for historical reasons. In the past, it stood for inductance):

- I (current) = V (voltage) / R (resistance)

This is equivalent to the following:

- R (resistance) = V (voltage) / I (current)
- V (voltage) = R (resistance) × I (current)

So, for two given values, you can calculate the third one. Ohm's law is the only formula you'll absolutely have to learn when learning electronics. When working with LEDs, it helps you calculate the size of the resistor you need.

If you look at an LED's data sheet, you will usually find two values: a forward voltage and a current rating. The forward voltage usually is between 1.8V and

3.6V, and the maximum current often is 20 mA (milliamperes). Let's say we have an LED with a maximum of 2.5 volts and a safe current of 20 mA. We also assume that we have a power supply delivering 5 volts (as most Arduinos do). What's the right size of the resistor we need to put in front of the LED?

We have to make sure that the resistor takes 5 − 2.5 = 2.5 volts from the circuit, so only 2.5 volts are left for the LED. This value is called *voltage drop*. Also, we want a maximum of 20 mA to flow through the LED. This implies that a maximum of 20 mA (0.02 A) should flow through our resistor also.

Now that we know that 2.5V and 0.02 A should pass the LED, we can use Ohm's law to calculate the resistance R:

R = V / I

In our case, we have the following:

R = 2.5V / 0.02A = 125Ω

This means we need a 125Ω resistor for our LED. If you do not have a 125Ω resistor, use a bigger one, such as 150Ω or 220Ω. It will still protect the LED and only slightly decrease its brightness. That's because we'd decrease the current even more:

I = 2.5V / 150Ω = 17mA

I = 2.5V / 220Ω = 11mA

Resistors

You'll hardly ever find an electronics project that doesn't need resistors. So, you'll need them often and should get more familiar with them. Usually you'll use carbon or metal resistors. Metal resistors are more precise and don't create so much noise, but carbon resistors are cheaper. In simple circuits, it usually doesn't matter which type you use.

The most important attribute of a resistor is its resistance value that is measured in ohms. Only a few vendors actually print this value on the resistor, because resistors are small parts, and it's hard to read text that is small enough to fit on them. So, they use a trick and encode the value using colored stripes.

Usually you find four or five stripes on a resistor (at least on through-hole parts; SMD resistors don't have them). One of them is separated from the others by a gap. (See the following figure.) The separate stripe is on the right side of the resistor, and it tells you about the resistor's accuracy. Gold stands for an accuracy of ±5 percent, silver stands for ±10 percent, and no stripe means ±20 percent. Using the remaining stripes, you can calculate the resistor value.

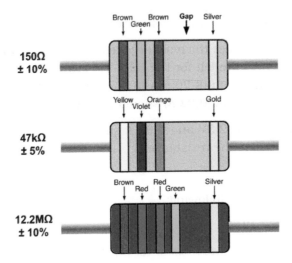

You read the stripes from left to right, and every color stands for a digit. (See the following figure.) The rightmost stripe—that is, the third or fourth one—stands for an amount of zeros to be added to the preceding digits. In the following figure, you can see three examples:

Color	Code	Zeros
Black	0	-
Brown	1	0
Red	2	00
Orange	3	000
Yellow	4	0000
Green	5	00000
Blue	6	000000
Violet	7	0000000
Gray	8	00000000
White	9	000000000

- On the first resistor we find four stripes: brown (1), green (5), brown (1 zero), silver (±10%). That means we have a resistor value of 150Ω.

- The second resistor has four stripes again: yellow (4), violet (7), orange (3 zeros), gold (±5%). So, this resistor has a value of 47000Ω = 47kΩ.

- The third resistor has five stripes: brown (1), red (2), red (2), green (5 zeros), silver (±10%), so the value is 12,200,000Ω = 12.2MΩ.

In the beginning, the color coding seems to be complicated, but you'll get used to it quickly. Also, you can find countless tools for determining resistor values on the Internet.[2]

For the book's projects, this is all the theory of electricity you need to know. To learn more about electronics, have a look at *Make: Electronics [Pla10]* or at http://lcamtuf.coredump.cx/electronics/, for example.

Learning How to Use a Wire Cutter

When working with breadboards and through-hole parts, you often have to shorten wires. Sometimes you have to cut plain wires that you need to connect parts in your circuit. Other times you have to cut the wires of a component like a resistor to make it easier to handle.

For these purposes, a wire cutter is indispensable.

Using a wire cutter is like using a pair of scissors. The only difference is that you usually cut different types of material. When cutting metal wires you should always wear safety glasses. Often, when I cut wires, the part I cut off flies right into my safety glasses.

Learning How to Solder

You can build nearly all of the book's projects by plugging parts into a breadboard or directly into the Arduino board. But sooner or later you'll have to learn how to solder if you want to become an expert in electronics. That's mainly because you'll learn the most by building projects, and even the simplest kits require some sort of soldering.

Many people think that soldering is difficult or requires expensive equipment, so they never try to do it. The truth is that it's cheap and pretty easy. It requires some practice, but after only a few solder joints you'll see that it's not rocket science.

In this book, we have one project that requires you to solder a pin header to an ADXL335 breakout board. We need it for building the motion-sensing game controller in Chapter 6, *Building a Motion-Sensing Game Controller*, on page 99. In this section, you'll learn how to do it, and you'll need the following equipment:

---

2. http://www.digikey.de/en/resources/conversion-calculators/conversion-calculator-resistor-color-code-4-band

- A 25–30W soldering iron with a tip (preferably 1/16-inch) and a soldering stand.

- A standard 60/40 solder (rosin-core) spool for electronics work. It should have a 0.031-inch diameter.

- A sponge.

Before you start to solder, prepare your work area. Make sure you can easily access all your tools and that you have something to protect your work area from drops of solder. Wearing safety glasses is always a good idea! Even seemingly simple and harmless activities such as cutting wires can be very dangerous! Also make sure that your room has good ventilation, because the solder fumes aren't good for your health.

Bring all parts into the correct position: attach the pin header to the breakout board, and make sure you can't accidentally move it while soldering.

People get very creative when it comes to locking parts into a certain position. But you have to be careful—don't use flammable materials to bring parts together. You also shouldn't use parts that distribute heat very well, especially if they're in touch with other parts. Duct tape might work in some cases, but be careful with it, too.

Try to find a piece of wood or something similar that has the right height: the height of the pin headers. Then you can put the breakout board on top of it and attach the pin headers. If you're planning to solder more often and build some electronics projects, you should always look for these little tools that make your life easier.

In the following figure, you can see how I've prepared all parts:

I've used a *helping hand*, a useful tool for locking parts into a position. Helping hands usually come with a magnifying glass, and they are cheap. If you plan to solder often, you should get one—they justify their name.

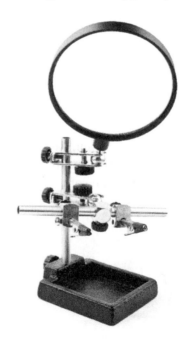

After you've prepared everything, it's time to heat up the soldering iron. The main purpose of soldering is to join metallic surfaces. In our case, we'd like to join the surface of the pin header with the metal in the breakout board. To achieve this, we'll heat up the metallic parts and then connect them using molten solder.

This process depends on a certain temperature, and having the wrong temperature is one of the most common soldering problems. If the temperature is too low, your solder joints might become fragile, and you also might have to touch the parts for too long, so you are liable to damage them. An extremely high temperature can damage your parts right away. Experts can debate for hours about "the right temperature," but 600°F to 650°F (315°C to 350°C) is a good compromise. Even with cheap soldering irons, you can adjust the temperature.

Dampen the sponge (it shouldn't be too wet) and clean the tip by wiping it over the sponge a few times. Then *tin* the tip by putting a small amount of solder back onto it. This helps protect the tip, and it also improves the heat transfer to components:

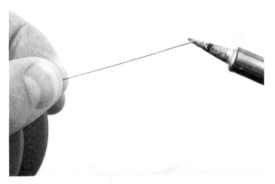

Soldering is mainly about heat distribution, and now it's time to heat the joint. Make sure the tip of the soldering iron touches the part (pin header) and the pad of the breakout board at the same time:

Keep it there for about a second, and then feed a small amount of solder between the tip and the pin:

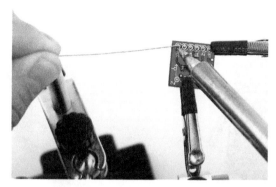

As soon as the solder starts to flow, you're safer, because the solder distributes heat automatically. Feed some more solder (not too much!) until you have a nice, shiny solder joint. The whole process shouldn't take more than two to three seconds. When you're finished, remove the iron tip quickly and give the joint a few seconds to cool down.

Repeat this for all six pin headers, and the result should look like this:

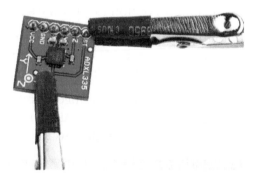

Test it by building the motion-sensing game controller, and play a video game to relax.

Congratulations! You have just finished your first soldering job!

Learning How to Desolder

Let's face it: even if soldering isn't that difficult, things can still go wrong. Sometimes you solder a part to the wrong place. In other cases you accidentally use too much solder and create unwanted connections. To correct such mistakes, you have to remove the excessive solder.

The following figure shows two of the most popular tools for desoldering. On the left you see a desoldering braid, and on the right you see a desoldering pump (also known as a *solder sucker*).

Both tools work the same in principle: you heat the solder you want to get rid of with the soldering iron, and then you use the tool to remove the molten solder. When you use the desoldering pump, you heat the solder until it melts, and then you press the pump's button to suck the solder.

To desolder using braid, put the braid on top of the solder joint you'd like to remove. Then press the soldering iron's tip to the braid and wait until the solder melts. The braid will suck the molten solder automatically.

Make sure that the distance between your fingers and the solder joint is reasonable, because the braid gets pretty hot. Also make sure you're using a part of the braid that isn't full of solder already.

This tutorial is only a starting point for your new shiny soldering career. You now know that soldering isn't too difficult, and as a next step, you can try to build some beginner's kits. All electronics stores offer them, and they usually come with soldering instructions, too. You can also find excellent tutorials and even videos on the Internet to build your skills.[3]

---

3. http://store.curiousinventor.com/guides/How_to_Solder

Advanced Arduino Programming

In reality, the Arduino programming language is nothing but C++, but it has some restrictions, and it uses a special tool suite. In this appendix, you'll learn what your options are. Also, you'll find a short section showing how bit operators work, because you need them often when working with sensors and other devices.

The Arduino Programming Language

The first sketches you'll write for an Arduino might seem to be written in a special Arduino language, but they aren't. To program the Arduino, you usually use plain old C/C++. Unfortunately, the Arduino doesn't understand C or C++ code, so you have to compile the code on your PC or Mac into machine code suitable for the Arduino's microcontroller. This process is called *cross-compiling*, and it's the usual way of creating executable software for microcontrollers. You edit and compile the software on your PC, and then you transfer the machine code to the microcontroller.

In case of the Arduino, these microcontrollers are often part of the AVR family produced by a company named Atmel. To make software development for Atmel microcontrollers as easy as possible, Atmel has developed a whole tool chain based on the GNU compiler tools. All tools work like the originals, but they have been optimized for generating code for the Atmel microcontrollers.

For nearly all GNU development tools, such as gcc, ld, or as, there's an AVR variant: avr-gcc, avr-ld, and so on. You can find them in the hardware/tools/avr/bin directory of the Arduino IDE.

The IDE is mainly a graphical wrapper that helps you avoid using the command-line tools directly. Whenever you compile or upload a program using the IDE, it delegates all work to the AVR tools. As a serious software developer, you should turn on a more verbose output, so you can see all command-line tool invocations. Enable verbose output for both compilation and upload in the Preferences menu, as described in *Changing Preferences*, on page 26. Then load your blinking LED sketch and compile it. (We did this back at the start of our journey in *Changing Preferences*, on page 26).

The command invocations look weird at first because of the names of the many temporary files that are created. You should still be able to identify all compile and link steps necessary to build even a simple sketch like our blinking LED example. That's the most important thing the Arduino team did: they hid all these nasty details well behind the IDE, so even people with no software development experience can program the Arduino. For programmers, it's a good idea to work in verbose mode, because the best way to learn about all the AVR tools is to see them in action.

Upload the program to the Arduino now to see avrdude in action. This tool is responsible for loading code into the Arduino and can be used for programming many other devices, too. Interestingly, the AVR tools even make it possible to use the Arduino IDE for non-Arduino projects.

There's another difference between Arduino programming and regular C++ code. When programming for the Arduino, you don't define main yourself, because it is already defined in the libraries provided by the Arduino developers. As you might have guessed, it calls setup first and then runs the loop function in a loop. Since Arduino 1.0, it also calls serialEvent at the end of the loop function.

Further restrictions when programming C++ on AVR microcontrollers include the following:[1]

- You cannot use the Standard Template Library (STL) because it's way too big for the small AVR microcontrollers.

- Exception handling isn't supported. That's why you see the -fno-exceptions switch often when the avr-gcc compiler is invoked.

- Dynamic memory management using new and delete isn't supported.

In addition to all that, you should keep an eye on performance. C++ automatically creates a lot of functions (copy constructors, assignment operators, and so on) in the background that are rarely needed on the Arduino. Even with these restrictions, the Arduino supports a powerful subset of the C++ programming language. So there's no excuse for sloppy coding!

---

1. http://www.nongnu.org/avr-libc/user-manual/FAQ.html#faq_cplusplus

Bit Operations

In embedded computing, you often have to manipulate bits. You sometimes have to read single bits to get some sensor data. In other cases, you have to set bits to turn a device into a certain status or to make it perform some action.

For bit manipulation, you need only a few operations. The simplest is the *not* operation that inverts a bit. It turns a 0 into a 1 and vice versa. Most programming languages implement the binary *not* operation with a ~ operator:

```
int x = 42; // In binary this is 101010
int y = ~x; // y == 010101
```

In addition, you'll find three binary operations named *AND*, *OR*, and *XOR* (eXclusive OR). Most programming languages call the corresponding operators &, |, and ^, and their definitions are as follows:

a	b	a AND b a & b	a OR b a | b	a XOR b a ^ b
0	0	0	0	0
1	0	0	1	1
0	1	0	1	1
1	1	1	1	0

With these operators, it's possible to *mask* bits in a number, so you can extract certain bits. If you're interested only in the lower two bits of a number, you can do it as follows:

```
int x = 42;        // In binary this is 101010
int y = x & 0x03; // y == 2 == B10
```

You can also set one or more bits in a number using the *OR* operation. The following code sets the fifth bit in x regardless of whether this bit is 0 or 1.

```
int x = 42;        // In binary this is 101010
int y = x | 0x10; // y == 58 == B111010
```

The bit shift operators « and » let you move bits to a certain position before you work with them. The first one moves bits to the left, and the second moves them to the right:

```
int x = 42;        // In binary this is 101010
int y = x << 1;    // y == 84 == B1010100
int z = x >> 2;    // z == 10 == B1010
```

Shifting operations might seem intuitive, but you have to be careful when shifting signed values.[2] Although they look similar, binary operators aren't the same as Boolean operators. Boolean operators such as && and || don't operate on the bit level. They implement the rules of Boolean algebra.[3]

Beginners are often afraid of bit operations, but there's no reason to fear them. Microcontrollers operate on a bit level, so you have to be able to make the bits obey your will. It takes some training, but it's not rocket science.

2. http://en.wikipedia.org/wiki/Arithmetic_shift
3. http://en.wikipedia.org/wiki/Boolean_algebra_%28logic%29

Advanced Serial Programming

In nearly all of the book's projects, we've used the Arduino's serial port. Sometimes we only emitted debug messages to monitor the current state of our sketches, but often we needed it to actually output information or to send commands. And the fact is, we've used the Serial class without explaining how serial communication actually works. We'll catch up on that in this appendix.

To communicate with an Arduino, we mainly used JavaScript, and in some cases we used Processing. But many developers prefer other languages, and in this appendix, you'll also learn how to use C/C++, Java, Ruby, Python, and Perl to talk to an Arduino.

Learning More About Serial Communication

In Chapter 2, *Creating Bigger Projects with the Arduino*, on page 23, you saw that you need only three wires for serial communication: a common ground, a line for transmitting data (TX), and one for receiving data (RX). (See the diagram on page 28.)

Data is transmitted as electrical pulses, so both communication partners need a reference for the voltage level, and that's what the common ground is for. The transmission line is used to send data to the recipient and has to be connected to the recipient's receiving line. This enables full-duplex communication where both partners can send and receive data simultaneously. (Wouldn't it be great if people could also communicate full-duplex?)

We now know how to connect two devices, but we still have to transmit some data. Therefore, both communication partners have to agree on a protocol, and on page 254, you can see what a typical serial communication looks like. The different states of a bit are represented by different voltage levels. Usually, a 0 bit is represented by 0 volts, while 5 volts stands for a 1 bit. (Some proto-cols use -12V and 12V, respectively.)

The following parameters control a serial communication:

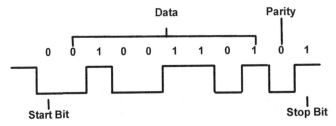

- A *start bit* indicates the beginning of a data word and is used to synchro-nize the transmitter and receiver. It is always 0.

- A *stop bit* tells us when the last data bit has been sent and separates two consecutive data words. Depending on the particular protocol agreement, there can be more than one stop bit, but that happens rarely.

- Information is transferred as binary *data bits*; that is, if you'd like to transmit the letter *M*, you have to turn it into a number first. Several character set encodings are available, but when working with the Arduino, the ASCII encoding fits best. In ASCII, an uppercase *M* is encoded as the decimal number 77, which is 01001101 in binary. This is the bit sequence that eventually gets transmitted.

- The *parity bit* indicates whether the number of 1s in the data has been odd or even. This is a simple error-checking algorithm that is rarely used and that stems from a time when network connections were less reliable than they are today. Parity control can be "none" (no parity bit is sent), "odd" (the parity bit is set if the amount of 1s in the data bits is odd; otherwise, it is 0), or "even" (the parity bit is set if the amount of 1s in the data bits is even; otherwise, it is 0). We chose odd parity for our data, and because there are 4 bits set to 1 in 01001101, the parity bit is 0.

- The *baud rate* defines the transmission speed and is measured in trans-mission steps per second. When working with the Arduino, typical baud rates are 9600, 14400, 19200, or even 115200. Note that the baud rate doesn't define how much data is actually transferred per second, because you have to take the control bits into account. If your connection settings are 1 start bit, 1 stop bit, no parity, and 8 bits per byte, then you have to transfer 1 + 1 + 8 = 10 bits to transfer a single byte. With a baud rate set to 9600, you can then theoretically send 9600 / 10 = 960 bytes per sec-ond—at least if every bit gets transferred in exactly one transmission step.

Serial Communication Using Various Languages

When working with the Arduino, you often have to talk to it using a serial port. In this section, you'll learn how to do that in various programming languages. For demonstration purposes, we'll use the same Arduino sketch for all of them:

SerialProgramming/AnalogReader/AnalogReader.ino
```
const unsigned int BAUD_RATE = 9600;
const unsigned int NUM_PINS = 6;

String  pin_name = "";
boolean input_available = false;

void setup() {
  Serial.begin(BAUD_RATE);
}

void loop() {
  if (input_available) {
    if (pin_name.length() > 1 &&
        (pin_name[0] == 'a' || pin_name[0] == 'A'))
    {
      const unsigned int pin = pin_name.substring(1).toInt();
      if (pin < NUM_PINS) {
        Serial.print(pin_name);
        Serial.print(": ");
        Serial.println(analogRead(pin));
      } else {
        Serial.print("Unknown pin: ");
        Serial.println(pin);
      }
    } else {
      Serial.print("Unknown pin name: ");
      Serial.println(pin_name);
    }
    pin_name = "";
    input_available = false;
  }
}

void serialEvent() {
  while (Serial.available()) {
    const char c = Serial.read();
    if (c == '\n')
      input_available = true;
    else
      pin_name += c;
  }
}
```

This program waits for the name of an analog pin (a0, a1,...a5) and returns its current value. So, all of our clients have to send data to the Arduino (the name of the pin), and they have to receive the result. In the following figure, you can see it working with the IDE's serial monitor.

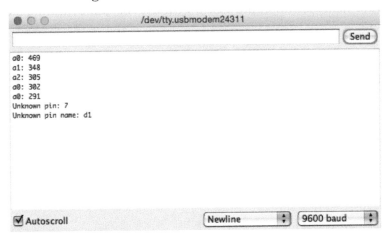

Although you have already seen a few Arduino programs using the serial port, you should pay special attention to the sketch above, because it uses one of the new features in Arduino 1.0: the serialEvent function. The Arduino calls this function automatically at the end of the loop function, and you can use it to process data arriving at the serial port. This nicely decouples your application's logic from the more or less mechanical task of performing serial communication.

Programs using serialEvent often follow the same pattern. They define a global variable for aggregating incoming data (pin_name in our case), and they define a global Boolean variable that indicates whether new data is available (input_available, in our case). Whenever we read a newline character from the serial port, we set input_available to true. So, when the Arduino calls loop the next time, we know that new data has arrived, and we also know that we can find it in pin_name. After we have processed the data, we set the input string to an empty string and set input_available to false.

Back to the clients we're going to implement. Although we use different programming languages to implement them, they all look similar: they expect the name of the serial port to connect to as a command-line argument; they constantly send the string "a0" to the Arduino to get back the current value of analog pin 0; they print the result to the console; they use a constant baud rate of 9600; and they wait for two seconds after opening the serial port, because many Arduinos reboot upon opening a serial connection.

Some Arduinos—for example, the Leonardo or the Micro—do not reboot upon opening a serial connection. If you're using one of these boards, your program should wait until the serial stream is open:

```
Serial.begin(9600);
while (!Serial) ;
```

For some of the clients, you need to install additional libraries. In some cases, you have to do that as an admin user on your machine. I won't mention that explicitly in the following sections. Also, you should make sure you don't have any serial monitor windows open when running one of the examples in the following sections.

Finally, you should keep in mind that all sample programs show the bare mechanics of serial port programming. In production code you'd at least check whether the data you read back from the Arduino has the right format.

C/C++

Although you program the Arduino in C++, you don't need to write clients talking to the Arduino in C++ or C. Still, you can, and it's easy if you use Tod E. Kurt's excellent arduino_serial[1] as a basis.

The project implements a complete command-line tool offering a lot of useful options. For our purposes, that's not necessary. It's sufficient to download the files arduino-serial-lib.h and arduino-serial-lib.c.

The arduino-serial library exports the following functions:

- serialport_init opens a serial port connection. It expects the name of the serial port to be opened and the baud rate to be used. It returns a file descriptor if everything went fine, and it returns -1 otherwise.

- When you no longer need the serial port connection, you should close it using serialport_close.

- With serialport_writebyte, you can send a single byte to an Arduino connected to your computer's serial port. Simply pass it the file descriptor returned by serialport_init and the byte to be written. It returns -1 if an error occurred. Otherwise, it returns 0.

- serialport_write writes an entire string to the serial port. It expects a file descriptor and the string to be written. It returns -1 if an error occurred. Otherwise, it returns 0.

---

1. https://github.com/todbot/arduino-serial

- Use serialport_read_until to read data from a serial port. Pass it a file descriptor and a buffer to be filled with the data read. The method also expects a delimiter character, the maximum length of the buffer, and a timeout value measured in milliseconds. serial_port_read_until stops reading when it finds the delimiter character, when the buffer is full, or when it times out. If it cannot read any more data before one of these conditions is met, it returns -1. Otherwise, it returns 0.

- To make sure that all data you've written gets actually transferred, call serialport_flush and pass it the file descriptor of your serial port connection.

Here's how to use the code for communicating with our analog reader sketch (note that the following code will run on your PC and not on your Arduino):

SerialProgramming/C/analog_reader.c

```
Line 1  #include <stdio.h>
   -    #include <unistd.h>
   -    #include <termios.h>
   -    #include "arduino-serial-lib.h"
   5    #define MAX_LINE 256
   -
   -    int main(int argc, char* argv[]) {
   -      int timeout = 1000;
   -
   10     if (argc == 1) {
   -        printf("You have to pass the name of a serial port.\n");
   -        return -1;
   -      }
   -      int baudrate = B9600;
   15     int arduino = serialport_init(argv[1], baudrate);
   -      if (arduino == -1) {
   -        printf("Could not open serial port %s.\n", argv[1]);
   -        return -1;
   -      }
   20     sleep(2);
   -      char line[MAX_LINE];
   -      while (1) {
   -        int rc = serialport_write(arduino, "a0\n");
   -        if (rc == -1) {
   25         printf("Could not write to serial port.\n");
   -        } else {
   -          serialport_read_until(arduino, line, '\n', MAX_LINE, timeout);
   -          printf("%s", line);
   -        }
   30     }
   -      serialport_close(arduino);
   -      return 0;
   -    }
```

First we import all the libraries we need, and we define a constant for the maximum length of the lines we are going to read from the Arduino. Then we define a main function.

After we've made sure that the name of a serial port was passed on the command line, we initialize a serial port in line 15. Then we sleep for two seconds to give the Arduino some time to get ready. After that, we start a loop in line 23 where we constantly send the string "a0" to the Arduino. We check the result of serialport_write, and if it was successful, we read the result sent by the Arduino in line 27. Let's compile our little program:

```
maik> gcc arduino-serial-lib.c analog_reader.c -o analog_reader
```

Determine what serial port your Arduino is connected to (mine is connected to /dev/tty.usbmodem24321) and run the program like this:

```
maik> ./analog_reader /dev/tty.usbmodem24321
a0: 495
a0: 376
^C
```

Everything works as expected, and accessing a serial port using C isn't that difficult. To embed this code into a C++ program, you should wrap it in a class named SerialPort or something similar.

Note that the arduino-serial library works on any POSIX-compatible system—in other words, it won't work on Windows.

Java

The Java platform standardizes a lot, and it also defines how to access a serial port in the Java Communications API.[2] But the API is only a specification that still has to be implemented. Unfortunately, there is no complete or even perfect implementation available at the time of this writing.

For many years the RXTX project[3] provided a good implementation, but it hasn't been updated for a while now.

Oracle's own implementation runs only on a few platforms, and the remaining solutions are commercial products you have to pay for.

Fortunately, the jSSC (java-simple-serial-connector) project[4] comes to the rescue. It doesn't implement the Java Communications API, but it follows a

---

2.   http://www.oracle.com/technetwork/java/index-jsp-141752.html
3.   http://rxtx.qbang.org/
4.   https://code.google.com/p/java-simple-serial-connector/

rather pragmatic approach. (Guess why we're using it?) Also, it doesn't have a lot of bells and whistles yet, but it runs on many platforms and works perfectly with the Arduino.

jSSC is completely self-contained—that is, you only need the jssc.jar file to get started with your first project. Download the most current release and make sure that jssc.jar is on your class path. Then enter the following code in your favorite IDE or text editor:

SerialProgramming/Java/AnalogReader.java
```java
import jssc.SerialPort;
import jssc.SerialPortList;
import jssc.SerialPortException;

public class AnalogReader {
  public static void main(String[] args) throws Exception {
    if (args.length != 1) {
      System.out.println(
        "You have to pass the name of a serial port."
      );
      System.exit(1);
    }

    try {
      SerialPort serialPort = new SerialPort(args[0]);
      serialPort.openPort();
      Thread.sleep(2000);
      serialPort.setParams(
        SerialPort.BAUDRATE_9600,
        SerialPort.DATABITS_8,
        SerialPort.STOPBITS_1,
        SerialPort.PARITY_NONE
      );

      while (true) {
        serialPort.writeString("a0\n");
        System.out.println(readLine(serialPort));
      }
    }
    catch (SerialPortException ex) {
      System.out.println(ex);
    }
  }

  private static String readLine(SerialPort serialPort) throws Exception {
    final int MAX_LINE = 10;
    final byte NEWLINE = 10;

    byte[] line = new byte[MAX_LINE];
    int i = 0;
```

```
    byte currentByte = serialPort.readBytes(1)[0];
    while (currentByte != NEWLINE) {
      line[i++] = currentByte;
      currentByte = serialPort.readBytes(1)[0];
    }
    return new String(line);
  }
}
```

Although this program defines a class named AnalogReader, it's not very object-oriented. We only define it because everything in Java has to live in a class context.

The main function implements the protocol for our Arduino sketch. First, we make sure that the name of a serial port was set on the command line. Then we use this name to initialize a new SerialPort object. To open the serial port, we call the openPort method. After a two-second pause, we configure the serial port's parameters.

In the loop that follows, we send the string "a0" to the serial port using Serial-Port's writeString method. Afterward, we read the result by invoking the readLine function and print it to the console.

Currently, jSSC doesn't offer a readLine function, so we have to write our own. The function reads the Arduino's response byte by byte using the readBytes method, because jSSC doesn't offer a method for reading a single byte. readLine appends all bytes read to the byte array named line until it detects a newline character (ASCII code 10). Finally, it converts the byte array into a String object and returns it.

Here's how to compile and use the program:

```
maik> javac -cp jssc.jar AnalogReader.java
maik> java -cp jssc.jar:. AnalogReader /dev/tty.usbmodem24321
a0: 496
a0: 433
a0: 328
a0: 328
^C
```

AnalogReader does exactly what it's intended to do: it permanently prints the values of the analog pin 0. Accessing a serial port in Java is a piece of cake if you use the right libraries.

Note that jSSC also allows you to write object-oriented code. It has a Serial-PortEventListener interface that makes it easy to decouple the handling of serial communication from your application's logic. Have a look at the project's examples to learn more about these features.

Ruby

Even dynamic languages such as Ruby give you instant access to your computer's serial port and to an Arduino connected to it. But before that, you need to install the serialport gem:

```
maik> gem install serialport
```

Using it, you can connect to the Arduino in just 30 lines of code.

SerialProgramming/Ruby/analog_reader.rb
```ruby
require 'rubygems'
require 'serialport'

if ARGV.size != 1
  puts "You have to pass the name of a serial port."
  exit 1
end

port_name = ARGV[0]
baud_rate = 9600
data_bits = 8
stop_bits = 1
parity    = SerialPort::NONE

arduino = SerialPort.new(
  port_name,
  baud_rate,
  data_bits,
  stop_bits,
  parity
)

sleep 2
while true
  arduino.write "a0\n"
  sleep 0.01
  line = arduino.gets.chomp
  puts line
end
```

We create a new SerialPort object in line 15, passing it all the usual parameters. After we sleep for two seconds, we start a loop and call write on the SerialPort object. To get the result back from the Arduino, we call gets, and then we print the result to the console. Here you can see the program in action:

```
maik> ruby analog_reader.rb /dev/tty.usbmodem24321
a0: 496
a0: 456
a0: 382
^Canalog_reader.rb:27:in `gets': Interrupt
  from analog_reader.rb:27
```

Using Ruby to access an Arduino is a good choice because you can fully
concentrate on your application. All of the ugly details you have to deal with
in other programming languages are well hidden.

Python

Python is another dynamic programming language you can use to quickly
create Arduino clients. For programming a serial port, download and install
the pyserial library first.[5] There is a special installer for Windows, but usually
it's sufficient to install it like this:

```
maik> python setup.py install
```

After you've installed pyserial, you can use it to create a client for our analog
reader sketch:

/SerialProgramming/Python/analog_reader.py
```
Line 1  import sys
   -    import time
   -    import serial
   -
   5    if len(sys.argv) != 2:
   -      print "You have to pass the name of a serial port."
   -      sys.exit(1)
   -
   -    serial_port = sys.argv[1]
   10   arduino = serial.Serial(
   -      serial_port,
   -      9600,
   -      serial.EIGHTBITS,
   -      serial.PARITY_NONE,
   15     serial.STOPBITS_ONE)
   -    time.sleep(2)
   -    while 1:
   -      arduino.write("a0\n")
   -      line = arduino.readline().rstrip()
   20     print line
```

---

5.   http://sourceforge.net/projects/pyserial/files/

We make sure that we have the name of a serial port on the command line. Then we create a new Serial object in line 10, passing it all the parameters we'd like to use for serial communication.

After sleeping for two seconds, we start an infinite loop. In the loop, we send the string "a0" to the serial port calling write. We read the result returned by the Arduino using the readline method and output the result to the console. Here's what a typical session looks like:

```
maik> python analog_reader.py /dev/tty.usbmodem24321
a0: 497
a0: 458
a0: 383
^C
```

Isn't that code beautiful? With about twenty lines of Python code, you get full control over your Arduino sketch. So, Python is another excellent choice for writing Arduino clients.

Perl

Perl is still one of the most widely used dynamic programming languages, and it has good support for serial communication. Some distributions come with libraries for programming the serial port, but usually you have to install a module first.

Windows users should have a look at Win32::SerialPort.[6] For the rest, Device::SerialPort is a good choice. You can install it as follows:

```
maik> perl -MCPAN -e 'install Device::SerialPort'
```

Then use it like this:

SerialProgramming/Perl/analog_reader.pl

```
Line 1  use strict;
     -  use warnings;
     -  use Device::SerialPort;
     -
     5  my $num_args = $#ARGV + 1;
     -  if ($num_args != 1) {
     -      die "You have to pass the name of a serial port.";
     -  }
     -
    10  my $serial_port = $ARGV[0];
     -  my $arduino = Device::SerialPort->new($serial_port);
     -  $arduino->baudrate(9600);
     -  $arduino->databits(8);
```

---

6. http://search.cpan.org/dist/Win32-SerialPort/

```
  -     $arduino->parity("none");
 15     $arduino->stopbits(1);
  -     $arduino->read_const_time(1);
  -     $arduino->read_char_time(1);
  -
  -     sleep(2);
 20     while (1) {
  -         $arduino->write("a0\n");
  -         my ($count, $line) = $arduino->read(255);
  -         print $line;
  -     }
```

We check whether the name of a serial port was passed on the command line. Then we create a new Device::SerialPort instance in line 11. We configure all serial port parameters, and in line 16, we set a timeout value for read calls. If we did not set it, read would return immediately, giving the Arduino no time to respond. read_char_time sets a timeout for the waiting period between two characters.

Then we sleep for two seconds and start an infinite loop. Here we send the string "a0" to the serial port and read the Arduino's response using the read method. read expects a maximum number of bytes to be read, and it returns the actual number of bytes read and the data it received. Finally, we output the result to the console. A typical program run looks as follows:

```
maik> perl analog_reader.pl /dev/tty.usbmodem24321
a0: 496
a0: 366
a0: 320
^C
```

That's it! It takes only about twenty lines of Perl code to create a client for the analog reader Arduino sketch. So, Perl is a good choice for programming Arduino clients, too.

Controlling the Arduino with a Browser

For many hardware projects, you'll need an application on your computer that visualizes some sensor data or that controls your device. In the Arduino scene, many people use Processing[1] for this purpose. Processing is a good choice. It's fast, it has excellent multimedia support, and it supports a lot of libraries because it uses the Java Virtual Machine (JVM).

Processing has some disadvantages, too. It is very similar to Java; that is, it's a statically typed programming language. As such, it isn't a good tool for building prototypes interactively and incrementally. Also, you have to install Java and the Processing environment to use it.

In many cases it's a better choice to use a regular web browser to write applications that communicate with the Arduino. Web browsers have excellent multimedia support, too, and the JavaScript programming language is easy to learn and widely available.

The only problem is that most web browsers don't support serial port programming. But fortunately, Google Chrome comes with native support for serial port programming. Due to security restrictions, you can access the corresponding library only in Chrome Web apps and not on regular websites. Fortunately, it's not difficult to create Chrome apps, and in this appendix you'll learn how.

What Are Google Chrome Apps?

Over the years, web browsers have evolved from simple applications used for rendering HTML documents to full-blown programming environments. They've become so powerful that you can barely distinguish them from operating

---

1. http://processing.org

systems today. Chrome OS,[2] for example, is an operating system that was designed for executing web applications.

Very early on, Google realized that applications made using standard web technologies such as HTML5, CSS3, and JavaScript could also work well on the desktop. So they invented Google Chrome apps, a technology for using web technologies to create desktop applications.

Google operates a web shop for Chrome apps.[3] Also, the company has released an application launcher that allows you to start Chrome apps without starting the browser.

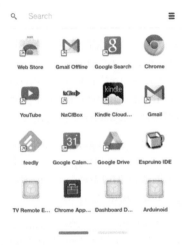

Unlike regular websites, you can use many Chrome apps when you're offline. You can even find complete office suites that were implemented as Chrome apps.

In contrast to native applications, web applications and JavaScript programs are often limited in a number of ways. Usually that's a good thing, because it prevents malicious websites from compromising your computer. Still, there are situations where a bit more freedom would be advantageous—for example, if you'd like to access serial devices from your browser.

Chrome apps address exactly this issue and provide APIs to access serial, USB, or Bluetooth devices. They also come with a mature permission management, so users can decide whether a certain application should get access to a particular resource.

---

2. http://en.wikipedia.org/wiki/Chrome_OS

3. https://chrome.google.com/webstore/category/apps

Creating a Minimal Chrome App

Chrome apps are zip files that contain all the assets you'd usually expect in a web application. They contain HTML files, JavaScript files, images, videos, and so on. In addition, each zip archive contains two special files: manifest.json and background.js.

manifest.json describes the Chrome app's metadata and typically looks like this:

```
ChromeApps/SimpleApp/manifest.json
{
  "manifest_version": 2,
  "name": "My First Chrome App",
  "version": "1",
  "permissions": ["serial"],
  "app": {
    "background": {
      "scripts": ["background.js"]
    }
  }
}
```

It uses JavaScript Object Notation (JSON)[4] and supports a lot of different options.[5]

Only name and version are mandatory. They specify the app's name and version. These attributes will appear in the Chrome Web Store, if you decide to make your application available to the public. So choose them carefully if you're going to release your application.

manifest_version contains the version of the manifest file's specification. Currently, you must set it to 2 for Chrome apps.

With the permissions option, your Chrome app can request permissions that applications do not have by default. We set it to serial so the Chrome app is allowed to access the computer's serial port. Users who install a Chrome app have to agree to all permissions it requests.

Eventually, manifest.json sets the Chrome app's background page to a file named background.js. Which brings us to the second mandatory file in each Chrome app: background.js.

Not only does every Chrome app need a starting point, but every app also needs some kind of lifecycle management. Like operating systems control a

---

4. http://json.org/
5. https://developer.chrome.com/apps/manifest

native application's lifecycle, the Chrome environment controls a web application's lifecycle. It provides the web applications with important events, such as alarms or signals.

The background.js file is where you connect your Chrome app to the Chrome runtime environment. You can register for many events, but you at least have to specify what happens when your application gets launched. Here's how you can do that:

ChromeApps/SimpleApp/background.js
```
chrome.app.runtime.onLaunched.addListener(function() {
  chrome.app.window.create('main.html', {
    id: 'main',
    bounds: { width: 200, height: 100 }
  });
});
```

The preceding file adds a new listener function to Chrome's runtime environment. Specifically, it registers a listener function for the onLaunched event—that is, the function will be called when the Chrome app gets launched.

The listener opens a new Chrome app window by calling the chrome.app.window.create function. This function expects the name of an HTML document to be opened and some optional arguments, such as the window's ID and its bounds. For our first Chrome app, the HTML document looks as follows:

ChromeApps/SimpleApp/main.html
```
<!DOCTYPE html>
<html>
  <head>
    <title>My First Chrome App</title>
  </head>
  <body>
    <p>Hello, world!</p>
  </body>
</html>
```

These three files (manifest.json, background.js, and main.html) are all you need for a basic Chrome app. In the next section, you'll learn how to run the application for the first time.

Starting the Chrome App

During development, it'd be tedious to create zip archives every time you wanted to try your latest changes to a Chrome app. That's why the Chrome browser supports the execution of unzipped applications. Point the browser to chrome://extensions or choose the Tools > Extensions menu. You'll see something like the following figure:

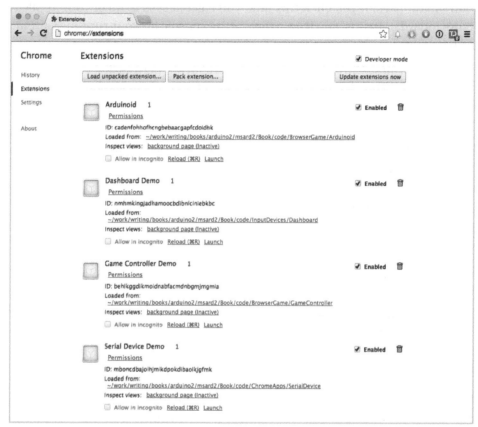

Make sure the Developer Mode checkbox at the top-right corner is checked. Click the Load Unpacked Extension button to load the Chrome app you wrote in the previous section. Click the Launch link belonging to the My First Chrome App application. Chrome will start a new Chrome app, which will look like the screenshot.

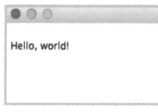

The Chrome app looks like a regular application in many regards. On Mac OS X, for example, it has a menu bar with a quit function, and it runs in a regular application window that you can minimize, maximize, and hide.

Exploring the Chrome Serial API

On Chrome's Extensions site, you'll see a link named background page next to each Chrome app. This link actually refers to a Chrome app's background page. If you click it, Chrome will open a console for the background page. Also, it automatically creates another link next to it, pointing to the application's main page. If you click this link, you'll get access to all of your application's innards—that is, you'll get a JavaScript console for your running Chrome App.

Because our first Chrome app's manifest requests permission for accessing the serial port, you can use Chrome's serial API[6] in the application's JavaScript console.

The following function prints the paths to all serial devices connected to your computer (to enter multi-line functions in the JavaScript console, press Shift+Enter at the end of each line):

```
chrome.serial.getDevices(function(devices) {
  devices.forEach(function(d) {
    console.log(d.path);
  })
});
```

On my machine this function outputs the following:

```
/dev/cu.Bluetooth-Incoming-Port
/dev/tty.Bluetooth-Incoming-Port
/dev/cu.Bluetooth-Modem
/dev/tty.Bluetooth-Modem
/dev/cu.usbmodem24321
/dev/tty.usbmodem24321
```

The last two lines represent the serial port connected to my Arduino. With the following statement you can connect to the Arduino from the JavaScript console:

```
chrome.serial.connect(
  "/dev/tty.usbmodem24321",
  { bitrate: 38400 },
  function(c) { console.log(c) })
```

chrome.serial.connect expects three arguments. The first is the path to the serial port to connect to. With the second argument, you can specify typical options for serial ports, such as the baud rate (named bitrate in this case) or the parity bit. Eventually you have to pass a callback function that gets called after Chrome tries to establish the connection.

---

6.   https://developer.chrome.com/apps/serial

The callback function receives an object containing all information about the connection. The statement above prints a text representation of the serial connection object that has been created:

```
Object {
  bitrate: 38400
  bufferSize: 4096
  connectionId: 13
  ctsFlowControl: false
  dataBits: "eight"
  name: ""
  parityBit: "no"
  paused: false
  persistent: false
  receiveTimeout: 0
  sendTimeout: 0
  stopBits: "one"
}
```

This object contains all properties you'd expect in an object representing a serial connection. It contains properties for the parity bit and stop bit settings. One of its most important properties is connectionId. If the call to connect was successful, its value is greater than zero.

In a next step, you can add a receive listener that gets called whenever data arrives at the serial port:

```
var listener = function(r) { console.log(r.data); }
chrome.serial.onReceive.addListener(listener)
```

This listener outputs the data it receives on the console. Its output looks like this:

```
ArrayBuffer {}
ArrayBuffer {}
ArrayBuffer {}
...
```

This probably isn't what you expected. The problem is that the Chrome Serial API stores the data it receives in an ArrayBuffer object. This is necessary because you can transmit not only textual, but also binary data over a serial connection. JavaScript doesn't support binary data out of the box, so you have to use a few helper classes, such as ArrayBuffer.

Using the following function, you can turn the content of an ArrayBuffer object into a JavaScript string:

```
function arrayBufferToString(buf) {
  var bufView = new Uint8Array(buf);
  var encodedString = String.fromCharCode.apply(null, bufView);
  return decodeURIComponent(escape(encodedString));
};
```

Although this function comprises only a few statements, it's very complex. It expects an ArrayBuffer object containing data encoded in UTF-8. That's why it creates a Uint8Array object first. An ArrayBuffer represents an arbitrary chunk of memory, and using view classes like Uint8Array, you can specify how the memory chunk should be interpreted. In our case, we want to interpret the data we've received as characters encoded in UTF-8.

JavaScript strings are usually encoded in UTF-16, so the next two statements convert the UTF-8 data we've received into a UTF-16 string. They use the function arrayBufferToString to turn ArrayBuffer objects into JavaScript strings.[7]

```
var listener = function(r) { console.log(arrayBufferToString(r.data)); }
chrome.serial.onReceive.addListener(listener)
```

This listener outputs the data received from the Arduino in a readable manner. Note that you'll see a lot of unexpected line breaks because the serial API doesn't look for newline characters. Whenever it receives a chunk of data, it hands the chunk over to the listener. It's the application's responsibility to interpret the data, and you'll learn how to do this in the next section.

You've learned how to create your own Chrome apps and how to talk to serial devices on the JavaScript console. But one of the great things about JavaScript and Chrome apps is that you can tinker so easily with APIs in the browser.

Writing a SerialDevice Class

Playing with a new library in an interactive environment is a great way to learn. Still, you eventually have to come up with some proper JavaScript code that you can actually use in your project.

JavaScript supports object-oriented programming, so it seems logical to put all code related to accessing the serial port into its own class. This way, you can reuse it in other projects, and if you have to fix bugs or improve the code, you have to do it only in one place. In addition, chances are good that there will be a cross-browser solution for accessing the serial port soon.[8] When this happens, you can replace the innards of your class with the new standard

---

7. At http://ecmanaut.blogspot.de/2006/07/encoding-decoding-utf8-in-javascript.html, you can find a detailed explanation of this function. It's not for the faint of heart!
8. http://whatwg.github.io/serial/

API, and your applications will work on all browsers automatically. At least the parts that access the serial port—all other parts will still be subject to browser incompatibilities, of course.

In this section, we'll create a SerialDevice class that we can use in many of our projects. It's based on one of the standard Google Chrome app samples,[9] and you should have a look at the other samples, too. Studying them is a great way to learn.

Creating classes in JavaScript isn't difficult, but it's completely different from most other object-oriented languages you might know. JavaScript's object system is based on prototypes, not classes. Instead of providing a template (class) for creating new objects, you create new objects immediately. Then you refine these objects and can use them afterward as a template (or parent) for other objects.

Despite all differences between class-based and prototype-based languages, you have to create your objects somehow. In JavaScript, you can use a constructor function:

ChromeApps/SerialDevice/js/serial_device.js

```
Line 1  var SerialDevice = function(path, baudRate) {
   -      this.path = path;
   -      this.baudRate = baudRate || 38400;
   -      this.connectionId = -1;
   5      this.readBuffer = "";
   -      this.boundOnReceive = this.onReceive.bind(this);
   -      this.boundOnReceiveError = this.onReceiveError.bind(this);
   -      this.onConnect = new chrome.Event();
   -      this.onReadLine = new chrome.Event();
   10     this.onError = new chrome.Event();
   -    };
```

Using this function you can create new SerialDevice objects like this:

```
var arduino = new SerialDevice("/dev/tty.usbmodem24321");
```

Note the frequent use of the this keyword. In JavaScript, this refers to the current function's execution context. You can use it for various purposes. When creating objects, you'll most often use it to create attributes and methods that are bound to a certain object. In lines 2 to 5, we use it to define a few instance variables, such as path.

In the following two lines, we use it to define two more instance variables. This time, we use this also on the right-hand side of the assignment and pass

---

9. https://github.com/GoogleChrome/chrome-app-samples/tree/master/samples/serial/ledtoggle

it to the bind method. bind creates a new function and sets the new function's this keyword to the value you passed to bind originally. Using bind, you can define a function now, but make sure that it has a certain context when you actually call it.

When working with event handlers, this is often necessary. Users of the SerialDevice class should be able to pass their own callback functions, but they should be executed in the class' context. You'll see how this works in a minute.

At the end of the constructor, we define three instance variables that are all instances of the chrome.Event class.[10] This class provides some nice features to define and dispatch events within Chrome apps. We use it to define the three events that users of our SerialDevice class can listen for. Now users can register for readLine events using the onReadLine property.

The next three methods of the SerialDevice class implement everything needed for connecting and disconnecting serial devices:

ChromeApps/SerialDevice/js/serial_device.js
```
Line 1  SerialDevice.prototype.connect = function() {
          chrome.serial.connect(
            this.path,
            { bitrate: this.baudRate },
     5      this.onConnectComplete.bind(this))
        };

        SerialDevice.prototype.onConnectComplete = function(connectionInfo) {
          if (!connectionInfo) {
    10        console.log("Could not connect to serial device.");
            return;
          }
          this.connectionId = connectionInfo.connectionId;
          chrome.serial.onReceive.addListener(this.boundOnReceive);
    15      chrome.serial.onReceiveError.addListener(this.boundOnReceiveError);
          this.onConnect.dispatch();
        };

        SerialDevice.prototype.disconnect = function() {
    20      if (this.connectionId < 0) {
            throw "No serial device connected.";
          }
          chrome.serial.disconnect(this.connectionId, function() {});
        };
```

---

10. https://developer.chrome.com/extensions/events

First of all, you should note that we define all methods on the prototype property of the SerialDevice object. I won't go into the details here, but you should know that this is one way to add new methods to objects in JavaScript.

The connect method delegates its work to the chrome.serial.connect function that you saw in the previous section already. The only thing worth noting is the callback function we pass in the function call. Again we use bind to set the callback function's context explicitly. This way, we make sure that onConnect-Complete has access to the properties of the SerialDevice object.

We benefit from that in the onConnectComplete method. Here we can set the connectionId property of our SerialDevice object as soon as we've successfully connected to a serial device. If we hadn't bound onConnectComplete before, this would have a completely different meaning in this function, and we couldn't access the properties of the SerialDevice object.

In lines 14 and 15, we use the same technique to add receive and error listeners to the chrome.serial object. Here we use the listeners we've prepared in the constructor function before. After we've established the connection successfully, we call the onConnect object's dispatch method to spread the good news to all listeners outside.

Eventually, we have to implement the actual listener functions that deal with incoming and outgoing data and with errors:

ChromeApps/SerialDevice/js/serial_device.js

```
SerialDevice.prototype.onReceive = function(receiveInfo) {
  if (receiveInfo.connectionId !== this.connectionId) {
    return;
  }

  this.readBuffer += this.arrayBufferToString(receiveInfo.data);

  var n;
  while ((n = this.readBuffer.indexOf('\n')) >= 0) {
    var line = this.readBuffer.substr(0, n + 1);
    this.onReadLine.dispatch(line);
    this.readBuffer = this.readBuffer.substr(n + 1);
  }
};

SerialDevice.prototype.onReceiveError = function(errorInfo) {
  if (errorInfo.connectionId === this.connectionId) {
    this.onError.dispatch(errorInfo.error);
  }
};

SerialDevice.prototype.send = function(data) {
```

```
  if (this.connectionId < 0) {
    throw "No serial device connected.";
  }
  chrome.serial.send(
    this.connectionId,
    this.stringToArrayBuffer(data),
    function() {});
};
```

onReceive basically works like the sample listener we implemented in *Exploring the Chrome Serial API*, on page 271. The only difference is that the new implementation looks for newline characters. Whenever it finds one, it passes the current read buffer to the function that is listening for onReadLine events. Note that more than one line can be transmitted in a single data chunk. Also note that onReceive checks whether it got data from the correct serial port.

The onReceiveError method also makes sure first that it got error information for the correct connection. In this case, it dispatches the event to the function that is listening for onError events.

For our purposes we don't need a send method, but it doesn't hurt to add it for the sake of completeness. This way, you have a SerialDevice class that you can use in many more projects.

Finally, we need our two helper methods for converting ArrayBuffer objects into strings and vice versa:

ChromeApps/SerialDevice/js/serial_device.js
```
SerialDevice.prototype.arrayBufferToString = function(buf) {
  var bufView = new Uint8Array(buf);
  var encodedString = String.fromCharCode.apply(null, bufView);
  return decodeURIComponent(escape(encodedString));
};

SerialDevice.prototype.stringToArrayBuffer = function(str) {
  var encodedString = unescape(encodeURIComponent(str));
  var bytes = new Uint8Array(encodedString.length);
  for (var i = 0; i < encodedString.length; ++i) {
    bytes[i] = encodedString.charCodeAt(i);
  }
  return bytes.buffer;
};
```

That's it! We now have a generic class for communicating with serial devices from a Chrome app. Let's use it right away and write a small demo application. This demo will be the simplest serial monitor possible. It will permanently read data from a serial port and display it in an HTML page. The HTML page looks as follows:

ChromeApps/SerialDevice/main.html

```html
<!DOCTYPE html>
<html lang="en">
  <head>
    <meta charset="utf-8"/>
    <title>Serial Device Demo</title>
  </head>
  <body>
    <div id="main">
      <p>The Arduino sends:</p>
      <p id="output"></p>
    </div>
    <script src="js/serial_device.js"></script>
    <script src="js/arduino.js"></script>
  </body>
</html>
```

In the HTML page, you'll find a paragraph element with its id attribute set to output. That's the element we'll fill with the data we read from the serial port. At the end of the document, we include our new JavaScript library for accessing the serial device. Also, we include a file named arduino.js:

ChromeApps/SerialDevice/js/arduino.js

```javascript
var arduino = new SerialDevice('/dev/tty.usbmodem24311');

arduino.onConnect.addListener(function() {
  console.log('Connected to: ' + arduino.path);
});

arduino.onReadLine.addListener(function(line) {
  console.log('Read line: ' + line);
  document.getElementById('output').innerText = line;
});

arduino.connect();
```

Here we create a new SerialDevice object named arduino. Then we add listener functions for the onConnect and onReadLine events. Both write a message to the console. The onReadLine listener puts the line it has read into the browser's Document Object Model (DOM).

Make sure you use the correct serial port in the first line of arduino.js. Then connect your Arduino to your computer and upload a sketch that permanently outputs lines of text on the serial port. You can use the sketch from *Building Your Own Game Controller*, on page 106. Start the Chrome app, and you should see something like the following figure:

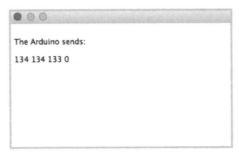

The Chrome app will update the HTML page whenever it receives a new line of data.

Isn't it fascinating how easy it is to combine modern Web technologies with microcontrollers?

There's one minor drawback, though. Support for the serial API in the Google Chrome browser is still a rather new feature. It might happen that your browser crashes from time to time, especially when you're starting or stopping Chrome apps that access the serial port, or when you're attaching or detaching devices while the browser is running. Apart from that, everything runs smoothly and is stable. The situation will probably improve with every new browser release.

Bibliography

[But09]   Paul Butcher. *Debug It!: Find, Repair, and Prevent Bugs in Your Code*. The Pragmatic Bookshelf, Raleigh, NC and Dallas, TX, 2009.

[KR98]   Brian W. Kernighan and Dennis Ritchie. *The C Programming Language*. Prentice Hall, Englewood Cliffs, NJ, Second edition, 1998.

[Mey97]   Scott Meyers. *Effective C++: 50 Specific Ways to Improve Your Programs and Designs*. Addison-Wesley Longman, Reading, MA, Second edition, 1997.

[Pin09]   Chris Pine. *Learn to Program*. The Pragmatic Bookshelf, Raleigh, NC and Dallas, TX, Second Edition, 2009.

[Pla10]   Charles Platt. *Make: Electronics*. O'Reilly & Associates, Inc., Sebastopol, CA, 2010.

[Str00]   Bjarne Stroustrup. *The C++ Programming Language*. Addison-Wesley, Reading, MA, 2000.

Index

Raspberry Pi and PC's

If you like the Arduino, you might really love the extra horsepower of the Raspberry Pi! And for top-performance, build your own PC from scratch.

Raspberry Pi: A Quick-Start Guide (2nd edition)

The Raspberry Pi is one of the most successful open source hardware projects ever. For less than $40, you get a full-blown PC, a multimedia center, and a web server—and this book gives you everything you need to get started. You'll learn the basics, progress to controlling the Pi, and then build your own electronics projects. This new edition is revised and updated with two new chapters on adding digital and analog sensors, and creating videos and a burglar alarm with the Pi camera. *Printed in full color.*

Maik Schmidt
(176 pages) ISBN: 9781937785802. $22
https://pragprog.com/book/msraspi2

Build an Awesome PC, 2014 Edition

Custom-build your own dream PC, have fun doing it, and save yourself a lot of money in the process. This book will give you the confidence to buy the best-of-class components and assemble them with clear, step-by-step instructions. You'll build your own PC capable of effortlessly running the most graphic and CPU-intensive games, graphics software, and programming compilers available today. And because it's a PC that you built yourself, you'll be able to keep it up to date with the latest hardware innovations.

Mike Riley
(119 pages) ISBN: 9781941222171. $17
https://pragprog.com/book/mrpc

The Joy of Math and Healthy Programming

Rediscover the joy and fascinating weirdness of pure mathematics, and learn how to take a healthier approach to programming.

Good Math

Mathematics is beautiful—and it can be fun and exciting as well as practical. *Good Math* is your guide to some of the most intriguing topics from two thousand years of mathematics: from Egyptian fractions to Turing machines; from the real meaning of numbers to proof trees, group symmetry, and mechanical computation. If you've ever wondered what lay beyond the proofs you struggled to complete in high school geometry, or what limits the capabilities of the computer on your desk, this is the book for you.

Mark C. Chu-Carroll
(282 pages) ISBN: 9781937785338. $34
https://pragprog.com/book/mcmath

The Healthy Programmer

To keep doing what you love, you need to maintain your own systems, not just the ones you write code for. Regular exercise and proper nutrition help you learn, remember, concentrate, and be creative—skills critical to doing your job well. Learn how to change your work habits, master exercises that make working at a computer more comfortable, and develop a plan to keep fit, healthy, and sharp for years to come.

This book is intended only as an informative guide for those wishing to know more about health issues. In no way is this book intended to replace, countermand, or conflict with the advice given to you by your own healthcare provider including Physician, Nurse Practitioner, Physician Assistant, Registered Dietician, and other licensed professionals.

Joe Kutner
(254 pages) ISBN: 9781937785314. $36
https://pragprog.com/book/jkthp

The Pragmatic Bookshelf

The Pragmatic Bookshelf features books written by developers for developers. The titles continue the well-known Pragmatic Programmer style and continue to garner awards and rave reviews. As development gets more and more difficult, the Pragmatic Programmers will be there with more titles and products to help you stay on top of your game.

Visit Us Online

This Book's Home Page
https://pragprog.com/book/msard2
Source code from this book, errata, and other resources. Come give us feedback, too!

Register for Updates
https://pragprog.com/updates
Be notified when updates and new books become available.

Join the Community
https://pragprog.com/community
Read our weblogs, join our online discussions, participate in our mailing list, interact with our wiki, and benefit from the experience of other Pragmatic Programmers.

New and Noteworthy
https://pragprog.com/news
Check out the latest pragmatic developments, new titles and other offerings.

Save on the eBook

Save on the eBook versions of this title. Owning the paper version of this book entitles you to purchase the electronic versions at a terrific discount.

PDFs are great for carrying around on your laptop—they are hyperlinked, have color, and are fully searchable. Most titles are also available for the iPhone and iPod touch, Amazon Kindle, and other popular e-book readers.

Buy now at *https://pragprog.com/coupon*

Contact Us

Online Orders:	*https://pragprog.com/catalog*
Customer Service:	*support@pragprog.com*
International Rights:	*translations@pragprog.com*
Academic Use:	*academic@pragprog.com*
Write for Us:	*http://write-for-us.pragprog.com*
Or Call:	+1 800-699-7764

CPSIA information can be obtained at www.ICGtesting.com
Printed in the USA
BVOW10s2023010315

389816BV00005B/10/P

31901056095336

9 781941 222249